State and Agents in China

State and Agents in China

DISCIPLINING GOVERNMENT OFFICIALS

Yongshun Cai

Stanford University Press
Stanford, California

Stanford University Press
Stanford, California

© 2015 by the Board of Trustees of the Leland Stanford Junior University. All rights reserved.

No part of this book may be reproduced or transmitted in any form or by any means, electronic or mechanical, including photocopying and recording, or in any information storage or retrieval system without the prior written permission of Stanford University Press.

Printed in the United States of America on acid-free, archival-quality paper

Library of Congress Cataloging-in-Publication Data

Cai, Yongshun, author.
    State and agents in China : disciplining government officials / Yongshun Cai.
      pages cm
  Includes bibliographical references and index.
  ISBN 978-0-8047-9251-6 (cloth : alk. paper) —
  ISBN 978-0-8047-9351-3 (pbk. : alk. paper)
    1. China—Officials and employees—Discipline.   2. Misconduct in office—China.   I. Title.
  JQ1512.Z13D536 2014
  352.6'8—dc23
                                      2014025802

ISBN 978-0-8047-9352-0 (electronic)

Typeset by Thompson Type in 11/14 Adobe Garamond

For My Parents

Contents

Figures and Tables		*ix*
Acknowledgments		*xi*
1	Introduction	1
2	Government Officials' Malfeasance in China	20
3	The Politics of Disciplining Government Officials	49
4	Disciplining Officials for Duty-Related Malfeasance	71
5	Punishing Corrupt Agents	104
6	The Politics of Blame Avoidance	134
7	Reform-Minded Officials, State Tolerance, and Institutional Change	159
8	Conclusion	181
Appendix: Data Collection		*195*
	3.1 *Collection of 111 Cases of Media Exposure*	*197*
	3.2 *Collection of 133 Cases of Officials' Duty-Related Malfeasance*	*198*
	4.1 *Cases of Disciplining Cadres in Conflict Management*	*199*
	5.1 *Cases of the Disciplining of 1,012 Officials*	*200*

5.2 Cases of High-Ranking Officials Given Serious Legal
    Punishment (N = 41)   203

Notes   205

Index   241

Figures and Tables

Figures

2.1	Number of Petitions and Number of Party Members Disciplined in Guangdong	23
2.2	Higher-Ranking Officials Investigated by Procuratorates	41
3.1	Party Members Disciplined in Guangdong Province in Selected Years	54
5.1	Predicted Probability of Imposing Different Types of Penalties on Officials of Different Ranks	127

Tables

2.1	Disciplining of Party Members in Guangdong Province in Selected Periods	22
2.2	Cases of Duty-Related Malfeasance Accepted by Procuratorates in China	24
2.3	Corruption Cases Accepted by Procuratorates in China	40
3.1	Examples of Campaigns in China from the 1950s to the 1970s	51
3.2	Pressure of Disciplining on the State Authority	59
3.3	Outcomes of Media Exposure	63

3.4	Modes of Discipline (N = 1,122)	65
4.1	Officials Disciplined (N = 898)	73
4.2	Mode of Discipline by the Administrative Rank of Officials (N = 1,122)	75
4.3	Disciplining of Local Officials in Cases of Conflict Management (N = 190)	80
4.4	Disciplining Local Officials in Tax Collection	82
4.5	Disciplining of Officials in Light of Their Responsibility as Leaders	91
4.6	Cases of Duty-Related Malfeasance Handled by Procuratorates in Yunnan Province (1998–2002)	101
5.1	Sources of Information on Corrupt Cadres	106
5.2	Reports Received and Cases Investigated by Disciplinary Agencies in Selected Years	108
5.3	Investigation of Cadres by Discipline Inspection Committees and Supervision Bureaus (1996)	117
5.4	First Agencies to Investigate Cases	121
5.5	Corruption Cases Handled by Procuratorates in Yunnan Province (1998–2002)	123
5.6	Ordinal Logistic Regression of Rank on the Severity of Punishment	126
6.1	Examples of Covering up Coal Mine Accidents	139

Acknowledgments

Many individuals have contributed to this book. Some parts of the manuscript were presented at the City University of Hong Kong, Sun Yat-sen University, Zhejiang University, Xi'an Jiaotong University, Chengchi University of Taiwan, and Tunghai University of Taiwan. I wish to thank the participants for their comments and suggestions. I owe special debts to the two anonymous reviewers whose constructive and insightful comments on the earlier version of the manuscript proved to be very helpful in the subsequent revision of the manuscript.

I am grateful to Zhu Lin, Huang Liang, Chen Jiayi, Wang Yanrong, Tian Yuan, Lin Chang, Zhao Hui, Chen Shulan, Cheng Chen, Liu Liwen, Chen Sirui, and Li Zhi for their help in data collection. Special thanks are due to those officials in China who were willing to participate in my interviews and who inspired my research over the past few years. I also wish to thank Zhou Titi, Wang Jia, and Wang Yige for their assistance in preparing the final manuscript. Research for this project was partly funded by Hong Kong University of Science and Technology.

At Stanford University, I would like to extend my sincere thanks to Michelle Lipinski and Frances Malcolm for their consistent support for this project.

My wife, Wang Chen, and my daughter, Xinyu, have always been the reliable source of support for my research, and I owe them the greatest gratitude for tolerating my spending much time on the research trips and writing. Over the years, my extended family has helped me in ways more than I can count, and I owe them the greatest debt.

Part of Chapter Four draws on materials published in "Disciplining Local Officials in China: The Case of Conflict Management," *The China Journal* (published by University of Chicago Press) no. 70 (2013), 98–119.

ONE

Introduction

In 2011, peasant protests in Wukan village in Guangdong province attracted the attention of the media in and outside China.[1] The protests were provoked by the village cadres, who had sold land without informing or asking permission from the villagers. Although the village cadres were suspected of embezzling a large amount of money obtained through land sales, the other villagers were barely compensated. In September, the villagers began to stage protests in their village and in front of government offices after repeated but unsuccessful petitions. The village representatives negotiated with the town- and county-level authorities but failed to reach a satisfactory solution. In December, the city government of Shanwei solved the dispute by removing the village party secretary and the head while arresting five village representatives for instigating the protests.

The way the city government handled this case is familiar. It disciplined the conflict-provoking cadres to appease the disgruntled villagers while punishing the leaders of the protests or the activists to deter other troublemakers.[2] Most protest incidents end this way, but the Wukan case did not. The county-level authority claimed that all of the major issues raised by the peasants, including the village finances, land issue, and village election, had been resolved, yet the villagers were disappointed because they felt that the government's declaration was untrue. The protests recurred, and the conflict intensified when one of the detained village representatives died in police custody. The government claimed that the representative died of heart disease, a conclusion that the family and other villagers did not accept. Instead, they believed that the representative had died of wounds.

The local government's failure to effectively solve the case and the constant attention of the media eventually led the provincial government to intervene. A team of around twenty high-ranking officials from about ten provincial Party and government agencies was sent to investigate the case. The team was headed by a vice provincial Party secretary, who was also a member of the central Discipline Inspection Commission; the deputy head of the team was a vice governor. When they took over the case, other detained representatives were released (two were on probation), and a reinvestigation into the cause of the representative's death was promised.[3]

The provincial leaders were dissatisfied with the local officials' performance. The head of the investigation team stated that the relationship between some cadres and the people was as incompatible as water and fire. Whether the people were facing difficulties was not these cadres' concern. The head of the team criticized the irresponsibility and irresponsiveness of some cadres, blaming them for failing to consider how the peasants who had lost land could make a living. He said:

> In some places, the government continues to ignore the problems that have long been raised by the people. If the problem can be suppressed, the government will take immediate and harsh measures to suppress it. The next step is to postpone the settlement as long as possible. In the cadres' view, leaving the problems to their successors is preferable. Once they are transferred, whatever happens next will no longer be their business. This mentality is common among local cadres.[4]

Nevertheless, although the criticisms made by the investigation head seemed to be based on what had happened in the Wukan case, the team's attitude toward the local officials involved in the case was not critical. Indeed, the local officials had been irresponsive in addressing this case because between 2009 and 2011, before the large-scale protests began, the Wukan villagers had repeatedly appealed to fourteen government agencies. Despite the lack of response from local officials, the head of the team was positive about the efforts of the county and the city governments, claiming that their earlier efforts created conditions for the ensuing solution to the disputes.[5]

The Wukan case, one of numerous social protests in China in recent years, reveals the issue of local officials' accountability in the country. The dispute occurred at the grassroots level between the villagers and the village cadres, but neither the town government nor the county- or city-level authority was able to handle it properly. Eventually, the provincial authority formed a team of high-ranking provincial officials to deal with it directly. This case also reveals the difficulties of using sanctions to ensure accountability. Although high-ranking officials were dissatisfied with the performance of the local officials, the former did not necessarily take punitive measures to deal with the latter.

In China, the performance of local officials is anchored to the fulfillment of their assigned responsibilities. For example, in the case of conflict management, government officials are assessed for their performance in maintaining social stability, and they will be disciplined if they fail.[6] If the threat of discipline is credible, local officials need to be more responsive, either to accommodate the demands of the disgruntled or to silence them. However, this does not always seem to be the case. Although the central authority prioritizes building a harmonious society and allocates resources for this purpose, social conflicts continue to increase. For example, incidents of collective action in China increased by 14.6 times, from 8,700 to approximately 127,460, between 1993 and 2008.[7] As the Wukan case shows, local officials may be exempted despite their failure in the management of social conflict.

Yet it would be misleading to conclude that Chinese local officials face little risk in failing to perform their duties. As a county Party secretary revealed, "Like scared birds, we are on high alert every day, worrying about production safety, sudden events, mass petitions, and other large-scale incidents that will result in punishment."[8] Others also admitted, "Given the various 'one-item veto' responsibilities, we wish we could keep one eye open even when we sleep. We are anxious all the time, fearing that we will be required to take responsibility."[9] Some local officials are punished or even jailed because of their failures in local governance.[10]

Why are some officials who fail to perform their duties tolerated, whereas others are punished? Answers to this question shed light on the issue of cadre management, governance, and state capacity in China.[11] This book addresses the issue of agent management in China by examining the political rationale behind the sanctioning of erring agents. Variations in the state's attitudes toward malfeasant officials reveal the political dilemma in disciplining state agents. On the one hand, unprincipled tolerance undermines regime legitimacy and the state's authority. On the other hand, disciplining can be costly because the government relies on its agents instead of electoral support to stay in power and to govern.

How does the Chinese party-state deal with this dilemma of disciplining malfeasant agents? This book shows that selective or differentiated discipline is a natural means of balancing the need for and the difficulties in disciplining agents on the part of the state authority. The issue then becomes the criterion that the state adopts in deciding whether and how an erring agent should be punished. Two factors significantly affect a malfeasant official's likelihood of being punished: the severity of the consequences of the official's failure in performing his or her duties or in governance and his or her role or responsibility in the failure. However, the effect of these factors can be mediated by the cost considerations on the part of the state authority or individual leaders.

The selective use of discipline has important implications for the behavior of government officials in China. Differentiated discipline inevitably leads to compromise and to the tolerance of certain agents, thus undermining the credibility of discipline. However, the effectiveness of disciplining in China does not depend on the capacity of the state authority to detect and punish each erring agent but on the non-negligible threat it creates for malfeasant agents when the state authority decides to mete out punishment.

Agents and Accountability

Solnick writes, "In any type of regime—from democratic to authoritarian—rulers need an apparatus to be able to rule. Before any set of leaders can think of governing a population, it must first resolve the problem of governing this state apparatus."[12] The state apparatus is operated by state agents. Skillful and loyal agents are an important component of state power because they determine the effectiveness of governance and thus affect the welfare of the public.[13] However, individuals work for the government for different reasons, so the state cannot rely on the agents' goodwill to ensure their accountability; instead, the state has to regulate the agents' behavior. As Grant and Keohane point out, accountability "implies that some actors have the right to hold other actors to a set of standards, to judge whether they have fulfilled their responsibilities in light of these standards, and to impose sanctions if they determine that these responsibilities have not been met."[14]

In political contexts that involve the delegation of power, accountability is tied to the interaction between the principal that delegates the power and the agents that are given the power and responsibility. Given that the delegation of power inevitably creates the agency problem, characterized by information asymmetries between the principal and the agents, on the one hand, and moral hazards on the other,[15] the principal must take measures to ensure the agents' accountability.[16] First, an alignment of interests can be formed between the principal and the agents, regardless of whether the alignment is based on material benefits or ideological attachment to the same cause. Second, the principal may design institutions *ex ante* to prevent agents from deviating from what the principal has planned. Third, the delegation authority may also take monitoring measures, such as the "police patrol," to detect malfeasance and supervise the agents.[17] Finally, the authority can monitor agents by assessing the outcome of their performance or use *ex post* measures to ensure that the agents fulfill their assigned responsibilities.

Regardless of the measures adopted by the delegation authority, the underlying assumption about the effectiveness of these measures is that agents with good performance will be rewarded and that agents with poor performance or rule-violating behavior will be disciplined. Hence, a political system defines not only to whom an agent must answer but also the types of punishment to be meted out if he or she fails to be accountable.[18] In other words, ensuring accountability requires two equally important measures: rewards and sanctions. O'Flaherty writes that "politics can be nothing more than meting out rewards and punishments, and doing so in a ham-fisted manner."[19] Dunn also reveals that "for accountability to sustain responsiveness, it must be supported by sanctions and awards."[20] Therefore, principals need to provide positive rewards for those who account well for their work[21] and to impose punishment on those who fail to perform their duties or deviate from the rules.[22]

Nevertheless, the use of sanctions to deal with erring agents is not an easy undertaking. In theory, democratic governments generally face a stronger need for disciplining malfeasant agents than their nondemocratic counterparts do. In a mature democracy with elections, a free press, and the rule of law, politicians have limited discretion in protecting erring agents because they and their parties face electoral pressure. As Key suggests, "The only really effective weapon of popular control in a democratic regime is the capacity of the electorate to throw a party from power."[23] Moreover, given the rule of law, agents who engage in serious malfeasance are subject to legal punishment that is beyond the control of politicians.

However, even in democracies, politicians may avoid punishment. One reason is that voters may not have sufficient information to make the right judgment.[24] People's understanding of government behavior is constrained by "the sheer complexity of the social world" and their own "limitations of time and cognitive capacity."[25] Moreover, as Maravall points out, "Governmental action is multidimensional, and voters may want to reject some policies but retain others that they value. Incumbents will fully play a balancing game, making popular and unpopular policies interdependent. Also, citizens may dislike the opposition even more intensely."[26] Another reason is that a society or its constituents can be divided. For example, in India, corrupt officials are not punished partly because of the divisions among the constituencies. Politicians who are corrupt but are able to bring benefits to their communities are still acceptable to their communities. Sondhi writes that, in India, "it is no surprise, therefore, that at times the corrupt political leaders walk majestically to the court and acknowledge their supporters' greetings as if they were to receive an award for public service."[27] Thus, Limaye concludes, "A badly divided electorate cannot be expected to devise effective corrective action against political immorality."[28]

AUTHORITARIAN GOVERNMENTS' DILEMMA

Although a democracy may not always ensure accountability, it is more conducive to accountability than alternative regimes.[29] Consequently, research on the monitoring of state agents in mature democracies tends to focus on the introduction of monitoring mechanisms such as "fire alarms," "police patrols," or other procedures that can prevent the agents' deviations.[30] It is generally assumed that the disciplining of agents who deviate from the rules or regulations is duly carried out.

Compared with democratic governments, authoritarian regimes face limited or no pressure arising from elections. Given their monopoly of political power and their control over the flow of information, authoritarian governments assume more autonomy or discretion in disciplining state agents. However, this discretion does not necessarily ease the issue of discipline. Authoritarian governments rely on their agents for governance and rule, and this reliance complicates the discipline. For one, the use of discipline demoralizes not only the disciplined agents but also their supporters. If the disciplining is not well institutionalized, consensus building is often needed in the decision making, which can be difficult because of factional politics. Furthermore, serious disciplining of certain agents means wasting the resources invested in them. Because of their reliance on their agents, authoritarian governments tend to be more concerned with these difficulties or the costs of discipline.

Yet, a lack of discipline inevitably results in serious consequences or creates concerns for the party-state. One is that a regime's legitimacy will be damaged if the state authority fails to discipline malfeasant agents. Although authoritarian regimes do not rely on legitimacy for survival, they still face the legitimacy constraint and have incentives to build and shore up legitimacy. Authoritarian states with a higher level of legitimacy not only have a better chance of surviving crises but also avoid the cost of imposing strict and constant control over society.[31] As Easton suggests, "A belief in legitimacy is necessary for the maintenance of support, at least for political systems that persist for any appreciable length of time," because legitimacy is a "belief in the right of authorities to rule and members to obey."[32] According to Gamson, "The existing trust orientation toward authorities . . . affects the means of influence a group will use."[33] In other words, people are less likely to take action to overthrow a regime if they still believe in its legitimacy. Therefore, Saxonberg writes, "Even if the Soviet-type regimes never gained complete legitimacy in the sense of gaining popular support for the system, they certainly tried."[34]

Moreover, tolerating malfeasant agents also weakens the state's authority or ability to enforce law and government policies, thereby directly undermining the effectiveness of governance and encouraging more misconduct.[35] An authoritarian government may be reluctant to pay the high cost of punishing its erring agents because the system is built on the support of such agents, but state agents can become predatory if they are not constrained and disciplined.[36] Worse, if the agents' malfeasance cannot be deterred in a timely manner, the state will lose control over the situation. A state's collapse is generally preceded by the unrestrained self-interested behavior of its agents. As Zartman writes, "Probably the ultimate danger sign [of collapse] is when the center loses control over its own state agents, who begin to operate on their own account. Officials exact payments for their own pockets, and law and order is consistently broken by the agents of law and order, the police and army units becoming gangs and brigands."[37]

Rampant corruption in the former Soviet Union highlights both the difficulties in disciplining agents and the consequences of failing to impose such discipline. Simis specifies two important reasons for the corruption in the Soviet Union. The first reason is the regime's fear of destroying the legend that was built up over sixty years by the propaganda machinery of the Soviet Union and the foreign Communist Parties. The legend concerned the infallibility of the Communist Party of the Soviet Union and its leadership, made up of chastely honest "servants of the people" whose personal needs were few and modest. The second reason is that there were simply too many corrupt officials to discipline, and it was too late for the government to stop the corruption:

> Why are the authorities so tolerant of a corruption that has penetrated their own ranks? This tolerance—in a regime that is so forthright and ruthless in punishing all other crimes—is due first and foremost to the fact that too high a proportion of members of the ruling elite is itself involved in the corruption. The proportion is so great that not even the all-powerful Politburo wants to risk a general purge of the ruling elite or the open confrontation with this elite that would result.[38]

Although the agents' malfeasance may not be sufficient to cause the immediate collapse of a regime, the emergence of a large number of malfeasant agents weakens the state's ability to govern and gradually removes its legitimacy. The long-term effects can be regime threatening. The collapse of the former Soviet Union was suggested to be related to the ineffective management of state agents. As Solnick argues, contrary to what is proposed in the extant literature, the Soviet system did not fall victim to stalemate at the top or to a revolution from below but rather to opportunism from within. He suggests that, even before Gorbachev, the mechanisms for controlling bureaucrats in Soviet organizations were already weak, giving these individuals great latitude in their actions. Once the reforms began, they translated this latitude into open insubordination by seizing the very organizational assets they were supposed to be managing. Therefore, the Soviet system suffered the organizational equivalent of a colossal bank run. "The decisive blow to the Soviet state and economy came from the disintegration of structural controls that kept 'the typical soldier or policeman or bureaucrat' loyal to the state. Once the *servants* of the state stopped obeying orders from above, its fate was sealed."[39] When the state lost control over its agents, "These officials were not merely stealing *from* the state, they were stealing the state."[40]

The experience of the former Soviet Union suggests that the state's loss of control over its agents, many of whom were self-interested, was self-defeating. An authoritarian government must properly handle the daunting challenge of managing its agents because the way it addresses this dilemma affects not only its governance but also the regime's survival.

Managing State Agents in China

Due to the large administrative structure and vast number of agents in China, the management of officials has been a challenging task for the party-state. Similar to its counterparts elsewhere, the Chinese authority has adopted both rewards and sanctions to manage state agents. Aside from the efforts to build an efficient and functional government through structural reforms,[41] the Chinese government has instituted rather comprehensive ways of assessing the cadres' performance. In the cadre evaluation system, the party authority is responsible for the selection, promotion, transfer, and removal of cadres using criteria such as qualifications, loyalty, and performance.[42] Research on officials' accountability has investigated the use of rewards, particularly promotion. A number of studies suggest that seeking promotion is an important reason for local officials in China to perform their duties or to achieve more than what is required.[43] Specifically, local officials who have succeeded in economic development, as measured by the growth of GDP or the generation of fiscal revenue, have a better chance of obtaining promotion.[44]

The central party-state uses performance criteria to control local officials' behavior.[45] Similarly, the cadre responsibility system is commonly used by upper-level local authorities to ensure their subordinates' accountability.[46] Under this system, leading officials are assigned responsibilities of varying importance and are under pressure to perform. Whiting showed that town and village officials promote rural industry either because of fiscal and political incentives or because they are under pressure to do so. The officials' performance in economic development, tax collection, and local development is connected to their personal income, promotion, and other consequences.[47] Edin suggests that the cadre responsibility system is not only a means to improve government efficiency but also a higher-level instrument to control lower-level agents and regulate central–local relations. She concludes that the Chinese state retains significant capacity to control and monitor lower-level agents.[48]

Nevertheless, the cadre responsibility system has limitations. Landry maintains that the Chinese Party authority "is proving less able to develop incentive mechanisms that reward ordinary officials and penalize officials who do not perform."[49] It has been found that most cadres are able to pass the performance assessment and are qualified for financial rewards.[50] Indeed, although performance assessment generates serious pressure on leading local officials, "the primary objective of evaluations was not to punish officials but to bring them in line with the policy and developmental requirements and to identify their problem solving capacity."[51] It therefore remains to be explained how the state authority applies sanctions in cadre management.

An analysis of the state authority's use of sanctions is crucial to understanding government officials' behavior in China. McCubbins, Noll, and Weingast point out that, when agents are given the discretion to choose, the "power to choose is the power to manipulate, hold up, and extract."[52] Chinese state agents who are assigned multiple responsibilities assume discretion in prioritizing their responsibilities in light of their careers or personal interests, resulting in selective policy implementation.[53] Policies that are perceived to be of low priority tend to be ignored by local officials. For example, a former deputy minister of the Ministry of Education lamented that "The most severe problem that China faces today is that policies are not being well enforced. Policies made in Zhongnanhai [that is, by the central government] are ignored outside Zhongnanhai."[54] Chinese officials can afford to ignore certain policies because they believe that doing so does not carry serious political risk.

Therefore, the Chinese state's ability to ensure the accountability of its agents is inconsistent. While the party-state retains power in pursuing certain policy goals,[55] various types of malfeasance persist among government officials. Examining how sanctions or disciplinary measures have been applied to erring agents sheds light on state capacity. This book explores agent management in China by focusing on the political rationale behind the state's use of selective or differentiated discipline.

USE OF SANCTIONS

For analytical convenience, Chinese government officials' malfeasance can be divided into two categories: (1) immoral and illegal self-regarding behavior and (2) duty-related malfeasance. Immoral and illegal self-regarding behavior refers to activities performed to achieve self-interests or illegal personal gains, such as corruption. Duty-related malfeasance refers to rule- or law-violating activities associated with an agent's performing of his or her duties, including failure to perform and dereliction of duties. Compared with duty-related malfeasance, illegal behavior for personal gains is less justifiable, either ideologically or legally.

Chinese local officials' malfeasance has persisted ever since the Communist Party came to power. Like other authoritarian governments, the Chinese government is under pressure to discipline erring agents for two reasons. The first is the legitimacy constraint. The Chinese party-state is motivated to shore up legitimacy and is more likely to do so when it already enjoys a relatively high level of legitimacy. Various surveys have consistently shown that the Chinese people have a rather high level of political trust in the government,[56] especially the central government.[57] The party-state's wish to gain and sustain legitimacy constitutes a pressure of accountability. When failing to discipline erring agents is believed to damage the regime's legitimacy, the state authority comes under pressure to mete out punishment.

The second reason is the state authority's concern over its authority. Specifically, the state needs to punish agents who violate laws, rules, or government policies or who fail to perform their duties, to protect its authority and deter deviations. In a political hierarchy, the top-level authority will lose its reputation and control over its agents if it fails to duly punish erring agents.[58] Relaxed discipline leads to the "leakage of authority" at lower levels of the hierarchy. Downs explains how the leakage of authority occurs as orders pass through the levels of a political hierarchy: Official A issues an order to B, but B's own goals indicate that his commands to his subordinate C should encompass only 90 percent of what he believes A actually has in mind. If C thinks in the same way, by the time A's order reaches level D officials, these officials will receive commands encompassing only 81 percent (90 percent of 90 percent) of what A really intends.[59] Such leakages cumulate when many levels are involved, which can have a striking effect on the effectiveness of orders issued by top-level officials.[60] In agent management, the leakage of authority may result in unprincipled tolerance of erring agents at lower levels.

These two needs or constraints constitute significant pressure on the party-state in agent management in China. Given that the Party monopolizes political power and is responsible for cadre management,[61] the operation of disciplinary agencies is influenced heavily by the Party authority or its leaders.[62] Decisions on important issues, including the punishment of important officials, are influenced or decided by important party and government leaders at each level, often through consensus building. However, power comes with responsibility. The need for disciplining agents generally translates into the *positional responsibilities* that decision makers, as the power holders, need to fulfill to meet the expectations of either the public (for central leaders) or the upper-level authorities (for local leaders) or both. Such positional responsibilities dictate that the state authority's tolerance of erring agents is conditional.

Nevertheless, the state authority at each level relies on lower-level agents for governance, and the leaders also face difficulties or costs in disciplining the agents. The leaders' cost considerations can be related to their personal and organizational interests. Decision makers can be connected to the erring agent because of patron–client relations or personal connections. Officials at different levels can also be connected because they are both responsible for an undesirable event or have engaged in corruption. At other times, the decision makers are constrained by considerations tied to organizational interests, such as protecting the agents' morale, maintaining the stability of institutions or unity among decision makers, or covering up and thereby tolerating agents' malfeasance to protect the regime's legitimacy.

Given the need for and cost of disciplining agents, both disciplining and tolerance are possible in agent management. Whether an erring agent is to be tolerated largely depends on the severity of the consequence of the agent's malfeasance (that is, consequence severity) and the agent's responsibility for the malfeasance (that is, blame attribution). State agents, including high-ranking officials, are most likely to be punished if their behavior directly causes severe consequences, such as damaging the regime's legitimacy, violating laws or rules, or challenging the state's policy priorities, or involves serious failures in governance or duties.

Agents who are not directly responsible for problems with severe consequences may still be disciplined if the authority faces pressure to show its accountability and to prevent similar problems from recurring. However, as there is an issue of fairness in blaming or attributing responsibility in such cases, there is room to manipulate the discipline. Agents who are held accountable for severe problems that are not directly caused by them may be forgiven or rehabilitated later on. In other words, their political careers may not be significantly and adversely affected.

Understandably, the state authority or its decision makers face substantially less pressure to mete out punishment if the consequences of an agent's malfeasance are not severe, regardless of whether the agent is directly responsible for the problem. In other words, when agents' malfeasance falls into the zone of tolerance of the state authority, they are generally exempted. State tolerance is the reason for the persistence of state agents' abuse of power and other types of malfeasance.

Depending on the degree to which an agent's malfeasance is perceived to be forgivable, the state authority may exercise leniency in meting out punishment through the use of various methods that can reduce the effect of discipline. One way is to give the agent a lighter punishment, which is possible because of the availability of multiple modes of discipline. Government officials are subject to party discipline, government or administrative discipline, organization-based discipline, and/or legal punishment (see Chapter Three). Each mode of discipline specifies varying degrees of punishment severity. Severe forms of discipline include expulsion from the Party, termination by the government, and prosecution in court. Once an official has been severely disciplined, his or her political career will probably be at an end. However, the availability of different disciplinary modes gives the authorities and pertinent leaders the discretion to mete out punishment, enabling them to protect agents they favor. For example, instead of criminal punishment, they may impose administrative or party discipline.[63]

Another way of reducing the effect of discipline on targeted agents, at least those who are not being punished because of their pursuit of illegal personal gains such as corruption, is to exercise *ex post* leniency. Specifically, this leniency is usually wielded when disciplined officials commit less severe malfeasance, commit malfeasance to fulfill assigned responsibilities, or shoulder the blame for upper-level authorities as scapegoats. Often, a punished official who has been removed from his or her post can later be assigned a new post of a similar or slightly lower administrative rank.

Thus, an agent's malfeasance can be ignored, covered up, or investigated, and the agent can be tolerated or disciplined depending on the severity of the consequences, the attribution of responsibility, and the decision makers' cost considerations. The coexistence of tolerance and discipline by no means implies that discipline has no credibility in China, because the pressure of accountability that the state authority or the leaders face can be beyond the anticipation of malfeasant agents. Although some agents have been exempted or given less serious punishments, whether a particular agent will be held liable may not be predetermined. Inconsistency in the disciplining of erring agents implies uncertainty. When the party-state decides to mete out punishment, the penalty can be harsh and career ending. For this reason, state agents in China are strongly motivated to avoid blame and punishment by adopting various strategies, from covering up their malfeasance to seeking help through personal connections (see Chapter Six).

Middle-Level Agents and Selective Accountability

To understand the disciplining of government officials in China, where the majority of state agents work for local-level state agencies, it is essential to understand the role of upper-level local authorities. In 2003, for example, there were about 6.4 million public servants in China. Of these, 7.5 percent worked for central state agencies, 8.4 percent for provincial agencies, 22.7 percent for city-level agencies, and 61.4 percent for county-level agencies (44.7 percent) and town authorities (16.7 percent).[64] The *nomenklatura* system also includes a large number of government-appointed cadres in non-administrative public agencies such as schools and hospitals and in state-owned businesses.

In this political hierarchy, direct monitoring and disciplining of the numerous local agents is beyond the capacity of the central authority. Consequently, the power and responsibility for monitoring local agents is inevitably delegated to upper-level local party and government authorities. These upper-level local leaders assume a double identity: They are agents of upper-level authorities, including the central government, and also the principals of lower-level officials. Given their position, the behavior of these middle-level principals significantly affects policy enforcement and the accountability of local governments and their officials.

EXCESSIVE EFFORTS VERSUS LEAKAGE OF AUTHORITY

The double identity of middle-level principals affects their interactions with their principals and their agents.[65] Local officials are delegated various responsibilities that they inevitably prioritize, and their prioritizing is significantly shaped by how they are assessed. Officials who are motivated to seek promotion devote more resources, energy, and attention to the responsibilities or "hard targets" that bear most directly on their tenure and promotion.[66] They extend fewer efforts to those that do not weigh much on their career. Such prioritizing may lead to the officials expending excessive efforts on outrunning their peers or to the phenomenon of "leakage of authority."[67]

Studies on the behavior of Chinese local officials show that China's rapid economic development is to a large extent due to the incentive structure instituted by the party authority. As elsewhere, agents who highly value their promotion goals find that "no matter how far one has climbed, there is always the same distance to go."[68] Promotion seekers resort to various means to achieve good performance or make up good performance to outrun their peers.[69] This promotion-seeking motivation and the adoption of excessive measures have a long history in China. Kung and Chen show that the radicalism during China's Great Leap Famine had much to do with the promotion-seeking desire of alternate members of the central Party committee.[70] In recent years, environmental pollution and social conflict in China have also been associated with local officials' motivation to achieve good performance.

Career-driven local officials have weak incentive to fulfill responsibilities that do not significantly affect their careers, especially when they believe that such responsibilities are not the priorities of the central authority either. When managing agents, local leaders or middle-level principals must fulfill their positional responsibilities to meet the expectations of the upper-level authorities and sometimes the public. However, local leaders are unlikely to put excessive effort into disciplining agents to outrun their peers, because such actions are costly and not a major criterion for assessing their performance. Compared with central leaders, local leaders face a different incentive structure in dealing with malfeasant subordinates. Specifically, protecting regime legitimacy is not the prior concern of local leaders because they are not the primary representatives of the regime.[71] As agents of the central party-state or upper-level superiors, local leaders' primary concern is to show their accountability to upper-level authorities. They come under pressure to punish their subordinates when the latter's malfeasance is known to the central- or upper-level authority and the public.

Leakage of authority occurs in the punishment of malfeasant agents when local leaders believe that disciplining officials is not a top priority of the central authority. Cost considerations sometimes serve as an incentive for local leaders to tolerate or even protect their subordinates. The possible leakage of authority constitutes a serious pressure on the central authority and prompts it to showcase the disciplining of some erring agents because unprincipled tolerance can only amplify the demonstration effect at the local level.

MIDDLE-LEVEL PRINCIPALS AND LOCAL INITIATION OF REFORM

The tolerance or leniency exercised by the state authority has important implications for officials' behavior. On the one hand, tolerance means that discipline is not a credible threat to some state agents, leading to the persistence of officials' malfeasance, such as corruption, abuse of power, and other forms of conflict-provoking behavior. At both the central and local levels, tolerance may also create a so-called protection umbrella that undermines people's confidence in the disciplinary institutions or even the political system.[72] These resulting problems are a serious concern of the party-state, indicating a strong need for the rule of law and the strengthening of disciplinary institutions.

On the other hand, flexibility in the disciplining of government officials or leniency on the part of the party-state also creates political space for rule-violating reform in the political system. Decentralization in China grants local officials both power and responsibility in local governance. Given that the central government's policies may not fit local situations and prevent local development, local officials have modified, adapted, or even distorted policies to deal with their respective situations. Local officials may also initiate reforms to change existing policies or institutions.[73] However, the problem faced by reform-minded officials is that their practices may break or violate existing rules or even laws. Without the tolerance or support of upper-level local leaders or middle-level principals, local officials' reform efforts are unlikely to succeed. Therefore, the flexibility embedded in the disciplinary institutions creates pockets of innovation or reform. Such pockets of reform have proved to be crucial to the economic and political development of the country, as evidenced by the important reforms initiated by local officials, such as the dismantling of the commune system and the trial of the tax-for-fee reform. Local initiations contribute to regime resilience because they can serve as solutions to certain serious challenges faced by the party-state.

Note on the Definition of Government Officials

The former Soviet Union adopted the *nomenklatura* system for managing state agents. This system encompasses state employees whose appointments are decided by a Party organ of appropriate seniority, from the district committee up to the Politburo and the Secretariat.[74] Most of those (that is, 60 percent of the 750,000) included in the *nomenklatura* are responsible for the management of industrial and agricultural production or are employed in the science and education sectors. Party and government employees account for about 33 percent and others for about 7 percent.[75]

The Chinese political system is modeled on that of the former Soviet Union, and the cadres are selected by upper-level authorities.[76] The concept of cadres, or *ganbu*, in China is also broader and includes Party, government, and army officials and also high-ranking employees in public enterprises, nonadministrative public agencies (for example, hospitals and universities), and mass organizations.[77] Only high-ranking cadres are included in the *nomenklatura* system.

As in the former Soviet Union, those who work in public enterprises account for the majority of the cadres in China.[78] In recent years, with the separation of public enterprises and nonadministrative public agencies from the government, lower-ranking cadres working in public firms and nonadministrative public agencies are no longer considered state cadres. The term *officials* is more frequently used to indicate cadres in party and government agencies. The revised Civil Servants Law that took effect in January 2006 states that civil servants in China include public employees who work in the government, Party, people's congress, political consultative conference, court, procuratorate, and organizations of democratic parties. This book focuses mainly on officials who hold administrative positions in Party and government agencies.

Organization of This Book

Chapter Two categorizes the officials' malfeasance into duty-related malfeasance and immoral and illegal self-regarding behavior. By examining government officials' malfeasance in different periods, this chapter shows that some types of malfeasance, such as corruption, have persisted in China ever since the Communist Party came to power, whereas others have existed only in certain periods because of the specific political environment. The persistence of agents' malfeasance highlights the need for the continued monitoring and disciplining of state agents.

Chapter Three addresses the political rationale for disciplining state agents in China by exploring how the officials who are responsible for the discipline balance their positional responsibilities with cost considerations in managing agents. It highlights the severity of the consequences arising from an agent's malfeasance and the way blame or responsibility is attributed. However, the effect of consequence severity and blame attribution can be mediated by the state authority's cost considerations. This chapter also discusses why differentiated discipline can still be credible in China.

Chapter Four illustrates the political logic of disciplining state agents for duty-related malfeasance. Consequence severity and blame attribution combine to affect a malfeasant agent's likelihood of being disciplined. Using the case of conflict management, this chapter explores why some agents who fail to prevent social conflict are disciplined while others are tolerated. It also discusses the circumstances under which high-ranking officials are disciplined for their duty-related malfeasance. This chapter demonstrates how the state authority exercises *ex post* leniency in disciplining erring agents and discusses the reasons for such leniency.

Chapter Five focuses on the punishment of corrupt agents. The state authority often faces two choices in dealing with corrupt agents, in the sense that corrupt agents can only either be tolerated or imposed criminal charges. The cost of discipline is therefore salient in handling corruption cases. By exploring the detection, investigation, and punishment of corrupt agents, this chapter shows that the Party is often cautious in dealing with corrupt agents, especially high-ranking officials. Nevertheless, once the state authority, especially the central authority, decides to investigate and discipline corrupt agents, the punishments are likely to be severe. In this way, the central authority tries to demonstrate its commitment to eliminating corruption, thereby reducing the leakage of authority at the local level.

Chapter Six explores the strategies that Chinese government officials use to avoid responsibility and punishment. Traditionally, Chinese government officials cover up their malfeasance from upper-level authorities and the public. Malfeasant agents may also try to avoid responsibility by using justifications or excuses or by finding scapegoats. They will also seek leniency or protection from pertinent leaders when they are unable to cover up their malfeasance or defend themselves. These blame-avoiding activities may complicate the disciplining of officials.

Chapter Seven discusses the political implications of the flexible disciplining of state agents for economic and political development in China. Given the countrywide variation in local conditions, local officials may introduce initiatives or new policy measures to solve the practical issues they face. However, doing so may carry political risks because some of these local initiatives violate laws or government regulations. Flexibility or relaxation in the disciplining of government officials creates political space for such initiatives to be possible. Some local initiatives serve as important solutions to the practical problems faced by the central or other local governments and thus contribute to the resilience of the political system in China.

Chapter Eight concludes by discussing the political rationale behind the disciplining of state agents in China, highlighting both the constraints and the pressures faced by the state authority in dealing with erring agents. This chapter also discusses the political implications of such discipline for state capacity and governance in China.

TWO

Government Officials' Malfeasance in China

In *Politics as a Vocation*, Weber suggests two ways of turning politics into a profession: One can either live for it or off it. Those who live for it make politics their life, either because they enjoy power or because they serve some cause. Those who live off it strive to make it their permanent source of income.[1] Therefore, some people work for the government or become politicians because they have certain policy preferences or are motivated by public interests, whereas others may be motivated more by self-interest. Downs writes that, in the United States, there are times when "every official acts at least partly in his own self-interest, and some officials are motivated solely by their own self-interest."[2] Similarly, Ames notes that in Latin America the main reasons for leaders wanting to stay in power are known only to themselves. Some simply covet the trappings of office; others hope to bestow benefits on a certain class, region, or ethnic group; and still others believe that they are building a better future for their nations or advancing the cause of liberty.[3] Regardless of their motivation, politicians must be (re)elected or fulfill other requirements to stay in power.

Government officials in China are not different from their counterparts in other societies in terms of their motivations for working for the party-state. Some work for the party-state because of their policy preferences, whereas others accept such jobs to make a living or pursue personal interests. Also like politicians elsewhere, Chinese government officials need to fulfill their responsibilities to stay in power or seek promotion. This pressure arises not because they face elections but because they must meet the performance assessment conducted by upper-level authorities.[4]

Government officials' self-interest and desire to stay in power may lead to their abuse of power. When officials are motivated or partly motivated by personal interests, they are likely to engage in the pursuit of illegal personal gain, such as corruption. Such malfeasance has been continuous in China ever since the Communist Party came to power. Furthermore, the pressure to demonstrate good performance has led government officials, especially those at the local level, to resort to all possible means, including illegal ones, to achieve the required performance levels. Such duty-related malfeasance may sacrifice the interests of the people, local communities, or the state. An examination of the different types of malfeasance committed by government officials reveals the continuities and changes in government officials' behavior in China.

Officials' Malfeasance in Socialist China

A reasonable assumption about Chinese government officials is that their primary goal is to stay in power so that they can pursue their policy preferences or personal interests. Therefore, the priorities of government officials in China can be assumed to be (1) keeping their positions and/or seeking promotion, (2) seeking personal and family welfare, and (3) serving the people or the community. Some officials may prioritize "serving the people" over "seeking personal welfare," but many other officials regard their own interests as a priority or pursue personal gains even at the expense of the interests of the people. Correspondingly, officials' malfeasance can be divided into two broad categories: (1) the pursuit of illegal personal gain (that is, corruption) and (2) malfeasance in performing their duties or responsibilities.

Government officials' malfeasance persists in socialist China.[5] Guangdong Province released relatively consistent statistics on the disciplining of Party members and public employees from the 1950s to the 1990s, with missing data during the period of the Cultural Revolution. Table 2.1 indicates the reasons for disciplining Party members in this province during three selected periods. Party members disciplined because of political charges or crimes accounted for approximately 22 percent of the total number of Party members penalized between 1956 and 1965. Political changes caused a dramatic decline in such political charges after the late 1970s and particularly during the 1990s.

TABLE 2.1.
Disciplining of Party members in Guangdong Province in selected periods.

Misconduct	1956–1965	1979–1993	1994–1995
Economic interests	22.7	17.0	36.1
Dissolute lifestyle	12.4	15.3	16.4
Failure of governance	17.1	3.0	5.3
Political mistakes/crimes	21.7	2.9	0.7
Violations of family planning		29.7	15.3
Miscellaneous	26.1	32.1	26.2
Total (percentage)	100	100	100
Total number	136,552	81,471	5,090

SOURCE: Compiled from the Discipline Inspection Committee and the Supervision Bureau of Guangdong Province (ed.), *Guangdong jijian jiancha zhi* (A record of discipline inspection in Guangdong province: 1950–1995) (Guangzhou: Guangdong renmin chubanshe, 1999), 138, 144, 150, 151.

Table 2.1 shows that the majority of Party members were disciplined because of malfeasance associated with their personal interests, such as embezzlement, accepting bribes, extracting bribes, and speculation. Such misconduct can generally be regarded as corruption. More Party members were punished for pursuing their own economic interests between 1994 and 1995 than in the two other periods, as indicated in the table. Some Party members were also accused of leading a dissolute life, often meaning that they were womanizing and leading a life of luxury, in striking contrast with the simple or poor lives of many people. Interestingly, a significant proportion of Party members in Guangdong were punished because they violated the family planning policy, which continued up to the 1990s.

Most government officials were Party members, but not all Party members held administrative positions in the Party or government organs. This could be why the number of Party members punished for governance problems, mainly the so-called bureaucratic working style that leads to the dereliction of duty, did not constitute a large proportion of cases except between 1956 and 1965.

In China, state–citizen disputes remain an important source of social conflict. However, statistics seem to suggest that only a limited number of Party members were disciplined for violations of citizens' rights. Among the cases concluded by the disciplinary agencies in Guangdong Province between 1979 and 1995, the number of people punished for such violations accounted for between 1 and 6.5 percent. However, this finding does not imply that violations of citizens' rights were rare. As Figure 2.1 shows, from the 1980s to 1995, Guangdong Province had a large number of petitions,

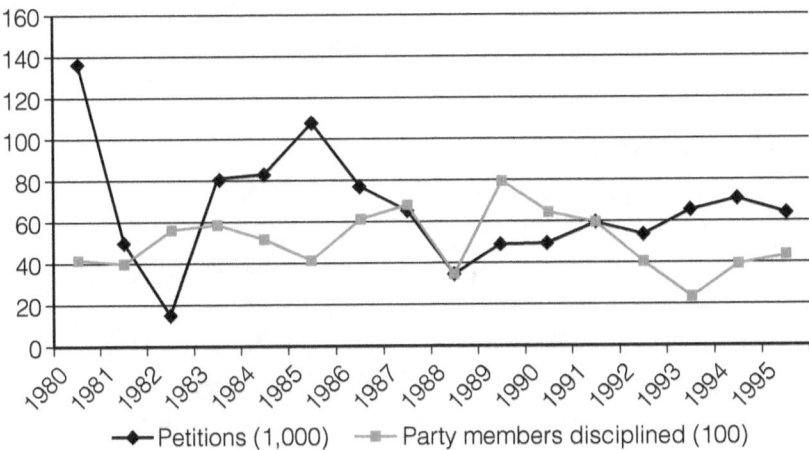

FIGURE 2.1. Number of petitions and number of Party members disciplined in Guandong.

SOURCE: The Discipline Inspection Committee and the Supervision Bureau of Guandong Province (ed.) 1999, 46, 150, 151.

much larger than the number of Party members disciplined. For example, the number of petitions received by the disciplinary agencies reached 137,000 in 1980, but only 4,100, or less than 3 percent, of cadres were disciplined. Figure 2.1 suggests no positive correlation between the number of petitions and the number of party members disciplined.

Several reasons account for the lack of a positive correlation. One is that not all grievances filed by petitioners involved government officials. Moreover, the state authority did not believe that individual government officials should be responsible for citizens' grievances, and thus they were not punished. For example, in the 1950s, some peasants who had joined rural cooperatives in various provinces, including Guangdong, demanded exit. When their requests were rejected, serious conflicts ensued between the peasants and local cadres. As the plan was a political issue, the peasants instead of officials were sometimes punished.[6] Another reason for the lack of correlation is that citizens' petitions against abusive officials are often ignored. Indeed, petitions are not an effective way of seeking justice because government officials who fail to address citizens' problems or who violate citizens' rights may not be disciplined despite citizens' complaints.[7]

The remainder of this chapter explores the two broad types of malfeasance of government officials, duty-related malfeasance and immoral and illegal self-regarding behavior. An examination of such malfeasance reveals not only the reasons behind it but also the operation of the political system.

Duty-Related Malfeasance

Chinese government officials have been blamed for their abuse of power for both personal gain and policy implementation. They have also been criticized for being irresponsible and irresponsive in performing their duties. Government officials can be given criminal penalties if their malfeasance breaks the state law. Official statistics report cases of duty-related crimes (*duzhi qinquan*) that include abuse of power (*lanyong zhiquan*), neglect of duty (*wanhu zhishou*), engaging in favoritism for selfish ends (*xunsi wubi*), and others. Table 2.2 reports such cases accepted by procuratorates in China between 1998 and 2010. The number of accepted cases declined by about 40 percent over this period; proportionally, however, cases concerning abuse of power and neglect of duty increased over the years.

Government officials can be accused of abuse of power when they use power for personal gain or fail to use their administrative power properly. In one example, a township official in Guangdong granted the use right of a piece of forestry land to a person who then illegally opened a mine on the land and destroyed the forest. The township official was accused of abuse of power and was sentenced to three years in jail in 2008. In another example,

TABLE 2.2.
Cases of duty-related malfeasance accepted by procuratorates in China.

	Cases	Abuse of power (percentage)	Neglect of duty (percentage)	Favoritism (percentage)	Miscellaneous (percentage)
1998	19,284	9.1	17.6	34.1	39.3
1999	19,801	13.1	20.1	31.9	34.9
2000	20,966	18.2	21.4	31.4	28.9
2001	20,710	22.2	22.5	31.8	23.5
2002	18,252	24.2	22.6	31.5	21.8
2003	15,699	25.8	25.7	27.7	20.8
2004	15,395	26.5	27.0	25.2	21.4
2005	14,331	28.8	30.4	22.8	18.0
2006	12,810	30.5	33.7	19.6	16.1
2007	12,803	30.7	36.1	17.9	15.3
2008	12,884	33.4	38.6	16.5	11.6
2009	12,589	32.9	39.7	15.3	12.1
2010	11,619	33.3	41.0	14.4	11.3

SOURCE: *Zhongguo jiancha nianjian* (Procuratorial Yearbook of China) (1999–2011).

in 2009, the former head of a district social security bureau in Guangzhou loaned 7 million yuan from the social security fund to a company that failed to pay back 6 million of the loan. This head was accused of abuse of power, misuse of public funds, and corruption and was sentenced to sixteen years in jail.[8]

Government officials also abuse power to achieve performance. Downs suggests that officials can be categorized into climbers and conservers. Climbers consider power, income, and prestige as all-important in their value structures, whereas conservers consider convenience and security as all-important. In contrast to climbers, conservers merely seek to retain the amount of power, income, and prestige they already have rather than to maximize them.[9] In China, both climbers and conservers face the pressure of fulfilling the requirements to keep their positions or obtain promotion. Although government officials may not always seek tenure and/or promotion by ignoring the interests of the public and the community, various types of malfeasance are associated with the achievement of performance on the part of government officials. Some types of malfeasance are illegal, whereas others cannot be defined as crimes.

ABUSE OF POWER AND PREDATORY BEHAVIOR

The primary responsibility of government officials, especially those at the local level, is to enforce policies made by upper-level governments. As local officials are held accountable to upper-level authorities instead of to the people, the officials may sacrifice the people's interests to fulfill their responsibilities when necessary. Local officials have interpreted government policies to their advantage, distorted policies, and abused power in policy implementation. When upper-level local leaders are under pressure to enforce certain policies, such pressure is also shifted to their subordinates.

Abuse of power by local officials is not rare in policy implementation, as exemplified by the enforcement of the family planning policy. As already mentioned, between 1980 and 1993, 24,140 Party members were disciplined in Guangdong for violating the policy.[10] Some Party members were punished because they violated the policy themselves, whereas others were punished because they failed to enforce the policy. For example, a county magistrate in this province was disciplined in 1991. This magistrate lied that his first child, a girl, had died; he then had a second child who was also a girl. He wanted a divorce so that he could father a boy.[11]

Some citizens have also violated this policy, and local officials have taken harsh measures in dealing with them. Birth control used to be the highest-priority national policy in rural China. To fulfill this "hard target,"[12] the so-called one-item veto system was introduced to ensure effective enforcement of the policy, which meant that the performance of major local leaders would be vetoed if they failed in this policy, regardless of their other achievements. In the face of such pressure, local officials resorted to almost all possible means, including pulling down homes, taking away property, detention, and forced abortion, to prevent the birth of extra children. To show their resolution, local governments used slogans such as "We would rather see a river of blood than an extra child" and "No ligation, no house; no abortion, no property."[13] Rural cadres might suddenly assault households with pregnant women and take them away for abortion, and some females who underwent surgery suffered long-term health problems. Local officials would even take away babies considered to have been born illegally.[14]

Local officials have also become predatory when faced with the pressure of fulfilling their responsibilities. For example, throughout the 1990s, numerous conflicts, including deadly confrontations, occurred between peasants and local cadres over the collection of fees and taxes.[15] According to the central government, at least seventeen peasants died in 1992, around forty-seven between 1994 and 1996, and thirty between 2002 and 2004.[16] Under the pressure of collecting enough revenue to fulfill their responsibilities, local officials, especially those at the township and village levels, resorted to various means, including violence. Township governments sent fee-collection teams to peasant households to confiscate grain, property such as television sets, and livestock. They also detained peasants who refused to pay or forced them to join the so-called closed-door training sessions, which essentially aimed to detain peasants until they agreed to pay. Local authorities also abused the legal system by putting peasants who resisted in jail. Some local cadres also abused their power in tax collection to line their own pockets.[17]

In recent years, local governments at each level have placed increasing emphasis on economic development and fiscal income. Fiscal revenue is important because it directly affects the operation of the government and public agencies (for example, schools). Unlike the report on the gross domestic product (GDP) growth rate, the generation of fiscal revenue cannot be easily manipulated.[18] According to a survey of twenty townships in ten provinces in the early 2000s, township leaders face two basic responsibilities: generating revenue to pay public employees and sustain the operation of the government, and maintaining social stability.[19] A major mode of revenue generation in many local governments across the country is land development. Given that most taxes and fees generated from land development are collected by local governments but are not shared with the central government, local governments have a strong incentive to lease land for commercial purposes. As a result, aside from taxes and fees, the rent generated from land leases has become a major source of local revenue. Nationwide revenues from land leases increased by 6,732 times, from 0.45 billion yuan in 1989 to 3,000 billion yuan in 2010.[20] Such land-dependent revenue generation is particularly obvious in more developed areas such as Shanghai, Beijing, Guangzhou, and Hangzhou but is also becoming increasingly important in less-developed areas.

Local governments can obtain land for development by nationalizing rural collective land or by carrying out urban renewal. Land use in both urban and rural areas has sacrificed the interests of citizens. Research based on province-level petition data suggests that petitions are more common in provinces where the government relies more on revenue from land development.[21] As a zero-sum game often exists between the government or other land users and residents, conflicts over land use are common. Local governments and other land users tend to minimize their costs by providing inadequate compensation to those who lose land. In urban areas, urban renewal or development usually involves the relocation of residents, and conflicts arise when residents who lose their homes are unreasonably compensated.[22] In rural areas, disputes arising from the nonagricultural use of farmland by external actors have been the major source of conflicts since the abolition of agricultural tax. An estimated 65 percent of the incidents of collective action in rural China were related to land in 2010.[23]

Given the priority of economic development and revenue generation, local governments have adopted or tolerated environment-sacrificing practices.[24] City and county governments commonly prioritize attracting external investment, and local officials are assessed based on their achievement of this task.[25] Local governments at the county and township levels usually assign an external investment quota to each government agency and each major government official, linking the fulfillment of this task to the official's salary, bonus, and/or promotion.[26]

Against this background, environmental protection is no longer a primary concern of local governments, even though some of the external investments become polluting projects. According to a 2006 survey by the provincial environmental protection bureau of Shanxi province, about 92 percent of officials (at the administrative level of city mayor) reported that environmental protection would negatively affect economic development.[27] The pressure to generate revenue and the competition between officials causes local governments to tolerate environmental deterioration and serious pollution. There have been a number of "cancer villages" in China. In 2000, the government of a township in Yancheng in Jiangsu Province attracted an investor who built a chemical factory. Within a few years, more than 100 people in three nearby villages died of cancer, and a number of domestic animals were killed by the pollution. Villagers who complained about the pollution were detained by the police. The township and county governments refused to close the factory for a simple reason: It generated a large amount of revenue that was crucial to the government's operations.[28]

When local officials are pressured to fulfill their assigned responsibilities, their abuse of power may be tolerated or even protected simply because they serve local interests or the interests of local leaders. Tolerated or protected abuse of power becomes possible also because local legal institutions are under the control of the local party-state. For example, in the enforcement of the family planning policy, courts were not allowed to accept citizens' lawsuits against local cadres or local governments. Therefore, the illegal use of power by local officials may not be corrected through legal means.

POLICY DISTORTION

According to Streeck and Thelen, rule takers do not just implement the rules made for them but also try to revise or manipulate them in the process of implementation.[29] Chinese local officials have also manipulated policy implementation to cater to local or personal interests. Again, one example is the enforcement of the family planning policy. In less-developed areas, some local authorities see the fines paid by households who want to have an extra child or extra children as a source of income. For example, a family planning office in a township in Henan province had as many as twenty-two employees in the early 2000s. The county family planning committee assigned an income-making task to this township office, requiring each employee to generate a non-negotiable income of between 1,500 and 2,000 yuan per month. This income was to be created by selling a quota for extra births at a price between 1,400 and 5,000 yuan each. Each employee was assigned to work in several villages and was expected to persuade or even encourage young or middle-aged peasants to have more children. In doing so, the cadres promised that there would be no ligation or abortion once the women became pregnant. An employee would be offered 300 yuan as a reward or bonus for each extra child beyond the regulated quota but would be forced to leave his or her position after failing to meet the quota.[30]

Policy distortion also occurs in revenue generation. In addition to abusing their power over land development, local officials also manipulate tax collection to generate assigned revenue. One example is the practice of "tax borrowing" among township governments. In this practice, if Township A has fulfilled its quota yet still has taxes to collect, while Township B does not have enough taxes to fulfill its quota, B may borrow taxes from A. If A agrees, it will allow its enterprises to pay taxes to B, and B in turn pays transaction fees to the tax collection department in A. In the future, when A needs to borrow taxes from B, the same system is practiced in reverse.[31]

Another practice—tax buying—may be more common, although it is illegal. In this practice, the township government invites external businesses to pay their taxes at a discounted rate. For example, if the rate for a certain tax is 5 percent, a township government may allow an external taxpayer to pay 3 percent (thereby lowering the tax rate), so that the latter will be willing to pay the tax to this particular township. The taxpayer's payment ticket or receipt still indicates that the firm has paid 5 percent. As the township government needs to remit an amount of the tax based on 5 percent, there is a 2 percent gap (that is $5 - 3 = 2$), which is the price paid by the township government for "buying tax." This 2 percent can be included in the cost of tax collection incurred by the township government. Buying tax is feasible because the tax payment ticket in some business sectors is unified across a province or a country, which enables some firms to pay taxes in different places.[32]

Township cadres mainly approach construction or transportation firms as targets for buying taxes because these firms often conduct business outside their headquarters. As a result, when construction projects are underway, township government officials sometimes approach the construction firms, usually through personal connections, and invite them to pay taxes to their townships.[33] If there is competition among township governments that intend to buy taxes, the taxpayer pays even less. The discount enjoyed by taxpayers can be as high as 40 percent.[34]

Although the township that buys the taxes incurs a loss, this has become a popular option in less-developed areas because it serves the more important interests of the township government. This measure was reportedly adopted in some places as early as 1996 but has become more common partly because the "tax-for-fee" reform and the abolition of agricultural tax in 2004 reduced the revenue of local governments. Township officials who buy taxes commonly report that they do so because of pressure from superiors. For example, in Gansu Province, the total amount of taxes collected in several townships was about 9 million yuan, but the assigned quota was as high as 40.8 million yuan. The large gap forced local officials to use all possible means, including buying taxes, to fulfill the quota. In 2006, a township party secretary commented, "Buying taxes is actually a means by which the government helps businesses to evade taxes. But by doing this, township cadres can be paid and their performance quotas are met. It is the state that suffers the loss."[35]

Similar to the cases of power abuse discussed earlier, a salient characteristic of officials' behavior in China is that they pay more attention to the outcome or goals than to the means to achieve the goals. Given that upper-level authorities rely on grassroots officials for governance and policy enforcement, these officials do not necessarily face serious risks when taking rule-violating measures to fulfill their responsibilities.

IRRESPONSIBLE BEHAVIOR

Local officials are deeply involved in economic development in China.[36] The question of involvement does not concern "how much" but "what kind."[37] Some local officials manipulate the presentation of their achievements by undertaking activities that waste public resources and fail to benefit local communities. Specifically, they carry out so-called face projects (*mianzi gongcheng*), image-enhancing projects (*xingxiang gongcheng*), or performance projects (*zhengji gongcheng*). A local official stated, "As the term of cadres is only a few years, they worry about their promotion prospects if they do not attain a good performance record. Some of them have to adopt 'image-enhancing projects.'"[38]

Image-enhancing projects have three characteristics. First, these projects are a means to an end, and they exist in a number of areas from infrastructure construction to mode of economic development. Second, as the aim is to establish projects of impressive appearance, their actual functions are not a major concern of those who launch them. As one report suggests, "Some cadres are only concerned with the number and appearance of the projects, as opposed to their quality and actual functions. Therefore, they carry out a number of projects that are unnecessary and are soon phased out, resulting in a waste of resources. Other projects are never completed."[39] Third, given the emphasis on the symbolic function of these projects, they often incur resentment because such activities may neglect the people's interests or produce negative externalities.

Leaders from the State Council have also admitted that some cadres do not carry out city construction in light of the fiscal situation and people's needs: "Instead, they launch projects without serious planning and compete meaninglessly with others, seeking to build 'a good record of performance' and so-called 'image projects.' The result is a waste of the resources and energy of the people, and the costs surpass the benefits."[40] Nevertheless, some local officials believe that such projects benefit their careers. As one city mayor admitted, "One of my predecessors was promoted because of his establishment of the development zone, and another was promoted because of his construction of the road. And all I can do now is to rebuild the old city."[41] "A new Party secretary, a new street; a new government, a new city" describes what occurs in a number of localities.[42] A cadre gave the following explanation for city construction:

> Image-enhancing projects are effective because they are observable. When higher-level officials visit, you do not need to say much if what they see are clean streets, lines of trees, and plots of grassland. This is proof of the performance of the local officials. Today, you do not expect many higher-level leaders to seriously collect comprehensive information about lower-level cadres. Instead, they are more likely to believe what they see during hasty visits. Even if you perform well, they may not see it. If they do not see it, your efforts will not be appreciated. The bottom line is that image-enhancing activities do not hurt you.[43]

There is nothing wrong with infrastructure construction if the local government has the financial resources and the projects are practical and desirable. However, image-enhancing activities are not based on such considerations. Instead, they are often large-scale and incur high costs but are not necessarily of much practical use and are often a waste of resources. One high-profile example is the airport in Zhuhai city in Guangdong province. In 1995, the government of this medium-sized city decided to build an airport. At that time, a number of large airports were located in Hong Kong, Guangzhou, Shenzhen, and Haikou, with smaller ones in other three nearby cities. Moreover, Macau and Hong Kong were also planning to build new airports at that time. Despite the many airports nearby and Zhuhai being a medium-sized city, the city government decided to build the largest and most advanced airport in China. The chief architect admitted that the length of the runway was originally designed as 3,000 meters but had become 4,000 meters by the time it was completed. An area of 25,000 square meters was plotted in the original design of the departure hall but was 92,800 square meters on completion. The architect questioned the builders on why they had changed the design and how they could obtain the funding. However, the architect was told that it was no longer his concern. Consequently, the investment increased from the original 1.5 billion to 6.9 billion yuan, of which the city government paid 3 billion.

However, since its completion, this airport has proved to be a waste of resources and a heavy financial burden on the city. Twelve million passengers a year were expected to use the airport, yet in 2000 the actual number was only 570,000, less than 5 percent of the designated capacity. The airport's poor performance caused the city government to incur a huge debt. The city government was unable even to pay the construction company, prompting the court to freeze its business income and part of its property. Citizens of the city commented with the following metaphor: "They [city officials] sowed the best seeds, used the best water, and applied the most expensive fertilizer, and then they bailed out. We waited, but the seeds did not sprout. Finally, we realized that they had chosen the wrong soil. The soil was suitable for lychees, but they chose to grow apples."[44]

The central government is aware of the image-building activities of local officials and has attempted to stop the practice. Local governments are required to follow the principle of "subsistence first and construction second." The central government points out that whether the leaders can appropriately handle the relationship between these two issues is a crucial indicator of their adherence to the principle of "seeking the truth from the facts."[45] Zhu Rongji, the former premier, repeatedly warned local officials: "Now, some cadres abuse their power, violate regulations, and launch projects without planning and research in order to build up a record of performance, focusing on the so-called image-enhancing projects. These projects are actually repetitions of previous constructions and burdens on the people. By doing this, they seriously encroach on people's interests."[46]

In 2001, the Central Party Committee issued a directive criticizing self-serving cadres:

We must use personnel, financial resources, and other resources in a way that can solve the most important needs of the people and the country. "Image-building projects" or "performance-record projects" that are of little practical use have to cease. We should establish and perfect sound and scientific criteria for judging the performance of cadres and stop the trend of establishing false records, hiding the truth from the higher-level authorities and the people, and seeking fame.[47]

This was not the first time the central government had issued such a directive. In the 1980s, the central Party repeatedly criticized cadres who sought only fame, fabricated records, reported good news and hid the bad, or listened only to the good news but not the bad.[48] In the early 1990s, the central Party authority instructed that a "scientific investigation and a comprehensive assessment be conducted before new projects are launched."[49] Repeated directives from the government and the Party suggest difficulties in curbing this phenomenon. In 2004, four central government agencies issued a joint directive requiring local governments to stop constructing large squares (that is, two hectares or larger) and roads (that is, eighty meters or wider) to stop image-enhancing projects. This detailed regulation by the central government reflects the seriousness of image-enhancing projects in China.[50] According to officials from the Ministry of Construction, image-enhancing projects such as wide roads, large squares, and grand offices exist in at least one-fifth of the 662 cities and more than 20,000 townships in China.[51]

Such image-enhancing activities also reveal the serious weakness of the budgeting process in China at every level. Despite the promulgation of the Budget Law in 1994, budgeting in China has remained beyond the control of the people's congress. Local leaders, rather than the people's congress, have an important or decisive say in local budgeting, which creates opportunities for them to allocate resources to high-priority projects on their agenda. This discretion is apparently a double-edged sword that can be used both to promote local economic development by focusing on profitable projects and to seek personal gains and implement image-enhancing projects. Such image-enhancing behavior is likely to persist as long as performance-seeking officials face soft budget constraints.

FAILURE IN DUTIES AND GOVERNANCE

Chinese government officials are assigned multiple responsibilities, and they (especially climbers) are unlikely to spend resources or energy on issues considered to have limited influence on their career advancement or performance assessment. Some of the important issues that may affect the interests of the people or local communities are not the major concerns or goals of government officials. The officials' irresponsible or irresponsive behavior may result in neglect of their duties or failure of governance. As Table 2.2 shows, proportionally more cases of neglect of duty were filed by procuratorates between 1998 and 2010. Local officials' dereliction of duty has had severe consequences. From 2005 to June 2010, procuratorates investigated 38,000 cases of duty crime involving 49,000 people. These cases claimed 32,000 lives, led 3,200 people to be severely wounded, and caused losses of 55 billion yuan.[52]

Government officials' failures in performing their duties and governance occur when they fail to follow the regulations and rules set by the government. For example, a deputy head of a government agency in Shenzhen was sentenced to eleven years in prison in 2009 because of his neglect of duty and corruption. The official had allowed an unqualified club to open for business, where a subsequent fire claimed forty-four lives and injured another sixty-four. In another case, also in Guangdong, a prison warden was accused of neglect of duty because it was disclosed on the Internet that a number of prisoners were using drugs. The warden was then sentenced to jail for eleven years for dereliction of duty and corruption.[53]

Government officials' failure in governance is reflected in various aspects of people's daily lives. One issue is food safety. Frequent cases of fake or poisonous food products, ranging from drinks to meat, have occurred in China in recent years. For example, twenty-seven people were poisoned to death and another 200 were hospitalized after drinking a fake alcoholic beverage in a city in Shanxi in January 1998. In 2003, 190 babies suffered malnutrition and twelve died after fake milk powder was sold in Fuyang city in Anhui province.[54] In 2008, milk containing melamine made about 300,000 children across the country sick, and some babies were believed to have died.[55] Poor-quality drugs are another serious problem in China. In 2001, around 192,000 people died after using fake or poor-quality medications.[56]

Although these incidents cannot be attributed entirely to the government, these tragic events indicate the government's failure in governance. For example, in Guangdong, a city government official issued a business license to an unqualified food processing plant that sold 600 tons of unhygienic pork on the market. The event was seen as harming people's health and producing highly undesirable social consequences. In 2010, the official was charged with neglect of duty and was sentenced to one year in jail with a one-year reprieve.[57]

Although government officials' failures or irresponsiveness in performing their duties are not always classified as crimes, this issue has long been a major source of grievance among citizens who encounter injustice. In the 1950s, the Party began recruiting peasants as activists to ensure there were enough people to implement the economic development projects. However, once these cadres came to power, some began to pursue personal gains (for example, through corruption and increasing their own pay), thus angering the peasants. Cadres were blamed for being undemocratic because they often made decisions without consulting other farmers. They were also blamed for assigning light workloads to their family members and were criticized for being indifferent to the peasants' problems. For example, in a commune in Tianjin, a seventeen-year-old girl who was sick approached the agricultural cooperative to seek financial help for medical care but was told to "solve the problem yourself." After the girl died because of the lack of medical treatment, the family asked for money from the cooperative to buy a coffin, but the cadres told the family to "use a reed mat instead."[58]

Officials' lack of response to citizens' grievances has persisted. State agents are responsible for the operation of conflict-redress mechanisms, and their willingness and capacity determine whether citizens can successfully seek justice. Thus far, state agents' unwillingness and/or weak capacity have disappointed a large number of citizens. One example is citizens' petitions. The head of the National Complaints Bureau admitted in 2003 that more than 80 percent of the petitions were reasonable or that petitioners had practical difficulties that should be solved. These problems could have been solved with the efforts of the Party and government authorities at different levels, and more than 80 percent of them should have been solved at the grassroots level.[59]

The lack of response on the part of local state agents forces people who are seeking justice to approach upper-level authorities. Take petitions in the legal sector as an example. Approximately 9 million petitions were submitted to the courts annually between 1998 and 2000, with about 75 percent made during personal visits and the rest by letter. The majority of these petitions pertained to the injustices encountered by the petitioners. During the same period, around 800,000 letters and visits were made to the procuratorates each year,[60] and the number of people lodging complaints with the Ministry of Public Security was about 50,000 to 60,000 per year.[61] An employee in the complaints bureau of the ministry admitted, "Most of those who approach us have suffered serious injustice. If their injustice fails to receive attention from us, it is very likely that it will never be addressed."[62] It is also true that the injustices suffered by some citizens have never been addressed. Chinese legal institutions are weak when they face the party-state, but they assume enormous power when dealing with citizens or social actors who do not have a strong political background. Without the help of the officials responsible for monitoring these agencies, such injustices can be ignored.

The irresponsiveness or failure of local officials in addressing the grievances of citizens has been a crucial factor in the numerous social protests in China in recent years. In a society replete with pent-up grievances, the continual irresponsiveness of local officials only worsens the situation. However, as discussed in Chapter Four, not all officials who have failed to maintain social stability have been punished.

Immoral and Illegal Self-Regarding Behavior

In democracies, some politicians seek power partly because of a motivation to implement specific policies or to encourage certain values; hence, "paying politicians very large sums would encourage exactly the wrong *types* to run for office—people motivated by financial gain rather than public interests."[63] This is not to say that corruption does not exist in democracies, as it is certainly rampant in countries such as Indonesia, India, and the Philippines. In communist regimes, the official ideology commonly fails to prevent state agents from turning their political positions into a money-making tool.

In the former Soviet Union in the late 1980s, the Communist Party "was butting out of people's lives, no longer telling them what to think, where to work, whom to vote, whom to hate."[64] In 1984, Voslensky noted, "It is in fact practically impossible to find a convinced Communist in the Soviet Union. They are to be found only in nonsocialist countries."[65] As a result, the state abandoned attempts to make people believe and instead tried to convince Soviet citizens that they must use a particular phraseology. Similarly, Kennan writes about the situation in Eastern European countries: "The officials of the regimes, not believing a word of [Communist ideology], said what they thought they needed to say. The people, also not believing a word of it, said the things they thought the regime wanted to hear. And the regime, knowing that they were pretending, pretended to be satisfied."[66]

In today's China, although faith in the official ideology has largely disappeared, Chinese government officials still have to issue public statements that "they themselves do not believe in."[67] Government officials commonly pursue personal gains or the welfare of their families. Some officials even claim that "there is no point in being an official if the position does not bring wealth with it."[68] As previously mentioned (Table 2.1), statistics from Guangdong province suggest that the pursuit of personal gain is the primary reason for cadres being disciplined.

Government officials' malfeasance for personal gain takes various forms. Some forms of behavior are immoral, while others are illegal. Regardless of the legality of the behavior, it severely damages the image and legitimacy of the party-state and government officials.

DISSOLUTE LIFESTYLE

In the former Soviet Union, the proverb "Live well and free, pay the Party fee" was used to describe government officials.[69] The proverb suggests that government officials in the former USSR could live well at the expense of the public as long as they remained in good standing with the Communist Party. Those officials enjoyed benefits not accessible to ordinary people. Writing in 1984, Voslensky noted of the former Soviet Union: "The *nomenklatura* is a class of privileged exploiters. It acquires wealth from power."[70] The *nomenklatura* class had actually become a class of outsiders, a group whose members lived like foreigners in their own country. As a result, "the masters of the *nomenklatura* [were] no Marxists," as "Marx would have turned away in disgust from the system they . . . established."[71]

Similarly, in the Chinese political system, the living expenses of leaders at certain levels are covered by public funds. Anecdotal evidence reveals that prior to the reform and opening up in China, high-ranking officials led a quite different life from the average person.[72] Burns shows how Chinese leaders at the top, unrestrained by democratic institutions, attempted to maximize their own incomes.[73] This remains true today. A county Party secretary publicly acknowledged that he did not need to spend his salary because everything was provided as a public expense. His case is by no means isolated; rather, it seems to apply to most top Party and government leaders at the county level and higher.[74]

Party and government officials may go well beyond a lifestyle that can be supported by public funds, pursuing a luxurious lifestyle supported by violating rules or even laws. Cadres have been accused of living a dissolute life ever since the founding of communist China, and they commonly use public funds for personal lives.[75] Although the central government has repeatedly warned government officials against using public funds for illegitimate purposes, such warnings are ignored. In 2011, for example, central government agencies spent 9.47 billion yuan on feasts, cars, and overseas travel, with the National Tax Bureau spending the largest portion (23 percent, or 2.2 billion yuan).[76]

Another type of misconduct that damages the image of the party-state and government officials is womanizing. An overwhelming majority of corrupt male officials who have been accused of misconduct had mistresses and/or were engaged in prostitution or even rape.[77] In my collection of forty-eight cases of officials reported to have mistresses, thirty-two had one mistress, five had between five and nine mistresses, and another five had ten or more mistresses. One provincial official in Jiangsu province kept a record that shows he had affairs with more than 100 women. Another county-level party secretary had affairs with more than 140 women. Ironically, some of these corrupt officials were caught because of their mistresses. In 2007, a vice secretary of the political and consultative conference of Shaanxi province was caught because of reports made by his eleven mistresses. On July 9, 2007, a woman driver was killed in a car explosion in Jinan, capital city of Shandong province. The woman was later identified as a mistress of the chairperson of the municipal people's congress. Believing that his mistress had become a burden and a threat, the chairperson sought the help of a relative who worked in the police department to kill the woman.[78]

Some officials also engage in gambling.[79] Scattered reports show that officials engaging in gambling are not isolated cases. In Hangzhou in 2000, 22 percent of the cases investigated by the city's discipline inspection committee concerned gambling by officials or Party members. The proportion was 27 percent in 2001, 32 percent in 2002, and 36 percent in 2003.[80] As gambling is illegal in China, government officials tend to go to overseas casinos, such as those in Macao.

Between 2003 and 2008, the discipline inspection commission of Guangdong province punished fifty-three officials who went to Macau to gamble. Between 1996 and 1999, a former vice mayor of Shenyang, capital city of Liaoning province, went to Hong Kong and Macao seventeen times to gamble. He once lost more than 10 million yuan within three days. The amounts involved in gambling can be surprisingly high. One township head in Guangdong province appropriated 11 million yuan of public funds for gambling in Macao between 1998 and 2004. His losses amounted to 9 million. Another official of the city government of Chongqing spent more than 200 million yuan of public funds on gambling in Macao and lost half of it.[81]

Such lifestyles are inevitably connected to corruption. Womanizing involves corruption either because a power–benefit exchange relationship exists between the official and his women or because maintaining such relationships entails money. In gambling, government officials either misappropriate public funds or have business people pay for their vice. For this reason, the state authority ruled in 2004 that those who gamble would be expelled from the Party. In 2007, the authority of Guangdong province pronounced that officials would be removed if they were found gambling in Macao.[82]

CORRUPTION OF OFFICIALS IN CHINA

Corruption in China is widely recognized to be rampant,[83] occurring in all public sectors from state agencies to public institutes such as universities and hospitals. Rampant corruption is not only a public perception but also common knowledge supported by consistent evidence. For example, whereas some corrupt officials have remained at large in China, others have escaped from the country. An investigation report by the People's Bank suggests that from mid-1990 to 2010 around 16,000 to 18,000 public employees fled China, taking with them 800 billion yuan.[84]

According to Chinese criminal law, an act is defined as corrupt if it involves (1) accepting or giving bribes; (2) embezzlement; (3) misappropriation; (4) failure to explain the sources of a large amount of income; (5) concealing deposits abroad; (6) privately distributing state-owned assets; and (7) privately distributing confiscated property. In other words, corruption in China takes different forms that may occur between citizens and officials or between businesses and officials.[85] Table 2.3 reports the cases accepted by procuratorates between 1998 and 2010. The statistics divide cases involving corruption into the following categories: embezzlement, bribery, misuse of public funds, dividing collective property, failing to explain a large income, and others. The table highlights a few changes in the cases filed by procuratorates. One is the decline in the number of cases filed, with a decrease of

TABLE 2.3.
Corruption cases accepted by procuratorates in China.

	Cases	Embezzlement (percentage)	Bribery (percentage)	Misappropriation (percentage)	Miscellaneous (percentage)[a]
1998	89,544	51.6	25.7	16.7	5.9
1999	83,555	53.1	24.3	19.0	3.6
2000	83,461	53.8	24.9	17.9	3.4
2001	76,530	54.2	25.7	16.4	3.6
2002	67,935	54.2	27.5	14.8	3.5
2003	55,333	52.9	29.8	14.9	2.4
2004	53,418	52.0	31.1	14.4	2.4
2005	48,722	50.0	33.3	14.4	2.3
2006	45,057	45.4	39.7	12.9	2.0
2007	41,175	44.1	41.9	12.2	1.7
2008	39,077	43.8	43.1	11.6	1.5
2009	39,279	43.3	45.3	10.0	1.4
2010	38,350	42.2	48.1	8.3	1.4

SOURCE: *Zhongguo jiancha nianjian* (Procuratorial Yearbook of China) (1999–2011).
[a] Includes "dividing public property," "a large amount of unexplained income," and others.

57 percent from 1998 to 2010. Second, proportionally more bribery cases were filed during this period, although the absolute number declined.

However, the decline in the number of cases filed by procuratorates does not necessarily mean significant progress in the party-state's anticorruption efforts.[86] Media reports and interviews with officials of disciplinary agencies suggest that corruption cases involving large amounts of money and/or higher-ranking officials have remained. The available statistics also seem to suggest this pattern. In the statistics released by procuratorates, "important cases" refer to cases involving cadres at the administrative level of county magistrate or higher. Figure 2.2 presents the number of higher-ranking officials who were involved in "important cases" investigated by procuratorates. From 1990 to 2010, the number of cases of embezzlement, bribery, and misuse of public funds investigated by procuratorates declined by 59 percent, from 61,929 to 25,336.[87] However, Figure 2.2 shows that the number of higher-ranking officials who were involved in "important cases" did not decline significantly during this period. Indeed, the number of higher-ranking cadres involved in bribery cases actually increased.

The persistence of corruption in China points to complex factors that prevent the party-state from effectively curbing corruption. Despite the various reforms, the Chinese state still monopolizes political power and controls important resources. Officials whose agencies control resources sought by others are natural targets for bribery. Hence, corruption tends

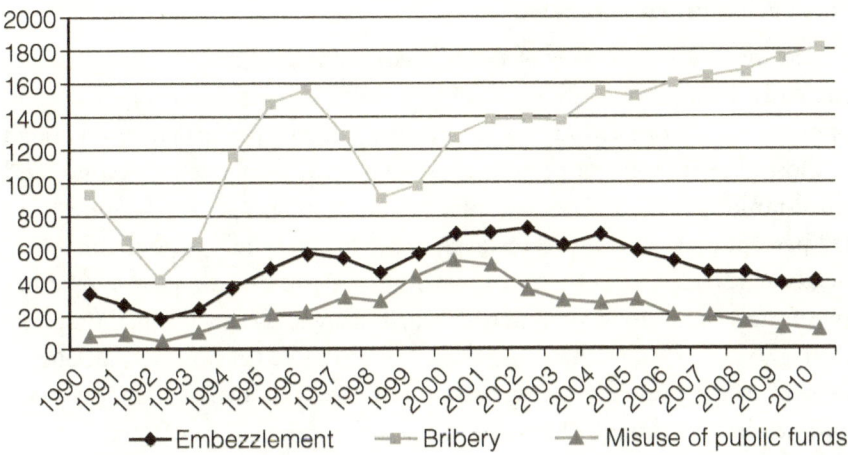

FIGURE 2.2. Higher-ranking officials investigated by procuratorates.

SOURCE: *Procuratorial Yearbook of China* (1991–2011).

to be more severe in agencies that have regulatory power or are involved in large-scale investments. For example, the construction sector is severely corrupt because of the large amount of investment involved.[88] Agencies in charge of construction projects remain the targets to which businesses offer bribes and other benefits. Many officials in agencies responsible for the construction of roads, highways, and railways are corrupt. Between 1996 and 2006, at least twelve provinces had their heads or deputy heads of the provincial bureaus of transportation arrested for corruption.[89] The recent arrests of several high-ranking officials from the former Ministry of Railways, including the minister himself, also highlight the severe corruption in the construction sector.[90]

The party-state's major concern arising from corruption has changed over time. For example, throughout the 1980s and 1990s, the loss of state revenue was seen as one of the major problems of corruption.[91] However, in the view of the party-state, it is the corruption within the Party and the government that causes most concern. Specifically, the implicit or explicit selling of posts among the cadre management weakens the state's legitimacy and capacity. Yang suggests that institutional reforms in China since the late 1990s have helped to improve the professional civil service and promote clean and efficient government.[92] Nevertheless, problems in cadre management persist. An analysis of the sales of posts reveals how political institutions in China may be plagued by corruption among state agents.[93]

CORRUPTION IN PROMOTION

According to a 1998 survey of 121 officials at the city level in China, among the eight factors that affect promotion (that is, performance, education, opportunities, connections, expertise, and others), performance was rated as most important by 52 percent of those polled, far above the second- and third-ranking factors of opportunity (23 percent) and personal connections (18 percent), respectively.[94] However, another survey of 570 government officials at the city, county, and township levels in an inland province between 2003 and 2004 reveals different findings. When given the opportunity to select more than one factor that affected promotion, about 75 percent of the respondents reported that promotion depends on "relations with leaders," although they also stressed the importance of "real capability" (63 percent), "age advantage" (48 percent), "mass support" (40 percent), "education" (23 percent), "gift sending" (20 percent), and "experience and seniority" (17 percent).[95]

Local officials complain about the lack of transparent and fair rules for promotion. The survey of 570 local officials found that 45 percent believed that the selection and promotion of cadres was distorted by "undesirable factors," including "networking and seeking posts" (identified as a factor by 75 percent), "personal connections or cronyism" (55 percent), "ineffective qualification review" (47 percent), "leaders' exclusive influence on selection or promotion" (43 percent), and "post sales and purchases" (28 percent).[96]

Although distorting factors may take different forms, a leader's attitude determines their effect. Whereas central leaders may pay attention to candidates' capability and political loyalty in deciding who to promote,[97] local leaders who do not control their own tenure and promotion and are customarily reshuffled every few years may pay more attention to the short-term or personal benefits of promoting their subordinates. As a result, when upper-level local leaders are motivated by amassing wealth, lower-level officials have to pay to keep their tenure or obtain promotion.

Selling of posts also occurred in other former communist countries. For example, a report by the first secretary of the central Party committee of Azerbaijan in 1970 revealed the selling of posts in the public sector. The secretaries of the district committee were in a highly lucrative situation because they had considerable power, and consequently opportunities, to reap benefits; thus, the price was high. In 1969, obtaining such a position cost about 200 thousand rubles. Cheaper posts were also offered in the Azerbaijan *nomenklatura*. Becoming a theater manager cost between 10 thousand and 30 thousand rubles, and a director of a research institute 40 thousand rubles; the title of Member of the Academy of Sciences of the Soviet Socialist Republic of Azerbaijan was priced at 50 thousand rubles. Understandably, purchasing such positions was generally beyond the ability of ordinary Soviet citizens. For example, a factory or office worker at that time was paid 150 rubles a month.[98]

In China, available reports from recent years suggest that selling posts is particularly serious at the grassroots level. My collection of cases on twenty city Party secretaries reveals that some Party secretaries accept bribes for local promotions, and others accept bribes from both business people and local officials.[99] The largest reported case of selling posts in socialist China occurred in Suihua city in Heilongjiang Province, where the Party secretary Ma De allegedly received an annual income of more than 20 million yuan, including more than 6 million in bribes from 265 lower-level officials in his city. The fifty top leaders of city state agencies all paid him to keep their jobs and to be selected for promotion.[100]

Selling posts is also common at the county level. My collection of cases on sixty corrupt county Party secretaries (including those in county-level cities or districts) caught in twenty provinces suggests that most of them were engaged in the selling of posts.[101] For example, eighteen county Party secretaries were imprisoned in Anhui province for accepting bribes for promotion and personnel reshuffles. In one case, a county Party secretary received 9 million yuan in bribes within four years. Around 210 local officials, including the leaders of thirty-one townships in the county, sent the county party secretary bribes in an effort to keep their jobs or be promoted.[102] When the top leader in a county is corrupt, corruption in the county becomes acute. In one Anhui county, the party secretary accepted bribes from 198 people who asked for help in job allocation and promotion, including the leaders of all thirty-seven townships. Unsurprisingly, another twelve local leaders in the county were also found to be corrupt.[103]

Those willing to pay bribes do so for different reasons. Some see bribes as investments. One corrupt official justified the decision this way: "Making more money is a condition for becoming an even higher-level official. Being promoted creates opportunities to make more money. Higher-level leaders also need money in order to be promoted, so I often send money to the leaders. When they are promoted, I will also be promoted."[104] Others offer bribes to keep their positions or to prevent leaders from vetoing their promotion. Some officials are forced to offer bribes because they believe that others have done the same.[105]

Quantifying how many local leaders have sold posts is difficult, but it is highly likely that many cases are not discovered. Selling posts is a criminal act involving both the buyer and the seller, and neither party has an incentive to report the case unless his or her corruption is revealed in the investigation of other cases. Moreover, some sellers accept bribes only from those already included in a pool of candidates for future promotion, publicly identified by the pertinent authorities. When such people are promoted, they are less likely to be suspected of having offered bribes.[106]

The twenty cases of city party secretaries and sixty cases of county party secretaries I collected suggest that selling posts is more rampant in less-developed areas, where corrupt local leaders do not have as many channels for amassing wealth. In less-developed counties, sometimes dozens or even hundreds of cadres are reshuffled at a time, and each affected cadre is pressured to pay. In more developed areas, corrupt local leaders tend to accept bribes from business people who have received their help in obtaining bank loans, land, and business licenses. This is not to say that officials in more-developed areas do not accept bribes for promotion; the difference between local officials in developed and less-developed areas is the degree to which they rely on the selling of posts for personal gain.[107]

The Politics of Promotion at the Local Level

The selling of posts reveals a fundamental cause of corruption among government officials in China; that is, local leaders assume considerable power without facing effective checks. In the case of promotion, as acknowledged by a former secretary of the provincial discipline inspection committee of Hunan province, if seeking office through networking with leaders or engaging in bribery is feasible, and if promotion can be achieved by telling lies and engaging in image-enhancing activities, then some officials will participate in these activities; if it is the top leader who decides the promotion, then some officials will court favor from the leader to win his or her trust and obtain promotion.[108] As Sun points out, despite the promulgation of many guidelines on the recruitment and promotion of cadres, and even when official procedures are earnestly followed, these can still end up as formalities for various reasons.[109] Therefore, the perceived significance of an official's "relationship with leaders" in promotion is reasonable.

The standing committee of the Party committee at each level is the most powerful organization that makes the most important decisions, including the promotion of important party and government officials. Standing committee members are influential political figures at each level of the political hierarchy. However, members of the standing committee do not enjoy equal power because the Party secretary has more power than other members. Consequently, top local leaders at each level have significant, even decisive, influence over the promotion of lower-level local officials. The considerable power local leaders wield over the selection and promotion of local officials can lead to the manipulation, distortion, or corruption of the regulated criteria for promotions.

Therefore, although the Chinese party-state stipulates complex procedures for selecting and promoting important officials at each level, these procedures do not diminish the influence of major leaders. Deng Xiaoping admitted that a system that is supposed to foster unified leadership often produces one-person leadership because power is usually concentrated in the hands of a few Party secretaries, especially the top Party secretary. He acknowledged that the so-called collective leadership at each level in China might result in one-person leadership. Although the Party has tried to limit the power of top leaders,[110] progress has been limited. In 1996, with the approval of the Politburo, the central Discipline Inspection Commission stipulated that "important decisions, the appointment or removal of important officials, the launching of important projects, and the use of a large amount of funds must be based on the discussion of the leadership as a collective."[111] However, to date, the state has not provided an effective means to ensure that decision-making power resides with the collective instead of with individual leaders.

For example, according to Party regulations, promotions to the positions of county Party secretary and county magistrate (*sheng guan gan bu*) are decided by the provincial Party authority instead of the city Party authority, which normally controls county-level affairs. A candidate should be nominated by the standing committee of the Party committee at the city and provincial levels and approved by the assembly of the provincial Party committee through anonymous voting. Therefore, on the surface, the city Party secretary appears unable to determine the promotion of the county Party secretary or county magistrate. However, in reality, the city Party secretary often has a crucial say in the nomination and recommendation of a candidate. The city Party secretary has the greatest influence over the promotion of other less important officials not administered by the provincial authority.[112] One city Party secretary admitted, "Those candidates for promotion will thank the Party and the Party organization for the promotion. But in a locality, the Party secretary becomes the representative of the Party and the organization, and thanking the Party and the Party organization becomes thanking the Party secretary, who has the final say in personnel affairs."[113]

Likewise, the county Party secretary assumes great power in promoting lower-level officials in his or her county, and the Party secretary is also responsible for assigning duties to other leaders. Because of his or her power, the county Party secretary is able to circumvent the regulations aimed at preventing the abuse of power in promotion.[114] Although important personnel affairs in a county are supposed to be discussed at the meeting of the standing committee of the county Party committee, evading this regulation is not difficult for the Party secretary. For example, the Party secretary and the head of the organization department in charge of cadre management prepare a list of officials to be reshuffled. The list is first discussed at the Party secretary's so-called work meeting, which is attended by the Party secretary and deputy secretaries. As the list has already been mapped out by the Party secretary and the head of the organization department, deputy secretaries usually do not have a strong incentive to oppose it. As the Party secretary, deputy secretaries, and the head of the organization department are also members of the standing committee of the Party committee, discussing promotion in the next meeting attended by all standing committee members can be no more than a ritual.

Promotion procedures vary across counties, but the influence of the county Party secretary often dominates all of them. A former Party secretary in a poverty-stricken county in Jilin Province reported how he controlled the appointment of lower-level cadres. Each time local officials in the county were adjusted, the organization department conducted a review of the officials affected and reported the results to the deputy Party secretary responsible for managing officials. After the deputy secretary's review, a report was sent to the Party secretary. With the latter's approval, the candidates were discussed at the meeting of the standing committee. However, before the review was conducted, the Party secretary set the rules for promotion. If the organization department failed to include candidates favored by the Party secretary, he rejected the list. As he explained, "Without my agreement, the list would not be submitted to the standing committee for a discussion. If I did not want to promote a person, he or she would not have a chance at all."[115] The concentration of power among the top leaders at each level naturally creates opportunities for corruption in promoting local officials.[116]

Selling of posts is a serious concern for high-level authorities. To prevent the corruption of local leaders in promoting officials, some local authorities have limited the number of officials who can be promoted at one time. In Jiangsu Province, for example, it was regulated in 2005 that a county Party committee could not promote more than thirty officials at one time or more than fifty people within two months. In a state agency above the county level, if the number of promotions at one time exceeds 15 percent of the total number of officials in the authority, or the number of promotions within two months exceeds 20 percent of the total number of officials, the authority must report in advance to the pertinent higher-level authorities. Otherwise, the promotions are invalidated, and responsible officials are punished.[117] At best, such regulations prevent local leaders from selling many posts at one time. As long as power is concentrated among top leaders intent on promoting their own interests, the practice of selling posts will continue. If more democratic procedures are less possible, making the process more transparent may be an option in addressing this problem.

Conclusion

What distinguishes Chinese government officials from their counterparts in mature democracies is that the former face fewer constraints than the latter in choosing the means to accomplish their assigned duties. The notion of "the end justifies the means" has led Chinese government officials to pay much attention to the achievement of assigned responsibilities. When government officials are answerable only to their superiors, making them respect the interests of the people is difficult. Consequently, conflicts between local governments and the people have increased in recent years. Moreover, some practices adopted by local governments sacrifice the long-term interests of both local communities (for example, polluting projects) and the state (such as illegal tax breaks). Government officials may ignore their duties if such duties are not high on their agenda, although performing these benefits local communities.

Compared with duty-related malfeasance, corruption is perhaps a more severe challenge faced by the party-state in China. Corruption has existed in China since the Communist Party came to power. Worsening corruption in recent years points to the declining influence of the communist ideology in the country. As early as 1991, a central leader admitted, "Some comrades in the Party now waver in their faith in the communist ideal, feeling that communism is out of reach. They suspect that socialism will soon come to an end."[118] Some corrupt Party members reported, "Our faith in communism is like a weakly ignited candle which can be put out by a fitful wind."[119] Against this background, the official ideology simply cannot induce officials to behave in a desirable way.

The persistence of government officials' malfeasance is certainly tied to the political system that not only shapes the officials' behavior but also affects the operation of the disciplinary institutions. As subsequent chapters reveal, disciplinary institutions in China have limited effectiveness in keeping government officials in check because they are under the heavy influence or control of the state authority. The various considerations on the part of those responsible for the disciplining have resulted in the tolerance of malfeasant agents or the relaxation of discipline in certain cases.

THREE

The Politics of Disciplining Government Officials

The Chinese state authority has taken various measures to deal with malfeasant agents over the years. Before the late 1970s, an important way of disciplining cadres was through political campaigns that often involved the participation of the masses. However, because such campaigns often targeted an excessive number of cadres, they ceased in the 1980s. The party-state has tried to institutionalize discipline through institution building, and a comprehensive network of disciplinary institutions has been established and staffed. By the early 2000s, China had about 300,000 officials responsible for discipline.[1]

Despite the changes in the modes of discipline, tolerance and discipline in cadre management continue to coexist because the disciplinary institutions are embedded in the political system, and their operation is under the heavy influence of the party authority and individual leaders. This chapter explains the political logic of the disciplining of erring agents in China by focusing on how the decisions made by the leaders responsible for discipline are affected by two sets of factors, their positional responsibilities and cost considerations. Positional responsibilities mean that the decision makers must mete out punishment to show accountability and protect the authority of the state as the power holder. Cost considerations imply that some erring agents are tolerated or given less severe punishment because (severe) punishment is seen as costly. The decision makers' positional responsibilities dictate that agents whose behavior directly causes problems with severe consequences will be disciplined. In other words, consequence severity and blame attribution significantly affect an erring agent's likelihood of being punished. However, the effect of these two factors can be mediated by the decision makers' cost considerations.

The coexistence of tolerance and discipline does not always weaken the credibility of discipline in China. For instance, the consequence of an agent's malfeasance can be beyond the anticipation or control of the agent. Consensus building among the decision makers is not always difficult or impossible, especially when the agent's malfeasance is perceived to be serious and the evidence is strong. In addition, disciplinary institutions assume more autonomy in dealing with less important or lower-ranking officials. Therefore, there is no guarantee that an erring agent can be exempted. Furthermore, the threat of discipline is not negligible because government officials have high stakes in their positions, and severe punishment threatens or even ends their careers. Thus, the credibility of disciplining state agents in China does not lie in the punishment of each erring agent but in the determination the state authority demonstrates when it has decided to impose the discipline.

Evolution of the Approach to Discipline

In dealing with malfeasant agents, the authoritarian government can impose due punishment on all malfeasant agents who are detected. This approach can produce a high deterrent effect because the probability of being punished is high, but it can be too costly if the number of officials to be punished is large. Another extreme method is to tolerate all malfeasant agents. This method involves little cost of discipline but produces zero deterrent effect and only encourages more malfeasance. If these two approaches represent the two ends of the spectrum of disciplining government officials, most governments tend to choose an approach between these two ends by considering both the scale and the severity of punishment.

In China, the evolution of the mode of discipline reveals the state authority's adjustment of its approaches considering the positive and negative effects of different modes. In the prereform period, a major mode of disciplining officials was the use of campaigns that often involved the participation of the masses.[2] As Table 3.1 shows, from the 1950s to the 1970s, various political and economic campaigns were carried out across the whole country. Not all of these campaigns targeted cadres or Party members. For example, during the initial stage of the consolidation of power, the Party

TABLE 3.1.
Examples of campaigns in China from the 1950s to the 1970s.

Period	Campaign
1950–1953	Repressing antirevolutionaries
1955–1957	Wiping out antirevolutionaries
1951–1952	Three oppositions (*san fan*) (i.e., embezzlement, waste, and bureaucratic style); five oppositions (*wu fan*) (i.e., bribery, tax evasion, stealing state assets, quality-sacrificing production, and stealing state economic information)
1957	Antirightists (*fan you*)
1959	Opposing the rightist tendency (*fan youqing*)
1958–1960	The Great Leap Forward
1958–1961	Opposing five tendencies (*wu feng yundong*) (i.e., common ownership, statistical inflation, high quota, misguidance, and mandatory orders)
1962	Four cleanings (*si qing*) (i.e., work points, accounting books, finance, and warehouses)
1964–1966	Socialism education movement
1957–1967	Opposing five types of people (*wu lei fenzi*) (i.e., landlords, rich peasants, antirevolutionaries, bad elements, and rightists)
1966–1976	The Cultural Revolution

SOURCE: Author's summary of county gazettes in twenty provinces.

focused mostly on the so-called antirevolutionaries who were claimed to be connected to the defeated Kuomintang (KMT) government.

Some of the campaigns were launched to discipline government officials who pursued illegal economic interests. For example, the "Three Oppositions" campaign was launched to target state employees who were believed to have embezzled public assets, wasted public resources, or adopted a bureaucratic or irresponsive working style.[3] The "Opposing Five Tendencies" campaign was carried out to discipline officials and rural cadres who pursued personal gains by, among others, accepting bribes or stealing state assets.[4] The frequent use of campaigns in dealing with cadres indicates the limited institutionalization of the management of cadres before the 1980s.

The most salient problem in the use of campaigns was that they often targeted an excessive number of people, sometimes including those who were not cadres. To address an issue through the use of a campaign, there had to be a sufficient number of targets to justify the use of the method. The negative effect of using campaigns was reflected in the treatment of cadres at almost all levels. For example, the Party authority in Shanglin county in Guangxi relaunched the "Three Oppositions" movement (that is, the new "Three Oppositions") in 1960, in which most cadres were involved. In April, about 6,300 cadres from the production-team level up to the county level went to the county seat for the meeting. To determine which cadres had problems (such as embezzlement, wasting, and bureaucratic working style), the authorities told the cadres to report each other's problems and mobilized the peasants to participate, thus "imposing psychological pressure on the cadres." As a result, most cadres were accused of embezzlement, misappropriation, and/or seeking petty personal gain. Specifically, about 87 percent of the 6,300 cadres were accused of having committed malfeasance, whereas almost all of the cadres at the brigade (99 percent) and production-team (92 percent) levels were accused of having committed malfeasance. However, as later acknowledged by the county authority, most of the cadres were innocent. Some cadres were forced to sell their family property to pay the funds they were accused of embezzling or misappropriating. In 1961, following an instruction from the higher-level authorities, the county Party authority reexamined and corrected some cases. For example, of the eighty-nine cases reviewed in five villages, the decisions on 79 percent of the cases were later found to be mistaken or inappropriate. The total amount of funds claimed to have been embezzled by the cadres in the five villages was 2,612 yuan, whereas the actual amount was 656 yuan (that is, 25 percent). Thus, some cadres were rehabilitated both politically and economically after the campaign.[5]

The number of mistreated cases peaked during the Cultural Revolution, when a vast number of people, including officials and their family members, were negatively affected. For example, by 1968, 75 percent of officials at the deputy-governor level and higher were investigated.[6] Not only were cadres purged in the Cultural Revolution, but some citizens were also targeted. For example, in a county in Guangxi, a peasant was charged with "antirevolution" and jailed for five years because he said that "it is not worthwhile learning from Lin Biao." Another peasant in the same county accidentally fell into a river. While trying to dry his clothes, he removed the badge with Chairman Mao's picture from his clothes and put in on his shorts. He was claimed to have "insulted the great leader Chairman Mao," was charged with "antirevolution," and was jailed for fifteen years.[7]

The party-state realized the problem of targeting an excessive number of people in campaigns and therefore required local governments to take rehabilitating measures after each campaign. Thus, the rehabilitation of cadres was conducted throughout the 1950s and up to the 1980s. For example, in Guangdong Province, 99.3 percent of the 36,800 rightists were later proven to be innocent. More than 94 percent of the 2,553 people who were claimed to be class enemies during the Cultural Revolution were rehabilitated after the movement.[8] Nationwide, in the "Antirightists Movement" of the late 1950s, around 552,900 people were claimed to be rightists, and around 547,880 of them (that is, 99 percent) had been rehabilitated by 1980.[9] The Party put tremendous effort into addressing the injustices suffered by officials and other people in the aftermath of the Cultural Revolution, with 3 million cadres being rehabilitated from 1977 to 1982.[10]

The serious lesson the Chinese party-state learned from the campaign-based discipline is that state agents are crucial to the operation of society. If many of them come under political attack, society will be in chaos, as evidenced by the Cultural Revolution. Therefore, disciplining state agents cannot be carried out on a massive scale with large-scale participation of the masses. After the Cultural Revolution, the campaign-based disciplining of officials with the active participation of the masses was ceased. As Manion points out, the anticorruption campaigns of the 1980s and 90s were no longer Maoist-style mass movements: "Chinese leaders clearly understand they must rouse ordinary citizens to report corruption to the authorities, but they explicitly reject the practice of mass mobilization to expose and punish corruption collectively."[11] The Party reverted to the policy whereby "the masses are to help keep the party on its toes, but their disciplinary role will be limited," which was adopted before 1949.[12] The power of disciplining local officials now resides with the party-state, which avoids "finishing off an erring comrade 'at one blow'" or with "ruthless struggles and merciless blows."[13] Certainly, the masses still actively participate in the disciplining of corrupt officials by providing tips.[14]

With the abolition of political campaigns, the disciplining of officials began to be institutionalized and is now procedurally managed by specialized agencies. The targeting of an excessive number of officials no longer occurs. As Figure 3.1 shows, in Guangdong Province, the number of Party members, including officials, who were disciplined fluctuated much more drastically between 1950 and 1965 (the data on discipline during the Cultural Revolution are missing) than after 1980. This change also indicates the relaxed political environment since the late 1970s. For example, in Jiangning County in Jiangsu Province, an average of ninety-nine Party members were punished each year between 1950 and 1956, and 141 between 1966 and 1976, compared with seventy-one between 1977 and 1985.[15]

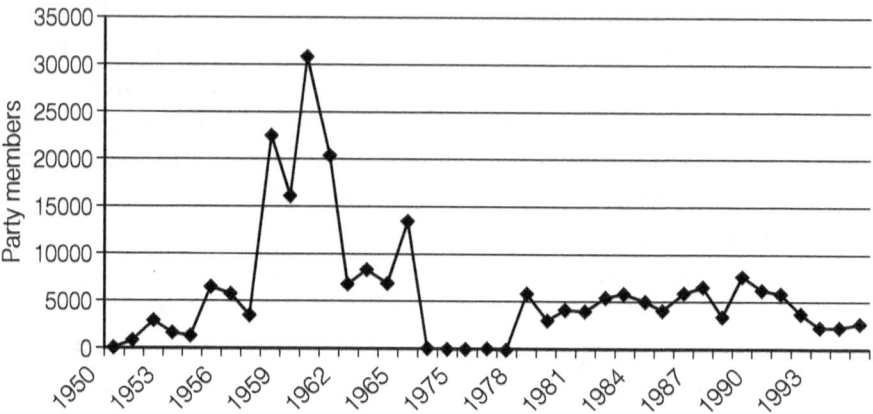

FIGURE 3.1. Party members disciplined in Guangdong Province in selected years.

SOURCE: The Discipline Inspection Committee and the Supervision Bureau of Guandong Province (ed.) 1999, 46, 150, 151.

INSTITUTIONALIZATION OF DISCIPLINE

China has established extensive disciplinary institutions in the Party and the government sectors since the end of the Cultural Revolution.[16] Depending on the type of malfeasance or failure on the part of government officials, the offenders are subject to the discipline of different agencies. Officials who commit crimes such as corruption are subject to the investigation and discipline of the Party, the government agencies, and the legal department when necessary. Others who fail in their duties but do not cause serious consequences are subject to the discipline imposed by the Party or government authorities.

In the Party system, discipline inspection committees, which were reinstituted in 1977 after the Cultural Revolution, are responsible for disciplining party members.[17] Each Party committee at the township level or higher now has a discipline inspection committee (DIC). In the government sector, the supervision bureau is responsible for disciplining employees in government agencies. At the central level, the Ministry of Supervision was established in the early 1950s (first as the People's Supervisory Commission in 1949), discontinued in 1959, and then reinstituted in 1986. Each of the county- and higher-level governments has established this agency.

To strengthen the disciplinary institutions, the party-state has expanded the disciplinary organizations and increased the number of employees over the years. In Guangdong Province, for example, the number of disciplinary agencies at the county level and higher increased from about 2,240 in 1985 to 7,960 in 1995 (that is, by 2.6 times), and the number of employees increased from 6,610 to 16,660 (that is, by 1.5 times).[18]

Since 1993, the DIC of the Party and the supervision bureau of the government have worked together (*heshu bangong*) to curb corruption while maintaining their respective organizational bases. The head of the supervision bureau is also a vice-secretary of the DIC, which automatically signals the DIC's leadership role in the joint task force. The secretary of the DIC is also a member of the standing committee of the Party committee, the supreme power center at each level. The DIC now participates extensively in the disciplining not only of Party cadres but also of government officials, including officials who are not Party members but are appointees of the government or its agencies.[19]

In dealing with cases of a criminal nature, such as corruption and serious dereliction of duties, the legal department assumes the responsibility of investigating the case and meting out legal punishment if a person is convicted. The procuratorate institutes the anticorruption bureau that specializes in dealing with corruption cases. DICs normally forward corruption cases to the legal department once they have gathered sufficient evidence and decided to impose legal punishment.[20] As discussed in the following pages, the political system in China determines that the disciplining of important officials is usually decided by the Party authority rather than the disciplinary agencies.

Aside from these regular agencies, ad hoc teams also investigate the malfeasance of government officials. These ad hoc teams can be formed by upper-level governments or upper-level government agencies in charge of the related affairs. For example, upper-level authorities in charge of food and production safety commonly organize teams to investigate cases that cause serious consequences. As these types of cases often involve different issues of governance, the investigation team consists of different government agencies. For example, to investigate the melamine-tainted milk incident in Hebei province in 2008, the central government's team included members from the Ministries of Health, Public Security, and Agriculture; the Bureau of Industry and Commerce; the Bureau of Quality Inspection; and the National Food and Drug Agency.

Similarly, on November 15, 2010, a fire in Jing'an district, Shanghai, claimed fifty-eight lives and injured seventy-one people, in addition to causing a loss of 158 million yuan in property. The State Council sent a work team consisting of officials from the National Bureau of Production Safety, the National Supervision Bureau, the Ministry of Public Security, the Ministry of Urban and Rural Housing Construction, the All-China Federation of Trade Unions, the city government of Shanghai, and pertinent city government agencies.[21] In the case of the protest in Wukan village that was presented in Chapter One, the team that was sent to the village by the provincial authority consisted of high-ranking officials from about ten provincial agencies, including the provincial Party committee, the provincial government, the Stability Maintenance Office, the Organization Department, the Propaganda Department, and the Supervision, Agricultural, Civil Affairs, and Land and Resource Management Bureaus.[22]

Note that these ad hoc investigation teams do not make decisions with respect to discipline or mete out punishment directly. The disciplining of officials in such cases is procedurally handled by the disciplinary agencies, although the decisions regarding the punishment of important officials are generally made by pertinent leaders in the Party and government based on the investigation reports of these teams.[23]

Disciplining State Agents

In China, because of the policy that the Party manages cadres,[24] the Party authority retains a significant or decisive influence on the disciplining of officials. The operation of disciplinary institutions is under the influence of Party and government leaders at each level.[25] The Party secretary and the head of the government at each level assume the most political power. For example, the Ministry of Organization, which specializes in the management of officials, stated in 2006 that the top Party and government leaders of the county authority hold important positions and are charged with important responsibilities. These leaders are also the focus of people's attention. Whether they use their power appropriately and whether they are incorruptible directly influences not only the reform, development, and stability of a place, but also the authority and image of the Party.[26]

Therefore, top leaders at each level play the key role in the decision making with respect to important issues. The leaders involved in disciplining important erring agents include top Party and government leaders, members of the Party standing committees, and members of the standing committee of the DIC. These decision makers need to take into account various factors in dealing with malfeasant agents. For analytical convenience, their decision making is believed to be affected by two sets of factors, their positional responsibilities and cost considerations. Positional responsibilities refer to those that decision makers need to fulfill as power holders (1) to show accountability and protect the regime's legitimacy and (2) to protect the state's authority.

At the central level, the leaders face more pressure arising from the legitimacy constraint because the central authority represents the regime more than local governments do.[27] They thus need to discipline erring agents to protect regime legitimacy and to show accountability to the public. Moreover, the central authority needs to protect its authority in ruling the country and has to mete out punishment to deter rule infractions. In a political hierarchy, the top authority's determination or reputation is crucial to deterring deviations because it affects not only errant agents' likelihood of being disciplined but also other agents' perception of risk if they commit malfeasance. Solnick uses the example of the former Soviet Union to explain this rationale. When officials at the top of the hierarchy were unable to control the activities of their subordinates, they invited doubts about what resources they still controlled: "These doubts spread the erosion of authority within the organizational structure, as local officials who were still loyal began to wonder whether their subservience might leave them completely disenfranchised if the center collapsed. Ill-fated attempts to reassert central control . . . only exacerbated the crisis by offering further proof of the center's weakness."[28] Hence, the possible erosion of the state's authority prompts the central authority to discipline erring agents to maintain its reputation.

At the local level, the leaders' positional responsibilities mean that they need to discipline malfeasant agents to ensure policy implementation and to show accountability to upper-level authorities and sometimes the public. Although regime legitimacy may not be the primary concern of local leaders,[29] they face the pressure of accountability when their subordinates' malfeasance is known to the upper-level authorities and the public.

Officials responsible for agent management must also accommodate cost considerations in dealing with malfeasant agents, and such cost considerations can be based on personal or organizational interests. Officials may tolerate erring agents to accommodate their personal interests to (1) protect their clients or supporters and (2) cover up their failure in monitoring agents or their own malfeasance (such as corruption). People usually become leaders, especially high-level leaders, because they have a patron or patrons in the upper levels of the political hierarchy. Such patron–client relations can be the basis of faction politics, which has always been present in Chinese politics at the central and local levels.[30] The support of their clients can facilitate the enforcement of policies made by the leaders, or the clients might offer political support to their patrons when necessary. Therefore, higher-level officials have the incentive to protect their clients or those agents with whom they have good personal connections.

Certainly, personal interests may also motivate the leaders to punish agents. Sometimes, the leaders punish agents to avoid responsibility or shift the blame to those agents, making them the scapegoats. At other times, they punish the agents in a rival's camp to weaken the rival's power base.

The leaders may also tolerate malfeasant agents to protect organizational interests, including (1) protecting the morale of agents, (2) maintaining institutional stability, (3) maintaining the unity among leaders, and (4) covering up malfeasance to protect the image of the state authority. At each level, the government has to rely on the agents for governance, and punishing agents demoralizes them. This is particularly true when agents commit malfeasance to fulfill the responsibilities assigned by their superiors. When the number of officials to be disciplined is large, leading officials may be reluctant to mete out punishment because doing so affects the operation of government agencies. Sometimes, tolerating malfeasant agents can be a compromise among officials to avoid faction politics and maintain the unity of the leadership. Finally, some agents are tolerated because the state authority does not want to disclose their malfeasance to the public, believing that disclosure will inflict greater harm on the regime's legitimacy.

Considering the decision makers' positional responsibilities and cost considerations, two factors significantly influence a malfeasant agent's likelihood of being disciplined. One is the severity of the consequences arising from the malfeasance. In duty-related malfeasance, severe consequences refer to the political, social, or economic effects of the malfeasance on the state, the people, or other social actors. Such consequences include heavy economic losses, deaths, ignorance of state policy priorities, governance crises, and strong public grievances or public attention. In corruption cases, the seriousness of consequences is generally determined by the amount of money involved in illegal transactions. The severity of the consequences is also related to the nature of the malfeasance. Criminal behavior is less tolerable or excusable than most types of duty-related malfeasance because the

TABLE 3.2.
Pressure of disciplining on the state authority.

Agent's responsibility	Consequence severity	
	Serious	Not serious
Direct	1. High pressure with limited space for manipulation	3. Less pressure
Not direct	2. High pressure with more space for manipulation	4. Least pressure

SOURCE: Author's summary.

former is simply unjustifiable. Ceteris paribus, consensus building among the decision makers is more likely when the consequences of an agent's malfeasance are severe.

The other factor is the substantiation of an agent's role in a case of malfeasance. In duty-related malfeasance, the substantiation of an agent's role means the attribution of responsibility or blame in a case. Some agents are directly responsible for the occurrence of events with undesirable consequences, whereas others are less directly responsible. However, officials who have not directly caused the problem may still be required to assume part of the responsibility if the consequences are severe. In criminal cases such as corruption, substantiation means obtaining evidence on the agent's corrupt activities. With strong evidence, ignoring or tolerating such criminal behavior is difficult for the state authority or pertinent leaders, although leniency in punishment is still possible.

Table 3.2 presents scenarios in which state authorities face pressure in dealing with malfeasant agents. The degree of pressure dictates an erring agent's likelihood of being disciplined. The state authority or leaders face the most serious pressure in meting out punishment when agent behavior causes serious consequences, and evidence of the agent's responsibility is strong (cell 1). In this circumstance, the agents involved are unlikely to be exempted. Yet, under special circumstances, tolerance is still possible if the state authority believes that the cost of discipline is too high.

One example is the central and local governments' tolerance of local officials' dereliction of duty or corruption in Sichuan. A political dissenter was imprisoned when he tried to disclose the poor quality of school buildings in Sichuan Province after the earthquake in 2008 that claimed the lives of a large number of students. Believing that an investigation would arouse strong accusations against the failure of local officials in performing their duties or corruption, the local government sentenced the dissenter to five years in jail under the charge of overthrowing the government, because he had earlier written articles about the 1989 Tiananmen incident and publicized them on overseas websites.[31] The central government did not intervene, perhaps because of its concern over the potential repercussions if an investigation was carried out.

Understandably, decision makers face limited pressure when the consequences of an agent's malfeasance are not serious (cells 3 and 4 in Table 3.2). Less serious consequences imply that the malfeasance is tolerable, regardless of whether an agent is directly responsible for the consequences. Equally important, less serious consequences are unlikely to draw much attention from the public, which significantly reduces the pressure on the state authority and creates much space for their tolerance and manipulation of the punishment.

A more complex scenario arises when the consequences are serious, but responsibility attribution is controversial (cell 2 in Table 3.2). In duty-related malfeasance, it can be difficult for the state authority to decide how to mete out punishment when identifying the responsible agents is controversial. The politics of blame or responsibility attribution exists in this circumstance. Given that the cost of discipline becomes salient when officials are not directly responsible for the consequences, *ex post* leniency is usually exercised in dealing with agents in such cases.

DISCIPLINING HIGHER-RANKING OFFICIALS

The party-state's cost consideration in dealing with agents is reflected in the way it handles cases involving high-ranking officials or officials who hold important positions. Both formal and informal procedures have been instituted to allow the state authority to exercise discretion or caution.[32] Caution is partly wielded through the political norm of consensus building. The introduction of these procedures and the use of consensus building imply veto points in the process of the decision making, which in turn allow some erring agents to be tolerated or exempted.

Several reasons motivate the state authority to exercise more caution in dealing with high-ranking officials or those holding important positions. One is the social and political connections of high-ranking officials with their even higher-level patrons. As already mentioned, it is unusual for a person to be promoted to an important or high-ranking position if he or she does not have political connections with upper-level leaders in the

Chinese political system. Such connections may affect consensus building among upper-level leaders when they decide on whether and how to discipline an erring agent.

Second, the political cost of punishing high-ranking officials is high. Serious punishment means the loss of investment in the disciplined agents. According to a vice minister of the Ministry of Supervision, the main purpose of disciplining officials is to keep the Party's organ healthy, rather than meting out punishment per se. He said that the Party should rely mainly on education to deal with the majority of cadres who have some common problems. Given that becoming a cadre or training one for the Party is not easy because it takes considerable time, money, and energy, the Party cannot turn a person into an official overnight. Therefore, if officials who commit mistakes can correct them, it means they still have some immunity: "As to those who commit mistakes *intentionally* and *repeatedly* [italics added], we should be strict with them. . . . We should stick to the party policy of being strict with those who refuse to acknowledge their crimes and of being lenient to those who are willing to acknowledge their misconduct."[33] Understandably, because the state invests more in training high-ranking officials, the cost of losing these agents is also higher.

Finally, high-ranking officials are very likely to have made a contribution to the Party and the state in the past, and they are the state's important human resources. Therefore, as Hollander puts it, they have accumulated more "idiosyncrasy credits," that is, "an accumulation of positively disposed impressions residing in the perceptions of relevant others; it is . . . the degree to which an individual may deviate from the common expectancies of the group."[34] In other words, high-status people with more idiosyncrasy credits may be better tolerated for their deviations than others in their organizations.

For these reasons, the procedures used to investigate and discipline high-ranking officials are more complex than those applied to lower-ranking or less important officials. As discussed in Chapter Five, consensus among major leaders (for example, members of the standing committee of the Party committee at each level) or the approval of major leaders (for example, the Party secretary) is often required for the investigation and punishment of important officials at each level. These formal and informal procedures imply that the investigation of malfeasant officials can be frustrated due to the lack of consensus among the decision makers or the lack of permission of major leaders.

The state authority's tolerance of malfeasant agents has led to the so-called nice man theory (*haoren zhuyi*) within the Party and the government. That is, major leaders are reluctant to punish their subordinates for infractions of laws or regulations. When Jiang Zemin was the General Party Secretary, he complained that some cadres adopted the nice man theory and stressed secular personal networks: "They are especially reluctant to punish the following people: their acquaintances, capable people, celebrities, people holding important posts, those with strong backgrounds, and their relatives."[35] This tolerance is also the reason for the phenomenon that "the people do not want me [a malfeasant cadre], but the Party does."[36]

One example of the state authority's caution and difficulty in dealing with higher-ranking officials is its response to the media exposure of local government malfeasance. Media exposure in China often generates pressure on the state authority to deal with the exposed problems, especially when these problems draw much public attention. My collection of 111 cases of media exposure between 1995 and 2010 (Appendix 3.1) provides some clues to the state's response to the media exposure of different levels of government. These cases are mostly related to the local governments' failure in governance (for example, food safety), abuse of power in dealing with citizens (for example, maltreating citizens), and failure in upholding justice (for example, mishandling legal cases). These cases were collected from the media, so the exposed issues are serious. Cases that involve high-ranking governments tend to be more difficult to address (Table 3.3). Of the 111 cases, 46 (41.5 percent) were completely solved, twenty (18 percent) were partly solved, and forty-five (40.5 percent) were not solved despite media exposure. Of the nineteen cases that involved city and provincial governments, thirteen (about 68 percent) were not solved. In contrast, proportionally more cases involving lower-level governments or nonstate agencies were solved once they were exposed. Similarly, despite media exposure, many officials, especially higher-ranking ones, were exempted in these cases. For example, none of the officials at the provincial level was punished, whereas proportionally many more lower-level officials at the township level or in the nonstate sector were punished when the cases were exposed and solved.

Nevertheless, as discussed in the next chapter, not all high-ranking officials who commit malfeasance are exempted. Depending on their role in a case with severe consequences, some high-ranking officials are disciplined by the party-state to avoid giving the impression that "the party is still on the side of the *nomenklaturist* class and not on that of the people."[37]

TABLE 3.3.
Outcomes of media exposure.

Authorities involved	Case	Solved (percentage)	Partly solved (percentage)	Cases involving the punishment of officials (percentage)
Province level	6	16.7	16.7	0
City level	13	23.1	7.7	23.0
County level	56	37.5	19.6	46.4
Township or lower level	12	41.7	25.0	66.7
Nonstate actors	24	66.6	16.7	75.0
Total number of cases	111	41.5	18.0	49.5

SOURCE: Author's collection.

As discussed in Chapter Four, high-ranking officials are disciplined when blaming lower-ranking officials is believed to be insufficient. Indeed, high-ranking officials are sometimes punished more severely than lower-level officials for similar malfeasance when the state authority wants to show its determination to curb malfeasance, such as corruption (see Chapter Five).

MODES OF DISCIPLINE

A deputy secretary of the central DIC said, "It is difficult to investigate officials' malfeasance and to collect evidence, but it is even more difficult to mete out punishment."[38] However, this difficulty can, to some extent, be reduced because of the availability of multiple modes of discipline in China. State agents, including those who work in public firms, are subject to four types of discipline: (1) Party discipline (*dangji chufen*), (2) administrative discipline (*zhengji chufen*), (3) organizational discipline (*zuzhi chufen*),[39] and (4) legal punishment.

Party discipline has five categories: (1) warned, (2) seriously warned, (3) removed from the position in the Party, (4) on probation with the Party, and (5) expelled from the Party. Agents who receive Party discipline will have their promotion frozen. Those who are warned or seriously warned cannot be promoted within one year, those on probation cannot be promoted within two years after the probation, and those expelled cannot rejoin within five years. Administrative discipline has six categories: (1) warned, (2) misconduct recorded, (3) misconduct highlighted, (4) demoted, (5) removed from position in the government, and (6) fired from the government agency. Those who are given any one of the first five modes of discipline will face a freezing period, ranging from six to twenty-four months, during which they will be denied any salary increase or promotion.

Organizational discipline, which is based on organizational rules, consists of the following: (1) criticisms and education, (2) publicized criticisms, (3) job transfer, (4) demotion, (5) forced resignation, and (6) dismissal. These modes of discipline do not necessarily mean the end of an official's political career. For example, an official who is dismissed or forced to resign may still be transferred elsewhere as an official. Moreover, dismissal does not affect an official's administrative ranking, salary level, or welfare.[40] Organizational discipline does not necessarily bear upon a government official's career because it may not appear in the disciplined official's file. For instance, when an official is dismissed, a notice of leaving the position is kept in the file, but the notice does not need to explain the reason for the decision. Therefore, dismissal sometimes becomes a way of protecting the agents.

Legal punishment means that an agent's misconduct is so serious that it is no longer appropriate for it to be handled exclusively by the Party or the government. Certainly, not all cases that are handled by the legal department result in the punishment of the accused agents. When a case is received by the procuratorate, it conducts a preliminary review and investigation. If there is evidence showing that an agent's behavior is likely to have broken the law, the procuratorate files the case for investigation. When the investigation is completed, the procuratorate decides whether to file a lawsuit against the agent in court. As discussed in subsequent chapters, many of the cases initially accepted by procuratorates are dropped in this process and do not reach the courts. Yet, agents who are tried and convicted are removed from their positions in the Party or the government, expelled from the Party if party members, and fired from the public sector.[41] Therefore, being expelled from the Party or government, or being tried in court, usually indicates the end of an official's political career. These are the most serious modes of discipline.

The severity of discipline is related to the type of malfeasance committed by an agent. In corruption cases, the agent is given legal punishment at the time of conviction. In duty-related malfeasance, administrative discipline and Party discipline are the major modes of discipline. Certainly, severe duty-related malfeasance will also lead to legal punishment. Table 3.4 presents the modes of discipline used on the 898 officials in the 133 cases of duty-related malfeasance collected for this study. These cases were collected from sanctioned sources in China (Appendix 3.2). Usually, only cases with severe consequences are reported, and these reports may provide detailed

TABLE 3.4.
Modes of discipline (N = 1,122).

Discipline	Officials	Frequency (percentage)
Party discipline	432	38.5
Warned	117	10.4
Seriously warned	155	13.8
Removed from the position in the Party	102	9.1
On probation within the Party	44	3.9
Expelled from the Party	14	1.2
Administrative discipline	497	44.3
Warned	63	5.6
Misconduct recorded	97	8.6
Misconduct highlighted	134	11.9
Demoted	50	4.5
Removed from the position in the government	148	13.2
Expelled from the public sector	5	0.4
Other organizational discipline	95	8.5
Warning talk	4	0.4
Written self-criticism	8	0.7
Resigning to take the blame	7	0.6
Dismissal	69	6.3
Forced resignation	7	0.6
Legal investigation or punishment	98	8.7
Total	1,122	100

SOURCE: Author's collection.

NOTE: Some officials were given more than one type of discipline, including being disciplined for corruption in addition to failing to perform their duties.

information on the disciplining of officials involved in the cases. In my collection, each of these cases involved more than one official being held responsible for the event. It is thus possible to gain basic knowledge about responsibility attribution and the use of discipline in cases of duty-related malfeasance (also see Chapter 4).

Some officials were disciplined in more than one way and were thus counted more than once (making a total of 1,122). Administrative discipline and party discipline are the two dominant modes of discipline in this collection of cases. About 25 percent of the 898 officials faced both Party and administrative discipline. Those who were most seriously punished by the Party (that is, "expelled from the Party") or the government (that is, "expelled from the public sector") accounted for less than 2 percent, and those who were investigated by legal departments or tried in courts accounted for 8.7 percent. The data show that only a small proportion of officials were seriously disciplined, which is also confirmed by available national statistics. In 2003 and 2004, fewer than two out of 1,000 party members, including those who did not hold administrative posts, were disciplined each year, and those who were tried in courts accounted for only 2.7 percent of the total number of officials disciplined.[42]

Chinese government officials rely on the government for their livelihoods and welfare benefits, and there is no easy way of exiting. These officials will lose their source of income and other welfare benefits (such as their pensions) if they are given legal punishment. Therefore, a salient characteristic of the disciplining of government officials in China is the wide use of nonlegal methods. Given the party-state's great discretion in disciplining state agents, some officials who should face legal punishment are exempted from legal responsibility and are made to face Party or administrative discipline instead. In other words, Party and administrative discipline may serve as substitutes for legal punishment. For example, an official's receipt of 5,000 yuan in bribes is now generally not considered a crime and will not be tried in court. Instead, the person will be warned by the Party or the government but will not be expelled from the Party or fired by the government.[43]

The significance of the availability of different modes of discipline is that it helps to reduce the dilemma faced by the state authority in balancing the need for and the costs of discipline. Given the different modes of discipline, the state authority can avoid the dichotomous choice between the exemption of malfeasant officials and the use of severe discipline by applying certain modes of discipline without seriously damaging the political careers of the agents. The availability of multiple modes of discipline also enables the party-state or the leaders to reward loyal agents by relaxing the discipline. As long as state agents do not receive severe punishments, their political careers do not come to an end. Rehabilitation is not rare for agents who commit less severe duty-related malfeasance. Some agents who are dismissed or removed from their responsibilities can be assigned new jobs or transferred to other places, still as government officials.

Credibility of Discipline

The disciplining of government officials in China is characterized by a combination of punishment and tolerance. Yet tolerance does not imply that disciplining has little credibility, because the threat of discipline and the potential consequence of punishment can be severe. First, consensus building among the leaders does not mean a lack of consensus on the need to punish erring agents. At both the central and local levels, if an agent's malfeasance is serious and the evidence is strong, defending the case or justifying an exemption is not easy for the patrons or supporters.[44] At the central level, concern over the leakage of authority may become an important reason for the disciplinary agencies and the leaders to strengthen their credibility in disciplining errant agents. The central party-state is essentially unable to keep state agents in check without the support of local leaders or midlevel principals. If the central state is reluctant to duly punish erring agents, there is no reason to believe that local leaders will do so. Therefore, the central authority is more motivated than local authorities to impose discipline, to create a deterrent effect or to reduce the effect of the leakage of authority (cf. Chapter One).

The central DIC is the primary agency responsible for disciplining government officials in China. Twelve of its twenty-seven departments focus on the investigation of officials mostly at the administrative rank of vice governor or vice minister and above.[45] In other words, the central DIC is designed to deal only with high-ranking officials and is unable to manage most local agents directly. Although the central DIC has intervened in the investigation of some lower-ranking officials, the number of such cases is inevitably small. Hence, the central authority has to rely on local leaders to monitor local agents and has to showcase its commitment to the disciplining of malfeasant agents. This political hierarchy dictates that the central authority needs to duly punish the agents under its supervision so that local authorities will follow suit.

Second, the Chinese party-state is now operating in a new environment, in which new information communication technologies make it easier to improve the flow of information. A better flow of information generates pressure of accountability on the state authority. As long as the central party-state still has the incentive to protect or enhance its legitimacy, it needs to pay attention to public opinion. Therefore, a better flow of information puts pressure on both the central and the local governments. At the local level, a better flow of information not only increases the difficulty for local authorities to cover up the malfeasance of their agents, but also generates pressure on them because they know that the central authority is aware of the agents' malfeasance. Thus, depending on the severity of the malfeasance, the pressure of accountability on the part of the decision makers can be beyond the expectation or control of the erring agent.

Third, the credibility of discipline in China is maintained because working for the party-state brings agents many benefits, and the loss of the position means the loss of these benefits. Working for the party-state is highly competitive in today's China.[46] It is no longer rare that hundreds, or even thousands, of people compete for one opening in state agencies. Many people are strongly motivated to work for the state because of the benefits associated with the positions. In addition to job security, welfare benefits, and steadily rising income, government officials also enjoy other benefits denied to non–office holders. Surveys repeatedly show that the Chinese people believe that Party and government officials have thus far benefited the most from the reform in China, followed by private business people, and actors and singers.[47] For example, one study of 15,800 residents in Guangzhou showed that, compared with other social groups, government officials not only have the highest but also the most stable hidden incomes (that is, off-the-books incomes). Government officials can accumulate significant amounts of hidden income and anticipate continued gains in the future. Officials who hold higher positions have significantly higher and more stable hidden incomes than those who work at lower levels.[48] To some extent, similar to their counterparts in the former Soviet Union, government officials in China belong to the "privileged class."[49] Given that Chinese officials have a high stake in their positions, discipline that may result in the loss of their positions remains a serious threat. As long as some agents are disciplined, malfeasant agents cannot ignore the possibility of being punished.

Finally, once created, organizations may have their own life and need to perform duties to justify their existence. Disciplinary agencies in China, such as the DIC, assume significant power in the Chinese political system. Although disciplinary institutions lack sufficient autonomy when dealing with the party authority, their role in disciplining state agents cannot be underestimated. Disciplinary agencies assume significant autonomy in dealing with lower-ranking officials, who are the majority of public servants.[50] Aside from the economic benefits associated with the investigation and settlement of certain cases (for example, corruption cases),[51] disciplinary agencies consider that they need to investigate and punish some state agents to achieve a record of performance. As a result, disciplinary agencies may sometimes abuse their power in dealing with officials or cadres of public firms or institutes.[52] Instances have occurred in which cadres suspected of corruption were beaten to death when detained by disciplinary agencies.[53]

Conclusion

Regardless of the political system, the government faces the issue of how to manage its agents. Solnick attributes the collapse of the former Soviet Union to its failure to keep its agents in check. Individual bureaucrats in the former Soviet Union were considered to be motivated by personal gain: "Their opportunism was chiefly limited by the authority of their bureaucratic supervisors, whose property rights over organizational assets were clear. When either authority relations or property rights were eroded, institutional collapse was unleashed."[54] What occurred in the former Soviet Union suggests that the state must introduce mechanisms to constrain opportunistic agents and prevent them from chipping away at the state's authority.

Compared with the former Soviet Union, the Chinese party-state seems to be better able to keep its agents in check,[55] although agents' malfeasance has persisted in China. The Chinese state authority is well cognizant of the malfeasance of state agents and has adopted a series of measures to address this issue. In the early years, a major form of discipline was political campaigns that often targeted and mistreated an excessive number of cadres. This mode was later considered inappropriate and was ceased after the Cultural Revolution because it not only demoralized cadres but also disrupted the operation of governance and even social stability. With the creation or reintroduction of disciplinary institutions, the disciplining of state agents has become more institutionalized in China.

The institutionalization of discipline means that disciplinary power is allocated to the disciplinary agencies. However, because these agencies are subject to the Party's control, their operation is heavily influenced by Party and government leaders. The party-state's control also implies its responsibility in monitoring agents. In dealing with malfeasant agents, the decision makers face both positional responsibilities and cost considerations. This chapter outlines the political logic behind the selective or differentiated disciplining of state agents in China. It suggests that the severity of the consequences of an agent's malfeasance and his or her responsibility significantly affect the likelihood of being disciplined. But the decision makers also face the cost of discipline. The state authority distinguishes government officials in terms of their administrative ranks and political importance when deciding whether and how to impose discipline. It should be stressed that differentiated discipline does not imply unconditional exemption or tolerance. As subsequent chapters show, government officials, including high-ranking ones, may face severe punishments when they commit malfeasance.

FOUR

Disciplining Officials for Duty-Related Malfeasance

Chinese local officials, who are responsible for daily governance and policy implementation, have committed various types of malfeasance in the performance of their duties (c.f. Chapter Two). Between 1998 and 2010, procuratorates in China filed 207,140 cases of duty-related malfeasance, and investigated 91,700 cases (that is, 44 percent) involving 112,300 people.[1] It is likely that some malfeasant agents are disciplined, whereas others are tolerated or excused. This chapter explores the political rationale behind the disciplining of government officials for duty-related malfeasance. In seeking to explain why some malfeasant agents are tolerated while others are not, two sets of factors are examined, the severity of the consequence of an agent's malfeasance and his or her responsibility for the malfeasance. Government officials are likely to be seriously disciplined if they are considered responsible for malfeasance or problems with severe consequences. For government officials who are not directly responsible for unwanted consequences, the likelihood of being disciplined and the mode of punishment are still tied to the consequence severity. The rationale behind the disciplining of officials is illustrated with the case of local officials' management of social conflict in China.

In the view of the state authority, some erring agents are more forgivable than others. Officials who are less directly responsible for an event are more forgivable than those who are directly responsible. Government officials who commit duty-related malfeasance without pursuing personal gains are more tolerated than those who abuse power for personal gains, if the consequence severity in the two scenarios is similar. When dealing with forgivable agents, the state authority may exercise leniency *ex post* by rehabilitating these officials to reduce the effects of the discipline on them. Some dismissed or removed officials can be reappointed or assigned new positions elsewhere. Despite such rehabilitating measures, punishment is still undesirable to officials because a disciplined agent cannot be certain whether he or she will be reappointed. It is also true that not all officials are reappointed, and most officials are not assigned positions as important as their original posts. For this reason, the threat of discipline cannot be ignored by state agents.

Disciplining Officials for Duty-Related Malfeasance: Characteristics

This section discusses the disciplining of agents for duty-related malfeasance based on my collection of 898 officials in 133 cases (see Appendix 3.2). These 133 cases occurred in twenty-six provinces or provincial-level cities between 1995 and 2010. All 898 officials held posts in government or party agencies. The 133 cases are divided into three categories: violations of national policies (for example, land use), incidents involving casualties (for example, coal mine accidents, traffic accidents), and problems with governance (for example, environmental pollution, food safety). On average, each case involved about seven officials. Given that most of these cases involved more than one official, it is possible to examine how the party-state attributes blame or responsibility when dealing with malfeasant agents.

There are some caveats regarding the data. First, the number of cases included in the analysis is limited because many of the cases that were handled by disciplinary agencies have probably not been reported or disclosed. The data collected for this study thus represent only a small portion of those who were not only disciplined but also disclosed.

Second, such cases can be selectively released by the party-state to show its accountability and responsiveness. In other words, cases in which irresponsible or abusive officials were tolerated might have been covered up, and cases involving senior officials or cases with less severe consequences may not have been released. In addition, information on the disciplining of officials in these cases might also have been selectively released to justify the way they were treated, whether exempted from punishment or given light punishment. These biases, if they exist, may mean that the state authority is more tolerant toward malfeasant agents than is indicated by these disclosed cases.

Nevertheless, because the media in China belong to different levels of state authority or businesses (for example, websites), different state authorities allow the exposure of officials' malfeasance for complex and varied reasons. The complex reasons may actually reduce the biases because not all cases were screened by a single state authority with a consistent criterion for selective exposure. Hence, although it is difficult to assess whether these 133 cases are representative, an examination of 898 disciplined officials can shed light on the political rationale behind the disciplining of officials in China. My collection shows several patterns or characteristics in the disciplining of state agents for duty-related malfeasance, which are also found in available national statistics.

THE DISTRIBUTION OF DISCIPLINED AGENTS

Table 4.1 presents the distribution of the 898 officials disciplined in the 133 cases. Fifty-three officials worked in central and provincial agencies, accounting for 6 percent of the total. Twenty percent of the officials worked for city agencies, compared with around 70 percent who worked for county and township authorities. The data also include thirty-two village Party secretaries and seventeen village directors. Although village cadres are not public servants in theory, they perform duties assigned by the state authority and behave as government officials. They are included to show the rationale behind the party-state's use of discipline.

Both high-ranking and grassroots officials were disciplined in my collection. The high-ranking officials include four ministers, one deputy minister, four governors, and nine vice governors. In addition, ten city Party secretaries and sixteen city mayors were disciplined. Top leaders accounted for only a small proportion of the officials disciplined at each level. At the

TABLE 4.1.
Officials disciplined (N = 898).

	Center	Province	City	County	Town	Village
Party secretary			10	46	75	32
Government head		4	16	68	72	17
Vice government head		10	38	81		
Head of the state agency	5	12	38	65		
Other officials		22	78	106	103	
Total	5	48	180	366	250	49
Frequency (percentage)	0.6	5.3	20.0	40.8	27.8	5.5

SOURCE: Author's collection.

provincial level, four governors accounted for 8 percent of the officials disciplined. At the city level, the city Party secretaries and mayors accounted for 14 percent of the city officials disciplined. At the county level, the Party secretaries and magistrates accounted for 31 percent of the county officials disciplined. This pattern does not continue to the township level, where township Party secretaries and township heads accounted for 58.8 percent of the officials disciplined.

The pattern of fewer higher-ranking officials being disciplined is also shown in the statistics released by procuratorates. For example, in Yunnan Province in 1998 and 2000, 403 people were investigated by procuratorates for "abuse of power," "neglect of duty," "engaging in favoritism for personal ends," and "violation of citizens' rights." Only seventeen out of the 403 officials (or 4.2 percent) were at the administrative level of county magistrate or higher.[2] Nationwide, between 1998 and 2010, about 112,300 people were investigated by the procuratorates for four types of duty-related malfeasance: "abuse of power," "neglect of duty," "engaging in favoritism for personal ends," and "miscellaneous." Officials at the administrative rank of county magistrate or higher accounted for 3.5 percent of the total number of people investigated.[3]

THE MODES AND SEVERITY OF DISCIPLINE

For analytical convenience, this study divides the modes of discipline into three categories based on their degree of severity: (1) less serious, (2) serious, and (3) most serious. Less serious punishment refers to disciplinary actions that do not seriously threaten the political careers of the punished officials. It includes "warned by the Party," "seriously warned by the Party," "warned by the government," "misconduct recorded," "misconduct highlighted," "warning talk," and "self-criticism." Serious punishment means that disciplined officials lose their posts but are not expelled from the Party nor fired by the government. It is possible that some of them will regain a post in the future. This mode of discipline includes "removed from the position in the Party," "placed on probation in the Party," "demoted," "removed from the position in the government," "dismissed," "resignation," and "forced resignation." The most serious punishment often means the end of the political careers of the disciplined officials and includes "expelled from the Party," "expelled from the public sector," and "legal punishment."

Table 4.2 presents the different categories of punishment imposed on the officials in terms of the seriousness of the discipline. It reveals several

TABLE 4.2.
Mode of discipline by administrative rank of officials (N = 1,122).

	Number[a]	Less serious (percentage)	Serious (percentage)	Most serious (percentage)
Ministry				
Minister	4	25.0	75.0	
Vice minister	1	100.0		
Provincial				
Governor	4	50.0	50.0	
Vice governor	10	90.0	10	
Head of the state agency	20	85.0	15	
Other officials	31	48.4	19.4	32.2
City				
Party secretary	10	70.0	10.0	20.0
Mayor	19	52.6	42.1	5.3
Vice mayor	46	67.4	26.1	6.5
Head of the state agency	56	57.1	37.5	5.4
Other officials	98	40.8	45.9	14.3
County				
Party secretary	47	80.9	8.5	10.6
Magistrate	82	74.4	23.2	2.4
Vice magistrate	96	65.6	20.8	13.6
Head of the state agency	90	43.3	42.2	14.4
Other officials	141	37.6	42.6	19.8
Township				
Party secretary	83	49.4	45.8	4.8
Township head	100	45.0	52.0	3.0
Other officials	130	41.5	50.0	8.5
Village				
Village Party secretary	33	33.3	48.5	18.2
Village director	21	28.6	66.7	4.7
Total/average	1122	51.3	38.1	10.6

SOURCE: Author's collection.

[a] Some officials were given two or more types of discipline.

features of the disciplining of malfeasant agents. One is that many officials were given less severe punishments. Overall, about 51 percent of the 1,122 officials (some were given more than one type of punishment) faced less serious discipline, about 38 percent faced serious discipline, and about 10 percent faced the most serious discipline. Legal punishments were not very common. Those who were investigated by legal departments or who were tried in court accounted for 8.7 percent.

Second, more lower-ranking officials were given severe punishments. At each level, excluding the central level, more officials at the lowest rank (that is, the category of "other officials") were given severe punishments (that is, a combination of the "serious" and "most serious" categories). From the provincial to the township level, more than 50 percent of such officials fell into the "serious" and "most serious" categories. The 400 lower-ranking officials (that is, "other officials," excluding village cadres) accounted for about 37 percent of the 1,068 officials. Among the 112 officials who were mostly seriously disciplined, lower-ranking officials accounted for 57 percent.

It is also worth mentioning that, at each level, many more government officials than Party officials were disciplined, except at the village level. No single provincial Party secretary was disciplined in my collection. Compared with government officials, Party cadres are less directly involved in daily governance. However, the Party secretary at each level assumes the most political power and has the final say in important issues, and he or she should in theory bear the most responsibility. As discussed in the following pages, the case of Meng Xuenong, who resigned twice, shows that it is often the head of the government rather than the Party secretary who is required to take the blame when serious problems arise in a locality. Intentionally or otherwise, the political system protects Party leaders more than it protects government leaders. However, such protection may be less obvious at the grassroots level (that is, township and village), where the division of labor between the Party committee and the government is less clear-cut.

BLAME ATTRIBUTION IN A HIERARCHICAL CONTEXT

More lower-ranking officials are disciplined for understandable reasons. First, there are fewer higher-ranking officials than lower-ranking officials. In China, more than 60 percent of civil servants work for county and township governments, whereas less than 10 percent work for central state agencies.[4] Similarly, in a state agency, the number of top leaders is much smaller than that of lower-level officials. As there are fewer higher-level officials, they naturally account for a smaller proportion of the total number of officials disciplined.

Second, and more important, more lower-ranking officials are disciplined because of their direct role in the malfeasance. Officials who commit duty-related malfeasance face different charges, depending on the responsibilities they are expected to assume. In determining an official's responsibility, the disciplinary authorities have a range of charges that they can make against agents. An official can be accused of assuming *the* responsibility, *certain* responsibility, the *direct* responsibility, the *leadership* responsibility, *certain* leadership responsibility, *important* leadership responsibility, or *major* leadership responsibility.[5] Malfeasant officials are accordingly given punishments of varying degrees of severity.

Officials who are directly involved in a problem with unwanted consequences are expected to assume direct and greater responsibility for the consequences. They are therefore more likely to be (severely) disciplined. In China, lower-ranking officials are more often and more directly involved in daily governance and policy implementation, so they are directly responsible for (severe) consequences or malfeasance. More blame or responsibility is therefore attributed to these lower-ranking officials.

In a bureaucratic context, lower-ranking officials are often deputy division heads or subdivision (deputy) heads of state agencies that specialize in certain responsibilities, such as ensuring production safety (that is, the bureau of production safety). In places where there is a coal mining industry, for example, local governments assign the responsibility of ensuring production safety to such supervisory agencies. Officials who work in such agencies are expected to prevent accidents, though this may be beyond their capability because whether or not a mine is worked is not necessarily within their purview.[6]

For example, in December 2005, a coal mine accident in a county in Tangshan city in Hebei Province claimed 108 lives, injured twenty-nine people, and resulted in the loss of 48.7 million yuan. The government arrested ten employees of the coal mine and disciplined twenty officials, including eight city officials. The city mayor, a vice mayor, and a bureau head were given "less serious" Party and government discipline. Among the other five city officials (that is, "other officials"), one was demoted, another was removed, and the remaining three were placed under legal investigation. At the county level, twelve officials were disciplined. The Party secretary, the magistrate, and a vice Party secretary were given "less serious" Party and/or administrative discipline, and a bureau head was demoted. Among the remaining eight "other officials," two were placed under legal investigation, two were put in jail, and another four were removed from their positions. Most of these lower-ranking officials were from the production safety agencies of the city and county governments, and they were accused of being directly responsible for the incident.[7]

In contrast, higher-level leaders are less directly involved in the handling of governance issues and are thus less directly responsible for undesirable consequences. Moreover, higher-level leaders are better positioned to avoid blame-generating situations because they can assign blame-generating responsibilities to lower-level agents. Lower-ranking officials sometimes abuse power and cause problems because of the pressure they face. As the case of tax collection in rural China shows, grassroots cadres, including village party secretaries and village heads, were often severely punished when their tax collection caused severe consequences, such as the death of peasants. However, these cadres were unable to avoid the tax-collection responsibility because it was linked to their performance assessment.

Yet, high-ranking officials can also be disciplined if they are directly responsible for severe problems. They may also be disciplined even if they are not directly responsible for a problem with severe consequences. In a hierarchical context, the administrative level and the number of the targets of blame are determined by the severity of the consequences of an event. If the event occurs at a lower level of the hierarchy, the responsibility assigned to the people involved decreases as responsibility attribution is exercised along the hierarchical ladder from lower to higher rungs. When the blame decreases progressively along the administrative ladder, high-level officials are better able to avoid severe responsibility. However, if the consequences are very severe, the level and the number of targets of blame will be extended to include high-ranking officials. But officials who are indirectly responsible for a problem tend to be less severely disciplined, if discipline is inevitable.

Therefore, consequence severity and an agent's role in an event determine how responsibility or blame is attributed and whether an agent is to be disciplined. This rationale implies that both high-ranking and lower-ranking officials may be disciplined if they are connected to severe problems. The remainder of this chapter explores the ways the state authority deals with officials, especially major local leaders, who fail in their duties, using the case of conflict management as an example.

The Case of Conflict Management

With social stability as a top priority for the central party-state, how the latter deals with local officials who have failed in maintaining stability illustrates the politics of selective or differentiated discipline or the variation in the use of discipline on the part of the state authority. The analysis presented in this section is based on a collection of around 190 cases of social conflict in China, mostly from 2000 to 2010, with another collection of thirty-eight cases of peasant–cadre conflict in the collection of taxes and fees prior to 2004 (see Appendix 4.1). Cases were collected based on the criterion that they contained the following information: the type of dispute (that is, civil disputes versus state–citizen disputes), the number of participants involved in the dispute, officials involved in the conflict and/or the management of conflict, the settlement of the dispute, and the manner in which upper-level authorities dealt with the officials, if they intervened in the case.

The Chinese state authority is concerned with social stability and regime legitimacy in dealing with social conflict. Cases of conflict with serious consequences tend to threaten social stability and/or regime legitimacy. My analysis of the gravity of consequences is based on the following factors: (1) the number of people involved in collective protests, (2) the casualties or economic loss involved, and (3) media exposure. Large-scale protests are considered serious incidents because these are likely to disrupt the social order. A protest involving a large number of participants is therefore seen as having a serious consequence. For analytical convenience, a case with 500 participants was used as the standard for distinguishing between incidents with serious or nonserious consequences.[8]

Serious casualties mean serious injury (*zhongshang*) or death, which indicates the tension in disputes. Moreover, if a case receives wide media attention, including the attention of Internet users, officials may also be disciplined because of the pressure on upper-level authorities to intervene in the settlement of disputes.[9] In other words, an incident is deemed serious when media coverage causes pressure on upper-level authorities, leading the latter to intervene in the case.

The decision to discipline and the type of discipline also depend on the role that local officials play in triggering or handling the conflict. There is an issue of responsibility attribution in social conflict. Some conflict can be directly attributed to local government policies or local officials' predatory behavior, whereas others, such as civil disputes, are not directly connected to the government or its policies. When local officials directly cause serious conflict, they are likely to be disciplined because their responsibility for the conflict is clear. They may also be punished when their mishandling of conflict results in serious consequences.

Similarly, local officials are less likely to be disciplined if there are no serious consequences arising from the conflict, regardless of whether they have directly caused the conflict. Given that many cases of social conflict arise from civil disputes in China, it is essentially impossible for local officials to be held responsible for such conflict, especially when it does not pose serious consequences.

TABLE 4.3.
Disciplining of local officials in cases of conflict management (N = 190).

	Consequences	
	Serious	Not serious
Directly caused	1. Cases: 58 Officials punished (*a*): 9 cases Participants punished (*b*): 22 cases *a* + *b*: 7 cases	3. Cases: 70 Officials (*a*): 1 Participants (*b*): 51 *a* + *b*: 1
Not directly caused	2. Cases: 36 Officials (*a*): 5 Participants (*b*): 16 *a* + *b*: 2	4. Cases: 26 Officials (*a*): None Participants (*b*): 16 *a* + *b*: None

SOURCE: Authors' collection.

The political rationale outlined in the preceding paragraphs is reflected in the cases collected in this study. Table 4.3 illustrates how local officials were disciplined in the 190 cases collected. Of these, twenty-five cases involved the punishment of officials. The reason for disciplining officials in sixteen of the twenty-five cases (or 64 percent) is that conflict was directly attributed to the official's behavior or local government policies and serious consequences ensued (that is, cell 1 in Table 4.3). In seven of the twenty-five cases, government officials were disciplined because they mishandled the conflict and their mismanagement resulted in the worsening of the conflict, although these officials did not directly cause the conflict (that is, cell 2). In the two remaining cases, officials were disciplined although the social conflict did not produce serious consequences (that is, cell 3). Predictably, if a conflict is not directly caused by the local government or its officials, and if the consequences are not serious, then officials are unlikely to be punished (that is, cell 4).

The following section illustrates the circumstances under which some government officials are punished for their failure in conflict management and the reasons some other officials are exempted.

PUNISHING OFFICIALS IN STATE–CITIZEN CONFLICTS

Local officials, especially grassroots officials, are directly responsible for daily governance; hence, they interact directly with citizens and other social actors. Under the pressure of fulfilling assigned responsibilities or achieving self-imposed development goals, local officials may create zero-sum games between themselves and citizens, in which conflict and the resulting contention become common or inevitable. Over the years, such predatory behavior of local officials has been an important source of social grievances and conflict in China. This has been reflected in conflict-laden issues such as the collection of taxes and fees in rural China prior to the abolition of the agricultural tax, and land development in urban and rural areas in recent years.

Local officials are most likely to be punished when their actions produce highly unwanted consequences, such as the deaths of citizens. One example is the collection of taxes and fees in rural China before the agricultural tax was abolished. There were multiple reasons for the peasants' financial burdens, but a crucial one was the fiscal reform that shifted the burden of financing local public goods such as rural education to the grassroots government. In agricultural areas where local governments did not have major nonagricultural sources of revenue, peasants often shouldered the burden. As a result, there were numerous conflicts between peasants and local cadres over tax or fee collection.[10] When serious confrontations occurred, township and village cadres were seen as directly responsible and were thus punished.

Some peasants died during confrontations with local officials; others simply felt hopeless and committed suicide after being pressured to pay taxes and fees. For example, in a township in Hunan Province in 1999, township officials and the county police went to a peasant household to collect taxes and fees. The peasant refused to pay, so the police arrested his son and beat the latter to death. Learning of the death of the peasant's son, over 100 villagers attacked the township government for two days and held a township leader hostage. The case caught the attention of both provincial and central authorities. Wen Jiabao, who was then vice premier, gave instructions to investigate the case. The three police officers involved were arrested and faced criminal charges, and the township leaders were transferred.[11]

Given the central government's intolerance of the use of force or violence in tax and fee collection, local officials became cautious. However, they were still liable to be punished if their actions led peasants to commit suicide. From 1993, the central government began to issue an annual document listing the number of such incidents arising from the collection of taxes and fees by local governments. Most cases involved the death of peasants. To warn local officials against abusing power in tax and fee collection, the state authority punished the officials involved in each of these fatal incidents. From the thirty-eight severe incidents collected in this study (not included in the 190 cases), a total of 236 officials were reportedly disciplined regardless of whether they directly caused the peasants' deaths. For example, a 1999 report cited eight cases wherein peasants committed suicide after being pressured by local officials to pay. One of these cases involves a household in Sichuan Province that owed fees amounting to 314 yuan. The couple, together with twenty-five other people who also owed fees, were brought to the township government to attend so-called study sessions, which actually meant detention. The husband promised to pay the fees and went to a relative to borrow money. Unable to borrow, he committed suicide. The local authority punished five township officials, removed the township head, and kept the township Party secretary under observation for two years. Four district officials, including the district Party secretary and the head, were subjected to Party and administrative discipline.[12]

Table 4.4 presents data on the disciplining of government officials at the county, town, and village levels in the thirty-eight cases of tax collection that occurred from 1995 to 2003. Each of these cases involved the death of a peasant. Local officials were grouped into those who were seriously disciplined and those who were less seriously disciplined. Serious discipline involved removal from office, expulsion from the Party, termination by the government, and prosecution in courts. Less serious discipline included subjecting cadres to Party or administrative discipline, mostly in the form of a warning or malfeasance recorded in personal files.

TABLE 4.4.
Disciplining local officials in tax collection.

Officials	Number	Less serious (percentage)	Serious (percentage)[a]
County Party secretary	17	100.0	
County magistrate	24	100.0	
Other county officials	15	100.0	
Town Party secretary	41	53.7	46.3
Town head	37	51.4	48.6
Other town officials	59	45.8	54.2
Village Party secretary	24	16.7	83.3
Village head	13	23.1	76.9
Other village cadres	6	16.7	83.3
Total	236	56.7	43.3

SOURCE: Author's collection.
[a] Including the "serious" and "most serious" categories.

The table clearly shows that grassroots officials at the township and village levels were more likely to be seriously disciplined than upper-level officials, because the former were often directly involved in collecting taxes and fees and in confronting the peasants. County officials comprised 23.7 percent of all officials disciplined in these cases, but none of the county officials was seriously disciplined. In contrast, around 46 percent of township Party secretaries, 49 percent of township heads, and 54 percent of other township officials were subjected to serious discipline. The situation was even more pronounced at the village level, where around 80 percent of the cadres were seriously disciplined.

The disciplining of officials over tax collection is conditioned by the attitudes of upper-level authorities. The thirty-eight cases all involved deaths of peasants; however, county officials were disciplined in only two of the thirteen cases that occurred in 1999 or earlier. When the peasants' grievances and resistance grew, the central government and upper-level local governments attempted to deter deadly confrontations by disciplining county officials or even higher-level officials. As a result, the remaining twenty-five cases that occurred after 1999 all involved the disciplining of county officials, including sixteen Party secretaries and twenty-two county magistrates, although the sanctions were not serious.

In recent years, officials have been punished as a result of conflicts arising from confrontations over land use and environmental protection. In one case, the local government of Dingzhou city in Hebei province constructed a power plant that needed a piece of land on which to store its coal ashes.[13] The construction of the ash-storage facility was contracted to a businessman who received strong support from the local government. In March 2004, when villagers from whom the land had been appropriated learned that the local government had retained more than half of the compensation funds paid by the land user, they began to petition authorities at different levels, but their appeals were ignored. A number of villagers were sentenced to jail for protesting. To block the construction, the peasants erected dozens of tents on the construction site where 100 to 200 of them stayed each night. Between March and July, the city government and the contracted firm made more than ten attempts to construct the ash-storage facility by sending police officers to remove villagers forcibly from the site, but they met strong resistance each time. Such resistance was becoming increasingly unacceptable to the local government and the contractor. Thus, in the early morning of June 11, 2005, more than 300 thugs attacked the peasants sleeping in the tents, killing six and wounding forty-eight. One peasant managed to videotape the fight at the cost of a broken arm. The five-minute footage became an important piece of evidence that was later shown on the Internet and by foreign television networks.

The casualties and media coverage generated serious pressure on the local authorities, including the provincial government, to investigate. The provincial public security bureau immediately formed a task force, which discovered that the thugs were hired by the contractor. The police department detained 106 people. Two days after the incident, the provincial authority in Hebei ousted the city mayor and Party secretary. In December, twenty-seven people who had assaulted the villagers were tried in court. Four suspects who organized the attack were sentenced to death, while three were sentenced to the death penalty with a reprieve, and another six, including the Party secretary and the contractor, were sentenced to life imprisonment. The Party secretary was accused of participating in the planning of the attack.[14]

Local officials were also punished when their behavior caused large-scale confrontation. One high-profile case occurred in Hanyuan County in Sichuan Province. In October 2004, approximately 100,000 peasants in Hanyuan protested the poor compensation they received for their farmland and homes that were lost due to the construction of a dam. After repeated but futile petitions to higher authorities, thousands of peasants marched to the construction site on the night of October 27, 2004, to halt work on the project. The government sent around 1,500 police officers to maintain order in the area. Violent confrontations ensued between citizens and police officers, resulting in deaths in both groups. As a huge number of residents were involved in the collective protest, the local government sent over 10,000 militiamen to help reestablish order. Both the provincial government and the central government intervened. The team sent by the central government concluded that the event was a "large-scale gathering of migrants who did not know the truth about the cause of the confrontation." Most of the participants were thus exempted from punishment. The provincial government assured the protesters that their homes would be relocated and they would receive better compensation for their lost property.[15]

At least eight local officials were detained on charges of corruption. The county Party secretary, who was also a vice mayor of the city government, was removed and investigated by the discipline inspection department.

Further investigations found that he was seriously corrupt; thus, he was sentenced to a lifetime in jail. Twenty-eight participants were also punished, with one executed for killing a police officer.[16]

Some local officials are disciplined, although the consequences of their actions are less serious compared with the abuse of power by their counterparts elsewhere, usually because their malfeasance is brought to the attention of the media and upper-level authorities. An example is the housing demolition in a county in Hunan Province. In early 2004, the government in Jiahe County in Hunan Province arrested three peasants for defending their homes. Without legal basis and without providing reasonable compensation, the local government tore down the residents' homes by force. Although the case was covered by Chinese Central Television, the county government refused to redress the violation. The case was posted online, and within three days more than 10,000 messages were posted on Sohu .com.[17] Some Internet protesters referred to local officials as "beasts." Others were more cynical: "Do not feel surprised. These are Chinese characteristics. Cadres are not held responsible to the people."

Despite the mounting furor, high-ranking authorities initially paid no heed. The lack of response from local authorities, including the provincial government, incited more resentment among Internet users, and they began accusing the provincial Party secretary and the governor of inaction. Interestingly, some homeowners from other places visited Jiahe County to express their support. The possibility of large-scale protests by homeowners from different localities pressured the central government to send a work team to Jiahe,[18] prompting the provincial government to pay attention to the case. The county government was found to have abused power in various ways during the demolition of houses. In the end, a number of officials were removed from office, including the county Party secretary, the county magistrate, a vice Party secretary who was also a deputy county magistrate, and the township Party secretary. The secretary of the county political and legal affairs committee was subjected to Party discipline. Other officials were placed under investigation by the legal department and disciplinary agencies.[19]

The preceding discussion reveals why some malfeasant officials are punished while others are not. The scale of public dissent, per se, is not the sole reason for disciplining officials. When a large-scale protest is quickly controlled without causing casualties or economic losses, local officials may be exempted from punishment. This is an important factor in the state authority's tolerance of the cases in cell 1 of Table 4.3. For example, only one official was disciplined in one of ten cases of large-scale strikes by taxi drivers. As these strikes often do not result in serious losses or confrontations, local officials who fail to prevent the strikes from happening tend to be tolerated. For example, on November 3, 2008, approximately 8,000 taxi drivers in Chongqing protested the excessive fees charged by taxi companies, low taxi fees, limited access to gas stations, and illegal taxis, among other problems. The city authority responded to the taxi drivers' requests quickly and positively, promising to address the issues they raised. With the swift and peaceful resolution of the case, no officials were blamed.[20]

Local officials are likewise less likely to be punished when their behavior causes less severe consequences. In cell 3 of Table 4.4, officials were disciplined in only two out of seventy cases. In one case in Jiangsu province in 2002, the county government seized land from peasants in a village to attract external investors. The villagers petitioned various levels of state authorities and, in 2003, more than forty villagers sent their petitions to the provincial government, while twenty-eight villagers went to Beijing to appeal. The National Complaints Bureau forwarded the case to the provincial authority, and the latter responded. As a result, a deputy county head and the director of the development zone were subjected to administrative discipline, while the township Party secretary was given party discipline.[21] The second case involved a village Party secretary in Hebei Province who sold land illegally to a firm. He was ousted in 2003 after sixty villagers petitioned the city government.[22]

INEFFECTIVE MANAGEMENT OF SOCIAL CONFLICT

Some large-scale protests or riots are not directly caused by local governments or officials, but local leaders face pressure or the threat of punishment because they are expected to maintain social stability and prevent incidents of collective action or reduce the consequences of the incidents. The occurrence of large-scale destructive action or incidents with severe consequences means that local officials have failed to maintain social stability. Responsible officials, including local leaders, are likely to be disciplined for the failure.

A high-profile case that occurred in Weng'an county in Guizhou province reflects the rationale behind the disciplining of important local leaders in conflict management. On June 22, 2008, a sixteen-year-old girl jumped into a river and drowned. Three young people who were at the site reported the case to the police department, and they were brought in for questioning. The police department conducted a medical examination that confirmed the girl had drowned and declared it to be a suicide. The girl's family doubted the reported cause of death, and thus a second medical examination was carried out. There was disagreement between the family and the police over the procedures of examination. As in many other riots, rumors began to spread that the three young witnesses were relatives of the county Party secretary and local police officials, and that the girl's family members and relatives were beaten, hospitalized, and mortally wounded.

On July 27, the police department informed the family that it was a suicide and advised the family to take the body and have it cremated. Around four o'clock in the afternoon, dozens of people petitioned the county government to reinvestigate the case. The number of participants exceeded 200 when some of the girl's classmates participated, in addition to over 1,000 bystanders. Failing to receive any response from the county government, the protestors marched to the county police bureau. A confrontation occurred between the police and the students, which angered more people. With around 20,000 people gathered, a riot started. Some people made their way into the office building of the county police bureau, destroying property and setting the building and police cars on fire. Around eight o'clock in the evening, the crowd moved to the county government. Some protesters set the buildings of the county party committee on fire. In this riot, at least 160 government offices and forty-two vehicles were burned, and more than 150 people were wounded.

After hearing the news, the central authority instructed the provincial authority of Guizhou province to address the case, and the county government established a headquarters for that purpose. A national official of the armed police in Beijing went to the county to supervise the settlement. When armed police forced the crowd to disperse, people began to leave, and order was restored.

Four days later, the provincial police bureau organized a third medical examination of the girl's body, proving that she had not been raped or injured. The local authority arrested a number of participants and jailed six of them for between two and sixteen years. The case clearly indicated the failure of local officials to handle the riot effectively. A number of local officials were punished; the county Party secretary, the county magistrate, another member of the standing committee of the county Party committee, and the head of the county police bureau were all dismissed.

In 2008, another deadly confrontation occurred in Menglian County in Yunnan Province.[23] The confrontation originated from a conflict between farmers and a local rubber manufacturer, which had lasted many years and triggered the farmers' strong resentment against the company and the local government for their failure to address the farmers' grievances. On July 19, local police officers came to the township to arrest five farmers who had previously participated in altercations with the company and the government's work team. These police officers soon found themselves surrounded by more than 500 villagers "who did not know the truth of the conflict" and were instigated by "a few people with a special motif." A violent exchange followed, in which police officers "opened fire in self-defense" after persuasion, retreat, and warning shots failed to stop the villagers. In this confrontation, two villagers were shot dead while nineteen villagers were wounded. Forty-one police officers were also wounded, and nine vehicles were damaged to varying degrees.

The provincial authority sent a team headed by a deputy provincial Party secretary to the county to handle the case. After some concessions with the farmers, the provincial authority punished several officials. The county Party secretary was removed, and his alternate membership in the provincial Party committee was revoked. The secretary of the city political and legal affairs committee was asked to resign owing to his poor handling of the case. The city Party secretary and the city mayor were required to submit written self-criticism reports. The city Party committee and the city government were required to discipline other major county and township leaders deemed responsible for the event. Disciplinary agencies investigated officials who were involved in the rubber company's business. Thirty-three officials, including the county Party secretary and his predecessor, were later found to be corrupt.[24]

The Menglian case shows that upper-level officials can be implicated when their subordinates fail to manage social conflict properly. In another case, in July 2010, a riot occurred in Suzhou after the township government demolished houses to construct an industrial zone and homeowners deemed the compensation to be unreasonably low, which is common in land usurpation or occupation.[25] The conflict culminated on July 14 when people attacked the township government and held the township party secretary hostage. The next day, over 10,000 people blocked traffic along the highway, leading to a confrontation between the participants and the police. On July 21, the upper-level district government issued an urgent notice to stop the demolition. Local officials were disciplined. The township Party secretary and the township head were both dismissed to appease the public. With the approval of the provincial authority, the city Party committee of Suzhou dismissed the district Party secretary.

The state authority considers certain types of malfeasance to be less forgivable than others, depending on the nature of local officials' failure in performing their duties. In one case, the city Party secretary, who was also a vice governor of Anhui province, was jailed largely because of his unacceptable failure in handling a riot.[26] In the city of Chizhou, Anhui Province, in 2005, a car carrying the owner of a private hospital crashed into a high-school student riding a bike. Instead of taking the student to the hospital to be examined, the businessman and his men beat the student and demanded compensation for the damage to his car. The businessman reportedly told his men, "300,000 yuan is enough for compensating his [the student's] life." The people present were angered. After the police came, the student was sent to the hospital. The businessman and his people were taken to a police station, and bystanders gathered in front of the police station and refused to leave despite persuasion from local officials. Later, a rumor spread that the student had died from his wounds, which brought at least 10,000 participants to the riot. Some participants burned a police van and looted a nearby department store.

Local officials could not contact the city Party secretary for instructions because he was with his mistress in another city. Annoyed by the phone calls from the local officials, he turned off his phone. The local officials had no choice but to report the case directly to the provincial authority. The provincial leaders instructed them to disperse the crowd and prevent further protests. The situation was brought under control with more than 700 police officers arriving at the site. As the city Party secretary was also a vice governor in charge of public security, the provincial authority believed that his dereliction of duty was unforgivable. Sanctioned by the central authority, the provincial DIC and the central DIC investigated the case and found that the city Party secretary was, in fact, with his mistress when the riot occurred. Furthermore, the city Party secretary was found to be seriously corrupt and was eventually sentenced to the death penalty with a reprieve.[27] Had he managed the riot properly, he would have avoided being investigated for corruption.

The party-state's reaction to local officials' failure in conflict management confirms their concern for their careers. As revealed in the preceding cases, local officials who fail to perform their duties may also be investigated for corruption and, if proven corrupt, face the end of their careers. Similar cases have occurred in other circumstances. For example, in the five years leading to 2012, the National Supervision Bureau investigated thirty-three serious incidents of production safety. Corruption was cited in thirteen cases, and seventy-two state employees were disciplined, sixty-five of whom were subjected to legal punishment.[28] Therefore, local officials can avoid being investigated for corruption if they are not negligent in performing their duties. In conflict management, when local officials manage tension properly or when the conflict is not serious, officials are less likely to be disciplined. Among the thirty-six cases collected on labor conflict, including protests, strikes, or demonstrations by workers, none revealed the disciplining of local officials.

The disciplining of local officials over conflict management reveals why social conflict has continued to grow in China despite the state's emphasis on social stability. Although local officials' performance is linked to their efforts in maintaining social stability, many of them have not been punished because not all social conflicts were caused by local officials and/or had severe consequences.

Punishing Higher-Ranking Officials

The case of Chizhou presented in the preceding pages suggests that high-ranking officials may also be disciplined if they are directly responsible for a problem with severe consequences. Even if high-ranking officials are not directly responsible for a problem, they may still be disciplined. When the state authority handles events with severe consequences, it may extend the list of targets of blame to include high-ranking officials to appease the public. However, the punishment for high-ranking officials in such cases is generally less severe.

My collection of 898 officials shows that an official's higher administrative rank, per se, does not always offer protection to the official. Table 4.5 compares two scenarios in which the officials held the same posts. In one scenario, the official (for example, a mayor) is the highest-ranking official in a group of officials responsible for an event (columns 2 and 3), and in the other scenario the official (such as another mayor) is not the highest-ranking official in a group of officials responsible for an event (columns 4 and 5). In other words, even higher-level officials (for example, city Party

TABLE 4.5.
Disciplining of officials in light of their responsibility as leaders.

	As the top leader		Not as the top leader	
	Number	Seriously disciplined (percentage)	Number	Seriously disciplined (percentage)
City Party secretary	5	40.0	5	40.0
Mayor	8	25.0	8	75.0
Vice mayor	14	7.1	24	54.2
County Party secretary	34	14.7	12	41.7
Magistrate	24	4.2	44	38.6
Vice magistrate	5	20.0	76	39.5
Town Party secretary	17	47.0	58	56.9
Total	107	19.6	227	46.7

SOURCE: Author's collection.
NOTE: If an official received two or more types of discipline, the most serious one is listed.

secretaries or vice governors) are blamed for the same event. In this second scenario, the official (that is, the mayor) becomes lower ranking when compared with the other, even higher-level, officials.

Given the way blame is attributed along the administrative ladder in a hierarchy, the highest-level official blamed tends to assume less responsibility and shoulders less blame when compared with lower-level officials. Among the 107 officials who were the top leaders responsible for their cases, about 20 percent were seriously disciplined. In contrast, among the 227 officials who were not the top leaders responsible for the events, almost 47 percent were seriously disciplined. This pattern holds true for officials at all levels included in Table 4.5, except city Party secretaries. For example, out of eight cases in which the mayor was the highest-ranking official deemed responsible for the event, two (25 percent) were severely disciplined. However, in other cases, in which the mayor was not the highest-ranking official responsible for the event, five of the seven mayors (71 percent) involved were severely disciplined. This difference is even more obvious for vice mayors and county magistrates.

The table seems to indicate a pattern of hierarchy-based blame attribution. The top leader who is not directly connected to the problem is often, but not always, given a less severe penalty. When the consequence is very severe, however, high-level officials may need to take significant blame to protect the regime's legitimacy. Indeed, even high-ranking officials sometimes become scapegoats of the party-state, as the case of Meng Xuenong, described in the following pages, suggests.

In my analysis, high-ranking officials include ministers, vice ministers, governors, vice governors, city Party secretaries, and mayors at the prefecture level. Provincial Party secretaries are excluded because no single provincial Party secretary was punished in the 133 cases. Officials whose administrative rankings reach these levels but who do not hold such administrative positions are also excluded from the analysis. Among the 898 officials, the forty-five high-ranking officials who were disciplined included four heads of central government agencies,[29] a vice minister, four governors, ten vice governors, ten city Party secretaries, and sixteen city mayors.

The punishment of these officials indicates that they were connected to severe problems in one way or another. In my collection, high-ranking officials were disciplined for accidents with severe casualties, violation of important national policies, and crises of governance. Although some were punished because they were directly responsible for severe problems, most were punished for problems that they were not directly responsible for. The forty-five high-ranking officials were disciplined in twenty-six cases. Eighteen of these cases (69 percent) were serious accidents that involved a large number of deaths. Five cases (19 percent) were crises of governance, and three cases (12 percent) were violations of important national policies.

INCIDENTS WITH SERIOUS CASUALTIES

The Chinese party-state has traditionally disciplined high-ranking officials connected to accidents involving large numbers of deaths. A vice premier was disciplined in 1979 because of an accident that claimed seventy-two lives.[30] In my collection of fifty-five accidents, including coal mine accidents, traffic accidents, and fires, the average number of deaths was forty-eight. In seventeen cases in which high-ranking officials were disciplined, the average number of deaths was 147. In six of these cases, the number of deaths exceeded 200, and in another six cases, the number exceeded 100. Only in five cases was the number of deaths fewer than eighty.

In recent years, production safety in the coal mining industry has been a serious concern for the central government and a serious challenge and worry for local governments. In May 2001, the governor of Shanxi was given the administrative discipline of "misconduct recorded" after three coal mine accidents occurred in that province in April that year. In my collection, six of the nine vice governors who were given administrative discipline were punished because of coal mine accidents. These vice governors were from Shanxi (an incident involving 148 deaths), Liaoning (214 deaths), Heilongjiang (171 deaths), Shaanxi (166 deaths), Guangdong (123 deaths), and Guangxi (81 deaths).

All of these incidents were directly handled by the central government. The State Council intervenes to investigate an accident when the number of deaths is large (that is, thirty or more), when the number of people who are seriously wounded is high, or when the economic loss is large.[31] Hence, if local governments are able to underreport casualties or losses, they may avoid direct investigation by the central government, although this is not always feasible (see Chapter Six).[32]

In my collection, the case that involved disciplining the most high-ranking officials was a ship accident in Shandong Province. On November 24, 1999, a ship sank as a result of both bad weather and the inappropriate operation of the ship by the staff, drowning 282 of the 302 people on board. As a result, seventeen people were punished, and four of them were tried in court. The provincial governor of Shandong Province was given an administrative warning, a vice governor was given "misconduct recorded," the minister of transportation was given an administrative warning, and a vice minister was given "misconduct recorded."[33]

Another high-profile case that led to the dismissal of a number of high-ranking officials was a mud-rock flow accident that killed about 270 people in a city in Shanxi Province in September 2008. The provincial governor, Meng Xuenong, who had already resigned as mayor of Beijing due to the severe acute respiratory syndrome (SARS) crisis in 2003, again resigned to take the blame, and a vice governor was dismissed. However, the provincial Party secretary did not take any of the blame for this incident. In the city, the Party secretary was temporarily relieved of his duty for self-criticism, and the mayor and a vice mayor were dismissed. Lower-ranking officials, including the county Party secretary, the county magistrate, and a vice county magistrate, were detained for legal investigations for their failure in preventing the incident and for their underreporting of the death toll.[34]

The fire in Jing'an district in Shanghai in November 2010 claimed fifty-eight lives and injured another seventy-one. The State Council sent a work team to investigate the case. Twenty-six people (most of them business people), including the director and deputy director of the district construction bureau, were given legal punishment. Another twenty-eight were given party or administrative discipline. A deputy head of the district government was removed, and another was given a serious warning. The head of the district government at the administrative rank of city mayor was removed, whereas the district Party secretary was given a serious Party warning. A vice mayor of Shanghai was given a discipline of "misconduct highlighted." The city government of Shanghai and the mayor were required to deliver self-criticism reports to the State Council.[35] As in other cases, the city Party secretary was exempted the responsibility.

CHALLENGING NATIONAL PRIORITIES

Some high-ranking officials have been punished because they failed to follow or enforce important national policies or they mistakenly ignored a policy considered to be a high priority of the central party-state. Local officials sometimes ignore or violate the policies made by the central government when they believe that such policies are not priorities of the central government.[36] But if the central authority is committed to certain policies, it has to impose exemplary punishment on certain agents to show its commitment. As a result, some high-ranking or important officials are punished, not because they violate national policies more seriously than their counterparts elsewhere but because they commit the misconduct at the wrong time.

One example is the nonagricultural use of farmland. In China, the nonagricultural use of farmland has given rise to a number of problems, such as endangering the preservation of land for grain production, threatening peasants' rights and thereby triggering protests, and contributing to a heated economy. The central government stipulates that the conversion of farmland for nonagricultural purposes requires the approval of the government at the provincial or central level, depending on the amount of land to be converted. However, this regulation has often been ignored or distorted by local governments. An official of the Ministry of Land and Resources acknowledged in 2006 that "almost all the serious law violations in land use involve [local] governments or leaders."[37] Local governments were responsible for 80 percent of the land illegally taken.[38]

An important reason local officials ignore the regulations of the central government is that the likelihood of being punished is not high. From 2000 to 2004, 616,360 cases of illegal or regulation-violating cases of land use were investigated, but only 4,705 people were disciplined by the Party or the government and only 521 people were tried in court for corruption related to land use.[39] While local governments regard occupying farmland as necessary to develop the local economy, attract investors, and raise revenues, the central government has been increasingly concerned in recent years because of the continuing loss of farmland. Against this background, the central government has punished high-ranking officials to show its determination.

Between 2003 and 2006, the city authority of Zhengzhou, the capital city of Henan Province, took 990 hectares of land for the construction of the so-called city of universities without applying for the approval of the use of the land. In 2004, a team from the central government decided to inspect the "city of universities" but was stopped by the provincial and city authorities under pretexts. In February 2005, central government officials eventually had a chance to investigate the case and found out the problem. The central government then ordered the provincial and city governments to recheck the project and punish the responsible officials. However, the local authorities ignored the instructions and continued to occupy more land, hoping to present a fait accompli.

The central government took action in 2006. The city Party secretary of Zhengzhou was seriously warned by the Party, the mayor was given the administrative discipline of "misconduct highlighted," and a vice mayor was demoted. The head of the provincial development and reform commission was also demoted. The secretary of the provincial Political and Legal Affairs Committee, who was a former vice governor, was seriously warned by the Party. Interestingly, although this construction plan was illegal, it had been approved by the provincial authority at the governor's working meeting in 2002.[40] Therefore, the governor, Li Keqiang (promoted to vice premier in 2008), should also have been found responsible, but he was exempted. Apparently, the central authority wanted to protect the top leaders in the province.

CRISES OF GOVERNANCE

A crisis of governance refers to the government's failure to address certain issues that threaten people's health and safety or endanger local stability. A series of such crises have recently occurred in China, and some high-ranking officials have been punished. One type of crisis of governance is large-scale social protests that seriously threaten local stability, as already discussed. Another type is the ineffective handling of issues that affect the well-being of a large number of people. In 2003, the SARS outbreak in China claimed about 350 lives. The Chinese government was blamed not only by the international community but also by the Chinese people for its initial mishandling of the outbreak. The government was heavily criticized for covering up the news and devaluing people's lives. Under this circumstance, the central authority dismissed Zhang Wenkang, the minister of health, and Meng Xuenong, the mayor of Beijing. However, the Party secretary of Beijing was not blamed. These dismissals were apparently a political strategy of finding scapegoats, but they also showed that, as in democracies, Chinese government officials may be held accountable for crises of governance.

Governance crises may also be caused by severe pollution, which has been a challenging issue in China.[41] On November 13, 2005, a chemical factory owned by the Jilin branch of PetroChina exploded, killing eight people and injuring another sixty. Furthermore, the explosion polluted the water of a major river. The water supply in Harbin, the capital city of Heilongjiang province and home to about 4.6 million people, was suspended for four days. Polluted water also flowed into Russia, which caused resentment there. Xie Zhenhua, the head of the National Bureau of Environmental Protection, resigned to take the blame. The head of the environmental protection bureau of Jilin Province was given a Party warning and an administrative discipline of "misconduct highlighted." The head of the environmental protection bureau of the city of Jilin was given an administrative warning.[42]

Another central government official resigned in 2008 because of a governance crisis arising from dairy factories adding melamine to fresh milk in Shijiazhuang city in Hebei Province and other provinces.[43] Four babies died after drinking the milk containing melamine, and more than 12,000 babies were hospitalized. Some milk products containing melamine had also been exported, causing strong resentment from the international community. The Chinese government had to respond. Dozens of business people were arrested. Initially, a vice mayor of Shijiazhuang was dismissed. As both domestic and international pressure mounted, more officials were disciplined. The city Party secretary, the mayor, and the heads of three city government agencies were all dismissed. The head of the provincial government agency responsible for product quality control was also dismissed, and the head of the National Food and Drug Agency resigned.

Ex Post Leniency

When disciplining erring agents, the state authority may believe that some agents are more forgivable than others. When the punishment of forgivable agents is inevitable, the authority may exercise leniency *ex post* to reduce the detrimental effect of the punishment. In a county in Jiangxi Province, the demolition of housing in 2010 led to a self-immolation case in which three people were burned, one of whom died. The city Party committee punished eight officials, including the county Party secretary and the magistrate. Although the city authority announced that these two major officials were to be investigated, the results of the investigation were never released to the public. In 2011, the two people were appointed heads of two city government agencies.[44] Similarly, in the Jiahe case previously mentioned, all of the leaders were assigned new jobs after being disciplined. The previous county Party secretary was appointed head of the city irrigation bureau, then the education bureau; the previous county magistrate was assigned a job in the city government, and the township Party secretary became the director of the county family planning bureau. Another deputy county head became a deputy head of another county. In the Weng'an case presented in the preceding pages, the dismissed county Party secretary was appointed deputy head of the city financial bureau seven months later.[45]

Similarly, in the melamine-tainted milk event in Shijiazhuang in Hebei province in 2008 presented earlier, a number of officials, including the mayor and two vice mayors, were disciplined. In 2011, the mayor was reappointed as vice head of the provincial bureau of industry and information. One vice mayor was reappointed vice mayor, and another became vice chairman of the city political consultative conference. Some other officials were also assigned new leadership jobs.[46]

Reappointing officials who have been removed from office is not limited to lower-level local officials. In 2003, Meng Xuenong, the then mayor of Beijing, was dismissed because of his alleged mishandling of SARS. He was then transferred to the State Council as vice director of an agency. In 2007, Meng was appointed governor of Shanxi Province, but he resigned in 2008 after being held responsible for the mud-rock flow accident that killed 270 people. In another case, Xie Zhenhua, the former head of the National Bureau of Environmental Protection, resigned because of the influential environmental pollution event in 2005. He was then appointed deputy head of the National Commission of Development and Reform in 2007.

According to the Regulations on the Appointment of Cadres, "If cadres who resign to take blame are required to resign or are demoted perform particularly well in their new positions for more than one year and are qualified for promotion, they can be appointed or promoted to leadership positions."[47] Thus, there is a rule regarding the reappointment of some dismissed or removed officials. Several political reasons account for the state's tolerance of agents who have been negligent in performing their duties. One, as mentioned earlier, is that it is costly to train a cadre and unrealistic to dismiss all agents who commit malfeasance. If the party-state can tolerate corrupt officials, it can certainly tolerate agents who have committed malfeasance when performing their duties. When local officials are believed to have broken rules for local benefits, such as local development, their behavior is deemed excusable or forgivable.

Second, upper-level authorities or leaders understand that local officials sometimes commit malfeasance under the pressure of fulfilling the responsibilities assigned by their leaders. The collection of taxes and fees in rural China before 2004 and the case of housing demolition reveal the pressure faced by grassroots officials in fulfilling the responsibilities assigned by their superiors. Thus, if local officials' rule-breaking behavior serves the interests of upper-level authorities or leaders, they can be tolerated, or they can be reinstituted *ex post* if they have to be disciplined.

Third, some problems are not directly caused by the officials who are punished. When officials are made to assume responsibility as scapegoats, they are normally promised reinstatement or reappointment after a certain period has lapsed. Should these disciplined officials not be reappointed, the pertinent authorities or leaders can be seen as failing to honor the promise, thereby violating political norms.[48] There is collective leadership in the Chinese political system. Intentionally or otherwise, this arrangement benefits the major leaders among the leadership, as they can claim the credit for good performance while avoiding assuming responsibilities when unwanted problems arise. In theory, collective leadership means collective responsibility, but in practice no individual leader is supposed to assume the responsibility for problems related to collective decisions. When the pressure builds to the extent that some officials have to take responsibility, less important leaders are likely to shoulder the blame to protect the major leaders or the collective leadership. In these circumstances, it is natural to reappoint the punished officials.[49]

An important method that local leaders use to protect their agents is having the case handled within the local leaders' jurisdiction, thereby preempting intervention from upper-level authorities. The rationale is simple: A case exclusively handled by local authorities allows the latter more discretion in deciding whether and how to discipline an agent. For example, in a case that occurred in a county in Hebei Province, the county Party secretary dismissed the township Party secretary because the township authority failed to prevent a petitioner from approaching national authorities in Beijing. The county Party secretary explained that the dismissal of the township Party secretary was meant to preempt the intervention of the upper-level authorities. By handling the case exclusively, the county authority would have had more latitude in reappointing the dismissed official afterwards.[50]

Understandably, the local governments' discretion is restricted when upper-level authorities intervene. An example is a riot that occurred in 2008 in the city of Longnan in Gansu Province, which caused heavy economic losses.[51] In 2006, the city government acquired land from peasants to construct an administration center or a cluster of city government office buildings based on a new development plan. Local residents, including the peasants, welcomed the plan because they would benefit economically from having the new administration center within their district. However, rumors spread that the city government had decided to relocate the administration center elsewhere, citing the geographic condition of this district as inappropriate for the project. The rumor gained ground with the 2008 earthquake in Sichuan and parts of Gansu. Local residents who were expecting the construction approached the city authority for clarification several times but were told that the rumor was unfounded.

On the afternoon of November 17, around 100 peasants from thirty households went to the city Party committee and sought clarification from the city Party secretary on whether the administration center would be constructed elsewhere. The city leader did not meet with the people, and the rumor began to spread that the city government had constructed temporary offices in other places. Participants spread the word to relatives and friends, and more people soon arrived. A vice mayor failed to persuade the people to leave. With more rumors spreading among the crowd, the participants became agitated. A riot ensued between participants and the police, in which 110 offices and twenty-two vehicles were smashed or burned, and seventy-four police officers and journalists were injured. Around thirty participants were detained.

Both the provincial government and the central government investigated the case by sending work teams to the city; however, the two authorities had different views on which officials should be disciplined. The provincial authority proposed that the major leaders of the Party committee and the government of the district where the riot occurred should be disciplined. This implied that city leaders would be exempted. Not surprisingly, the lower-level officials became resentful because the case was not directly handled by them but by the city authority. The central government, in contrast, believed that higher-level officials should take responsibility. Eventually, the city Party secretary was transferred and assigned as director of the agricultural office of the provincial Party committee.[52]

Local authorities may also protect their agents by allowing an investigation to drag on until it receives diminishing attention. In 1994, a woman was murdered in Hebei Province, and a suspect was caught. The suspect confessed to the crime after being tortured, was sentenced to death, and was executed in 1995. Nevertheless, when another suspect was caught in 2005, he confessed that he had killed the woman, in addition to various other crimes. However, the court dismissed his confessions, claiming that his murdering of the woman was irrelevant to the crimes he was charged with. In recalling how he decided the case, the judge said, "It was based on the leaders' decision. I made the ruling based on what the leaders said."[53] When the case was covered by the media, the provincial authority came under pressure. The provincial political and legal affairs committee formed a team to investigate the case, and the provincial authority initially promised to release the result of the investigation to the public. However, by 2014, the result had still not been released, and it is unclear whether it ever will be. As the provincial court was involved in the ruling, the investigation became complicated. If the interests of the local leaders and their agents are aligned, malfeasant agents are unlikely to be disciplined without pressure from above.

The state authority can protect their agents in other ways. Local authorities may not include records of discipline in the files of disciplined officials. Without a record of discipline, the official can be treated as not having been disciplined. In Shaanxi province, party or administrative disciplinary actions given to about 1,330 people were not enforced between 1997 and 2002. The disciplinary action taken against some cadres was not

TABLE 4.6.
Cases of duty-related malfeasance handled by procuratorates in Yunnan Province (1998–2002).

Cases	Cases	Frequency (percentage)
Accepted	2,420	100.0
Investigated	726	30.0
Investigation completed	631	100.0
a. Transferred for prosecution	344	54.5
b. Transferred not for prosecution	119	18.9
c. Revoked	168	26.6

SOURCE: *Yunnan jiancha nianjian* (Procuratorial Yearbook of Yunnan Province) (1999–2003).

made known to their agencies, some disciplinary decisions were not included in the personnel files of those disciplined, and some cadres who were sentenced to serve time in jail were even paid during their imprisonment.[54] Organizational support reduces disciplined agents' worry because organization-based endorsement has a legal and procedural base and protects their careers.[55]

Ex post leniency may also mean that accused officials are exempted from legal punishment or are given less severe punishment. From 2005 to June 2009, of the 17,670 people convicted of duty-related crimes, 9,707 (55 percent) were exempted and 5,390 (30.5 percent) were placed on probation.[56] Table 4.6 presents the settlement of cases of duty-related malfeasance in Yunnan province between 1998 and 2002. The duty-related malfeasance includes the following four types: abuse of power, neglect of duty, resorting to favoritism for personal ends, and abusing public power to violate citizens' rights. Only about 30 percent (726) of the cases filed (2,420) by procuratorates were investigated. Of the 631 cases with investigations completed, 54.5 percent (344) were transferred for prosecution, whereas others were not pursued. In other words, only about 14 percent of the filed cases (344 out of 2,420) were pursued. Certainly, some cases were dropped because of the lack of sufficient evidence, but a number of officials have been exempted because of the tolerance of the state authority and problems with the existing law. For example, the law stipulates that agents will be disciplined if his or her behavior causes "severe consequences," but the definition of severity is subject to different interpretations.[57]

Nevertheless, *ex post* leniency does not always undermine the credibility of discipline. Despite such leniency, punishment is still highly undesirable to government officials. First, not all disciplined agents will be reinstituted or reappointed; second, discipline may still affect the likelihood of punished agents being promoted or offered important positions.[58] Therefore, discipline even with *ex post* leniency is a threat to government officials in that not all officials will be exempted or can anticipate the exemption.

Conclusion

State capacity is crucial to governance and regime survival. Several decades ago, Huntington wrote, "The differences between democracy and dictatorship are less than the differences between those countries whose politics embodies consensus, community, legitimacy, organization, effectiveness, stability, and those countries whose politics is deficient in these qualities."[59] A government with strong capacity is effective in governance and is able to achieve important policy goals, based on the condition that the state authority retains effective control over its agents. The state's loss of control means it is unable to make its agents behave as desired. In explaining the "spontaneous privatization" in the former Soviet Union that led to the serious loss of state assets, Solnick writes, "Once it became clear that the ministerial supervisors were unable (or unwilling, given the rent-seeking potential) to stop enterprise managers from claiming de facto ownership rights over assets, the pace of spontaneous privatization accelerated."[60]

In China, the party-state is still able to achieve its important policy goals, such as economic growth and maintaining social stability. The party-state has used rewards as an important mechanism to induce local officials to achieve economic development. This chapter suggests that the imposition of sanctions is another important mechanism that allows the party-state to deter agents' severe deviations. Consequence severity and blame attribution are two crucial factors that affect a malfeasant agent's likelihood of being disciplined. To a large extent, the party-state has indicated its bottom line in terms of tolerance: Erring agents whose malfeasance directly causes severe consequences are less likely to be tolerated by the state authority, and vice versa. These two factors also dictate that grassroots officials are more likely to be (severely) disciplined because of their direct role in governance.

What merits emphasis is that blame attribution in China is not limited to grassroots officials. High-ranking officials have also been disciplined if they are connected to problems with severe consequences. Solnick writes that, based on the experience of the former Soviet Union, "the loss of confidence in the institution makes its demise a self-fulfilling prophecy."[61] In China, the disciplining of high-ranking officials enhances the credibility of discipline or at least signals to state agents the lack of guaranteed exemption.

While the Chinese party-state's power to discipline remains a threat to erring agents and enables the state to achieve important policy goals,[62] the state's discipline is selective. Government officials whose malfeasance did not cause severe consequences have generally been tolerated, regardless of whether they were directly responsible for the malfeasance. Hence, the state authority's dealing with erring agents in duty-related malfeasance reveals its cost considerations. In the view of the party-state and pertinent leaders, many agents who commit malfeasance are still forgivable, and those who have been removed or dismissed may be reappointed. This tolerance, though conditional, explains the persistence of state agents' irresponsive, irresponsible, and abusive behavior.

FIVE

Punishing Corrupt Agents

The previous chapter shows that selective or differentiated discipline, together with the availability of multiple types of discipline, alleviates the dilemma that the state authority faces when dealing with agents who commit duty-related malfeasance. The state authority tends to encounter a different situation when it comes to dealing with corrupt agents. Corruption is defined as criminal conduct that cannot be justified legally, morally, or ideologically, and the state authority often must choose between tolerance and punishment when handling corrupt agent cases. As corruption is illegal, the state authority must impose legal sanctions when it decides to punish agents. However, legal punishment generally ends the political careers of errant agents, and the cost or consequence of discipline is therefore obvious to the state authority. For this reason, compared with duty-related malfeasance, corruption cases may better reveal how the state balances the cost of discipline with the need to punish.

Corruption continues to breed strong resentment among the population and damages the regime's legitimacy in China. While anticorruption is a policy goal of the Chinese party-state, effective anticorruption is highly conditional. As Rose-Ackerman writes, the "deterrence of criminal behavior depends on the probability of detection and punishment and on the penalties imposed—both those imposed by the legal system and more subtle costs such as loss of reputation or shame."[1] In other words, a timely investigation of corrupt agents and due punishment are crucial to effectively curbing corruption and enhancing the government's reputation for anticorruption. Yet, as Solnick writes, "Maintaining a reputation for discipline requires an administrative apparatus that is willing and able to recognize potential threats early and alert political leaders to their existence."[2]

In China, the Party controls anticorruption agencies and enjoys a "first-move" advantage in terms of collecting information, carrying out investigations, and meting out punishments.[3] Such control necessitates responsibility. Although the Party authority and leaders recognize the need to punish corrupt agents, they face constraints in making punishment-related decisions (see Chapter Three). Both the investigation and punishment of corrupt agents have been affected by the party-state's cost considerations.

This chapter examines the state authority's tolerance and punishment of corrupt agents in China by exploring the access of disciplinary agencies to sources of information on corrupt agents, the investigation of suspects, and the imposition of punishment on convicted agents. It suggests that the Chinese state authority differentiates the processes involved in investigating officials of different administrative ranks or political importance by exercising more caution when dealing with higher-ranking officials. The formal and informal procedures introduced to differentiate the disciplining of state agents have inevitably resulted in inconsistencies in the punishment of corrupt officials. Although such inconsistencies compromise the credibility of discipline, corrupt agents still face serious threats due to the lack of an exemption guarantee. The threat is non-negligible because a large number of officials, including high-ranking officials, have been severely punished, and their punishments have brought an end to their political careers.

The Collection and Processing of Information in Anticorruption

In most societies, the government is unable to prevent corruption *ex ante* entirely, and *ex post* measures must be instituted to detect and punish corrupt agents. Obtaining reliable and accurate information on corrupt agents is the precondition for fighting against corruption *ex post*. The capability of anticorruption agencies to obtain and act on accurate information determines whether corrupt agents are detected and punished in a timely manner. It also indicates to state agents the probability that a corrupt agent will be caught and therefore affects the state's ability to deter corruption.[4] For this reason, how information is collected and used has a direct effect on the effectiveness of anticorruption.

THE IMPORTANCE AND LIMITATIONS OF TIPS

Anticorruption agencies in China rely on several information sources. One comprises citizen reports,[5] which can be signed or made anonymously. Another major source is the information revealed by other corruption cases under investigation (that is, implications). Other sources include inspections, audits, and media exposure. Citizen reports or tips in the forms of letters, visits, online reports, e-mails, and phone calls remain the most important channel of information on corruption cases. These reports are estimated to account for 60 percent to 80 percent of the corruption cases investigated by the legal department. Although some cases are revealed by other cases, these earlier cases are initially reported by the public.[6]

Of the more than 1,000 cases collected for this study, 547 reported the ways in which corrupt officials were detected (Appendix 5.1). Table 5.1 reports the sources of information on corrupt cadres. Although tips from citizens or other social actors constituted about 34 percent of the information sources, the actual number could have been larger. The second-largest source (33 percent) comprised clues disclosed by cases under investigation (that is, implicated), and many of these cases could have been reported by the public.[7]

In China, many corrupt cadres work in nonadministrative public agencies or firms. Table 5.1 shows no substantial difference between officials and other cadres in terms of the ways they were caught. However, being implicated or revealed by other cases seemed to be more common among state officials. Reporting on government officials is difficult, either because they are protected by some leaders or because their corruption is not known

TABLE 5.1.
Sources of information on corrupt cadres.

	Total (percentage)	State sector (percentage)	Nonadministrative public sector (percentage)	Business sector (percentage)
Reported	33.6	33.1	40.8	32.0
Implicated	32.7	39.0	24.5	14.6
Detected by agencies	13.2	16.4	8.2	3.9
Self report	4.4	2.8	6.1	9.7
Miscellaneous	16.1	8.7	20.4	39.8
Total[a]	547	390	49	103

SOURCE: Author's collection.

[a] Five of the 547 cases are not included because they do not belong to any of the three categories.

to the average person. However, when their corruption is revealed as an implication of other cases under investigation, corrupt agents are likely to be investigated due to strong evidence.[8]

State authorities in China are clearly aware of the importance of citizens' anticorruption reports. In 1988, the procuratorate of Shenzhen established the first reporting center in China to receive citizen reports on corruption. Since then, more than 3,600 reporting centers have been established by procuratorates across the country. Within ten years, the procuratorates received about 1.5 million reports of public-employee corruption, including embezzlement (57.7 percent), bribery (26.8 percent), misappropriation of public funds (9.4 percent), and dereliction of duty (3.3 percent).[9] In 1998, the Supreme Procuratorate reported that citizen reports accounted for 80 percent of the corruption cases investigated. In 2001, the figure remained as high as 70 percent.[10] Citizens' tips are indisputably crucial to the detection of corrupt agents.

Nevertheless, while tips remain an important source of information on corruption, they also have a severe limitation: Tip-turned cases account for only a very small portion of the total number of tips received by disciplinary agencies. Table 5.2 shows that a large number of tips were sent to DICs and supervision bureaus.[11] After the DICs and supervision bureaus screen the reports they receive, some of the cases are put on file for investigation and prosecution. If the cadres involved in a case are proven to have engaged in corruption, they are subjected to Party or administrative discipline. If the corruption is serious, the case is forwarded to the procuratorate for legal prosecution. All of these cases belong to the category of "cases put on file for investigation and prosecution." Table 5.2 shows that only about 7.3 percent of the 13.9 million reports made were pursued by DICs and supervision bureaus. During the five years between 1993 and 1997, procuratorates received about 1.8 million tips, and the number of pursuable cases based on tips accounted for about 15 percent of the total.[12] Procuratorates received 1.035 million tips between 2003 and June 2007, and the number of pursuable cases constituted about 13 percent of the total.[13]

Several factors account for the limited number of tips turning into pursuable cases. First, not all of the tips provided to disciplinary agencies relate to the corruption of officials. A significant portion of the tips involve complaints about other issues that cannot be categorized as corruption. Second, tips are not pursued because they fail to provide adequate information or

TABLE 5.2.
Reports received and cases investigated by disciplinary agencies in selected years.

	Reports (A)	Cases investigated (a)	a/A (percentage)
DICs and SBs			
1996	1,807,577	168,389	9.3
1997	1,826,100	174,320	9.5
1998	1,612,000	142,000	8.8
2002	1,488,061	171,066	11.5
2003–June 2008	7,169,000	360,000	5.0
Total	13,902,738	1,015,775	7.3

SOURCES: *The Yearbook of the People's Republic of China* (1997–1999, 2003).
DICs: discipline inspection committees; SBs: supervision bureaus.

are simply false accusations. Because corruption often takes the form of discrete transactions, it is difficult for outsiders to be aware of important detailed information. Third, political or cost considerations may also account for some tips not being pursued. These factors reveal not only the problems with tips but also the broad problems with anticorruption agencies and the political system.

UNRELATED ISSUES

Tips sent to anticorruption agencies do not always relate to cadre corruption. Procuratorates received 730,000 tips from 1988 to 1992, but 28.8 percent (that is, 210,000) of these tips related to issues that were beyond the purview of procuratorates.[14] As mentioned previously, procuratorates received 1.8 million citizen tips between 1993 and 1997. However, only about 38 percent (that is, 686,347) of the tips fell within the purview of procuratorates, and 39 percent (that is, 268,710) of the cases were filed for investigation based on these tips.[15]

Citizens may send tips to as many state agencies as possible to help draw attention to certain reported cases regardless of the duties of the agencies. At other times, tip providers may not be clear about the responsibilities of the state agencies to which they send tips. Some of the tips comprise citizen complaints about the malfeasance of officials, such as abuses of power or violations of citizen rights. For example, in one city in eastern China I visited, the DICs received more than 2,100 tips in 2012, but only about 10 percent (that is, 207) became pursuable cases. Hence, of the 670 cases of cadre corruption investigated, about 31 percent were based on tips, 24 percent were forwarded by other state agencies, and another 21 percent were revealed by other cases under investigation.[16]

Of the 2,108 tips received by the DICs in this city, about 72 percent related to the corruption of officials. Other tips comprised complaints about local officials' abuse of power in their interactions with citizens (10 percent), as in the cases of housing demolitions or land seizures. Such tips are similar to or the same as petitions presented to complaint bureaus. Still others related to the work style of officials (12 percent), blaming them for being irresponsible, irresponsive, or abusive in performing their duties. Again, such malfeasance cannot be categorized as corruption.

LIMITED RELIABILITY OF TIPS AS A SOURCE OF INFORMATION

Tips are limited in becoming pursuable cases also because the information provided by tip providers is not useful. Tips about corruption are understandably inaccurate because most people do not have enough information on the corruption, which is generally conducted discretely. Tip providers may thus base their reports on speculation. According to disciplinary agency officials, some tips are not processed because they are too vague or do not present a target for investigation.[17] Other tips are not useful because they accuse specific people but contain "obviously" distorted facts or are believed to overstate the problem. Still other tips simply make false accusations against government officials. In 1996, for example, disciplinary agencies in Sichuan cleared the names of 8,250 party members and cadres who were reported by others.[18] In the city I visited, about seventy to eighty of the more than 2,100 tips comprised false accusations made against reported cadres.

The reliability of tips as sources of information is further undermined because most tips are unsigned. When tips are signed, they are more pursuable and the tip providers are more committed. In China, disciplinary agencies pay more serious attention to signed tips and often notify tip providers of the settlement results of reported cases.[19] However, signed reports account for only a very small proportion of tips. In 2000, the Supreme Procuratorate reported that about 60 percent of reports were submitted anonymously. However, various local sources show that 70 percent or more of reports have been submitted anonymously in recent years.[20] For example, anonymous reports accounted for about 76 percent of the reports received by procuratorates in Jiangsu Province between 2006 and 2007 and about

77 percent between 2007 and 2008.²¹ In Hubei Province, the proportion was around 74 percent between 2000 and 2005. In Shanghai, it was 71 percent in 2005 and 77 percent between 2006 and 2007.²² In the city I visited, only about 10 percent of the more than 2,100 tips received by the DICs were signed.

Anonymity makes it difficult for anticorruption agencies to gain more information for further investigation. For example, from 2010 to June 2013, procuratorates in Beijing received 12,000 tips on the malfeasance of officials. Of these tips, 1,214 cases involving the corruption of officials, and 231 cases involving officials' dereliction of duty were filed for investigation. Therefore, about 12 percent (that is, 1,445) of the tips became pursuable cases. According to an official of the Procuratorate of Beijing, the pursuable cases were at a lower rate partly because about 15 percent of the tips were beyond the purview of the procuratorates. Although some tips were not processed because they were false, about 70 percent of the tips were unsigned, a major contribution to the low rate of pursuable cases. Unsigned reports often fail to provide helpful information. The official said that "under these circumstances, a tip is pursuable only if the tip provider can be reached for further information. But the procuratorates can barely find anonymous tip providers."²³ He acknowledged that most of the 1,445 pursuable cases were based on signed tips.

In the city I visited, the DIC officials reported that pursuable cases are founded on 20 percent to 30 percent of the signed tips. Although other signed tips are not necessarily false, they may overstate problems that are not serious enough to warrant investigation or discipline. In contrast, only a very small proportion (that is, far less than 10 percent) of the unsigned tips can be turned into pursuable cases.²⁴

The experience of the Independent Commission Against Corruption (ICAC) of Hong Kong also points to the positive correlation between signed tips and pursuable cases. In Hong Kong, signed reports facilitate the investigation of reported cases because they allow the ICAC to contact tip providers for verification and further information if necessary. Of the 64,460 cases received by the ICAC between 1989 and 2006, about 69 percent were signed. During this period, as the proportion of signed tips increased, the proportion of pursuable cases likewise increased. Between 1989 and 1995, while about 67 percent of the tips were signed, the proportion of pursuable cases was about 66 percent. Between 2001 and 2006,

72 percent of the tips were signed, and the proportion of pursuable cases increased to 77 percent.[25]

In theory, rampant corruption indicates a large number of corruption cases. As a corollary, there must be a non-negligible number of people who have knowledge of some of the corruption cases. Although some of these people may provide anonymous tips, others may be unwilling to do so. Reported officials may be able to identify tip providers if the number of people who know about a particular corruption case is limited. Hence, even unsigned tips may carry risks if the corrupt agents who are reported are not investigated or convicted. If people lack confidence in the state agencies' ability to offer protection to tip providers, they have little incentive to provide informative tips, not to mention signed tips.[26] People's worry about their personal safety has been borne out by the experiences of some tip providers.

Given the high stakes in their positions and the potential serious consequences that accompany being caught,[27] corrupt officials are strongly motivated to protect themselves and silence tip providers. Corrupt agents can identify tip providers due to their personal connections in state agencies or because the number of people who know about the corruption is limited. In addition, some people may submit the same tips to different anticorruption agencies such as DICs or procuratorates at the central, provincial, city, or county levels to maximize their chances of receiving attention from pertinent authorities. However, this mode of reporting increases their chances of being detected by the reported cadres because one or more of these agencies may expose the identities of the informants. Another common practice of upper-level anticorruption agencies is to forward such reports to lower-level state authorities or their anticorruption agencies. Although some of these forwarded cases may be acted on, others may be ignored. Corrupt cadres have better access to reporting materials if they are forwarded to local authorities.[28]

Once reported corrupt agents become aware of a tip and its source, they may use every possible means to take revenge. They can do so because the protection for tip providers is either very weak or altogether absent. For example, the threats posed by reported agents to tip providers are not specified as crimes under criminal law. Only when tip providers are seriously hurt or have their rights seriously encroached upon will the legal department investigate a case. Further, the punishment for officials who retaliate against tip providers is far from serious. For example, the legal department investigated 1,835 cases in 1991 that involved corrupt agents retaliating against the tip providers who reported them. Only 569 people (one person per three cases) were eventually sanctioned. Of these people, only thirty-nine were subjected to legal punishment, and the others were subjected to party or administrative discipline.[29] In each year during the early 2000s, procuratorates received more than 1,000 cases in which tip providers were retaliated against. However, less than 5 percent of these cases were eventually put on file for investigation. Understandably, many other cases were not submitted to the procuratorates.[30]

Therefore, although anticorruption agencies rely heavily on citizen reports, protecting the personal safety of informants is not the top priority of the party-state in lawmaking or enforcement. Against this background, retaliation against tip providers is not uncommon, and the costs paid by tip providers can be very high or even fatal. They may be fired by their employers if they report on leaders at their workplaces. They may be harassed by those they report or put in jail on false charges by local authorities or politically powerful officials. Some citizens have been wounded or even killed by hired thugs. In the 1990s, an average of about 500 cases per year involved tip providers or witnesses being disabled or killed. This number recently rose to 1,200 cases per year.[31]

For example, a city leader in Henan Province hired several people to murder a person who reported his corruption in 1996. The informant was seriously wounded, and his wife was killed.[32] In another Henan county, an employee at a county bureau reported on the corruption of his leaders. As a result, five officials, including the bureau head and a deputy head, attempted to murder the employee and his family in a 1999 explosion that killed three of his family members. The five leaders were eventually caught and executed in 2000.[33]

Some leaders abuse their power to deal with citizens who report on their corruption. In one case, an official reported the corruption of the provincial Party secretary of Hebei Province in 1995. The next year, he was expelled from the Party, charged with violating the personal honor of the major provincial leader, and placed in a labor camp. In another case, a township cadre reported the corruption of a city official. In 1996, the cadre was imprisoned for one year under the false charge of embezzling 3,000 yuan. After he was released, he continued to report on the city official's corruption.

In 1999, two thugs went to his home, killed his wife and son, and seriously wounded him in an attempted murder.[34]

Media coverage of such incidents tends to discourage some citizens from providing tips, especially signed tips. In 2007, an official of the Supreme Procuratorate reported that about 60 percent of tip providers did not have direct conflict of interests with the cadres they reported: "Many people who initially want to submit reports will give up when they find the miserable ending of tip providers. The whole society will have a sense of moral frustration . . . If tip providers are not protected, those 60 percent may stop reporting, and a large number of clues would be lost. This is very harmful to the investigation [of corruption cases]."[35] Despite the possible consequences, disciplinary agencies have not been able to significantly strengthen protections for tip providers.

The persistently high proportion of unsigned tips in Mainland China is in striking contrast to the high proportion of signed reports in Hong Kong.[36] When the ICAC was first established in Hong Kong in 1974, citizen reports on the corruption of public or private employees were mostly anonymous due to the risks involved. However, citizens gradually began to realize that the ICAC could provide sufficient protection and was determined to curb corruption. According to a survey of citizens in 1977, 38 percent believed that the majority of government agencies harbored corruption. This figure decreased to 7 percent in 1986.[37] Given their trust in the ICAC, more citizens became willing to submit signed tips or reports to the commission. The proportion of signed reports increased to over 70 percent from the initial 35 percent. The trust of citizens in the ICAC is also reflected in the willingness of the majority to appear in court as witnesses.[38]

POLITICAL CONSIDERATIONS AND SCREENING

Some tips may not be pursued due to political considerations. First, the reported problems may be perceived to have no serious consequences even if they are investigated. Second, the timing may not be appropriate for investigating the reported problems. Third, because other factors may make investigating reported cases inappropriate, these cases may be (temporarily) shelved with the permission of pertinent leaders.[39] Political considerations are also reflected in the different procedures used to deal with government officials. When disciplinary agencies receive information on the corruption of officials, they distinguish between cases that are based on the officials' administrative ranks. Cases involving lower-ranking officials are normally forwarded to lower-level state authorities to handle, sometimes with the requirement that the result be reported to the upper-level authorities. Cases involving high-ranking officials are handled directly by high-level disciplinary agencies.[40]

Both high-ranking and lower-ranking officials can be excused. When cases involving lower-ranking officials are handled exclusively by lower-level agencies or leaders, upper-level authorities do not always require the former to report the result. Upper-level authorities may restrain themselves from intervening too often in the settlement of cases to avoid upsetting lower-level authorities.[41] Nonintervention grants discretion to lower-level authorities when they come to dealing with their malfeasant agents, and tolerance or exemption become possible.

One city DIC official reported in an interview that DICs pay serious attention to the tips they receive. When asked why corruption has been so rampant in China if DICs have been functioning properly, he replied that "high-level officials are corrupt."[42] This explanation reflects that anticorruption efforts targeting high-level officials who have more political resources and strong political connections are ineffective. One provincial official responsible for the disciplining of state agents in the legal sector in his province reported that when he first assumed the position in 2013, the central authority was claiming that both "flies" (lower-ranking officials) and "tigers" (high-ranking officials) would be punished if they are corrupt. However, one of his colleagues told him that "if you want to beat a tiger, you need to be careful enough not to be eaten by the tiger."[43]

The state authority and disciplinary agency officials tend to exercise more caution in dealing with high-ranking and important officials. Different procedures have been applied to deal with officials of different administrative ranks and/or political importance. At the central level, when the central DIC receives information about a case, its standing committee or the central party authority decides whether the case should be pursued.[44] The central DIC normally needs to obtain the agreement of the members of the Politburo Standing Committee to investigate an official with the administrative rank of vice minister. The central DIC requires the approval of the politburo meeting to investigate an official with the administrative rank of minister (*zheng bu ji*). For example, the investigation of Chen Liangyu, the former Party secretary of Shanghai, was approved by the members of the Politburo Standing Committee.[45]

Similar procedures have also been used at the local level due to institutional isomorphism in the political hierarchy. The investigation of important local officials is also decided by local leaders. At the provincial level, the DIC has the discretion to investigate officials with the administrative rank of county magistrate (*chuji*). However, in investigating officials with the administrative rank of city mayor (*tingji*), the provincial DIC must submit reports to the provincial Party committee for approval. Therefore, the investigation of an official with the rank of city mayor or higher must be formally authorized by the standing committee of the provincial Party committee.[46]

In dealing with high-ranking officials, it is necessary for pertinent leaders to build a consensus, the process of which may create veto points. A former secretary of the DIC of Hunan Province acknowledged that when a case is discussed among the standing committee members of the provincial Party committee, a member who is reluctant to investigate an official may defend the official, indicating the said member's preference for other members. A lack of consensus may lead to the case being shelved. Various reasons, such as personal connections, may affect leaders' attitudes toward malfeasant officials.[47]

At the grassroots level, there is also a political norm to consider when dealing with important officials. At the county level, the DIC reviews the tips it receives and shelves some of them. Some of reported cases are submitted to the standing committee of the DIC for discussion. The investigation of an official at the administrative level of township head (*ke ji*) or even deputy township head (*fu ke ji*) often requires the agreement of the county Party secretary. Some of these cases must be discussed by the standing committee of the county Party committee. At the city level, the investigation of an official at the administrative level of county magistrate (*chu ji*) or deputy county magistrate (*fu chu ji*) requires the agreement of the city party secretary. These cases would also be discussed at the meeting of the standing committee of the city Party committee.[48]

Therefore, if the top local leader is not active in disciplining corrupt agents, disciplinary agencies are likewise not active. One county Party secretary said, "We have to be cautious in investigating cadres because doing it affects local stability and work. When I was the county party secretary, I told the DIC and the procuratorate not to investigate cadres without sufficient caution. So, not many officials were investigated and disciplined during my terms."[49]

Consequently, although the state authority sometimes receives information about a particular corrupt agent, taking action may be difficult. The authority may have to wait for the right time to lessen the repercussions or quell any opposition. One city DIC official made the following statement in an interview: "When investigating an official suspected of corruption, we are dealing with a person with power and resources. We need to think about how to conclude the case once we start the investigation. If we are not clear about how to conclude a case, it is better not to investigate it in the first place."[50]

Disciplinary agency officials acknowledge that some pursuable tips are dropped or tabled, although the number is generally limited. Some officials attribute this tolerance to local protectionism:

> Some local leaders may worry that investigating reported officials may affect the stability of their localities or agencies, thereby influencing local governance and their performance record. Others worry about local economic development effects and are thus reluctant to investigate officials who have made contributions to local economic development. Still others refuse to investigate reported officials so that they may protect their connections.[51]

Cost considerations on the part of pertinent leaders or the state authority make it possible to tolerate some corrupt agents. In 2005, the provincial Party secretary of Hebei province complained that such tolerance was a "virus" undermining the "immunity" of the Party. If this virus spreads, it would obscure the difference between the good and bad and demoralize Party members and officials. The secretary pointed out that "as a result, ugly, evil, and wrong practices would not be regarded as ugly, evil, and wrong, and the solidarity of the Party would be seriously eroded."[52]

Against this background, it may not be surprising that the processing of tips about corrupt agents varies among different groups of officials. Table 5.3 reveals that proportionally fewer high-ranking officials (that is, at the administrative level of county magistrate or higher) have been investigated compared with lower-ranking officials. In 1996, only 2.5 percent of the cases on higher-ranking officials were investigated, compared with 10.7 percent of those on lower-ranking officials. Therefore, although reports on corruption involving high-ranking officials accounted for 16.6 percent of the total reports, cases on the same accounted for only 4.4 percent of the total cases investigated.

TABLE 5.3.
Investigation of cadres by discipline inspection committees and supervision bureaus (1996).

Type of reports	Reports received (A)	Cases investigated (a)	a/A (percentage)
On lower-ranking cadres	1,508,201	160,986	10.7
On high-ranking cadres[a]	299,376	7,403	2.5
Total	1,807,577	168,389	9.3

SOURCE: *The Yearbook of the People's Republic of China 1997*, 216.
[a]Refers to cadres with an administrative rank of county magistrate or higher.

The difficulty involved in investigating government officials, especially high-ranking officials, has also been reflected by the common public practice of repeatedly reporting on cadres to draw the attention of anticorruption agencies to the cases. Some citizens have reported corrupt cadres for years, yet these cases remain on the back burner. Many officials who hold important positions are investigated not because people report their problems to the discipline agencies but because their problems are revealed by the other cases under investigation, which may yield details that leaders cannot ignore.[53]

For example, in a county-level city in Shanxi Province, 128 retired officials, including a former deputy county magistrate and heads of government agencies, began to report on the corruption of the city Party secretary from 2003, but with only one person signing his name the first time. They tried a second time after their first report was ignored. In addition to sending the materials to pertinent state agencies, they also submitted a copy directly to an official in Beijing who urged them to sign their names because anonymous reports were not handled seriously. Although seventeen people signed their names the third time, their report did not receive any response from the state agencies. Some of them then went to the provincial capital to report on the secretary's corruption, while a few representatives went to Beijing and stayed there for five months to present the case. But their efforts were unsuccessful. A sympathetic official of a central agency told them, "Do not feel frustrated. It generally takes five years to file a successful case against a county Party secretary." This corruption case was not investigated until 2006 when a murder case occurred in the city, involving people who were connected to the corrupt Party secretary. Eventually, the party secretary was sentenced to twelve years in prison in 2008.[54]

IMPLICATIONS OF THE SELECTIVE USE OF TIPS

Lü may be correct in stating that "there has not been a lack of leadership resolve to root out corruption, nor has there been any shortage of detailed, technical, even hairsplitting regulations regarding corruption."[55] However, intentionally or not, the selective and ineffective use of information undermines the effectiveness of anticorruption. Citizen tips can be seen as "fire alarms" sent to the state authority. However, as McCubbins and his coauthors suggest, "The effectiveness of the fire alarm depends on the credibility of political officials when they threaten to punish an agency that is not complying with the wishes of its overseers."[56] In China, the state authority's selective use of tips casts doubt on its credibility of anticorruption.

Frustrated people may resort to extreme measures when dealing with corrupt cadres. In an extreme case involving a village in Shanxi Province, a villager killed fourteen people and wounded another three in October 2001. The casualties comprised village cadres, their family members, and other villagers. The killer said in court that he was not sorry for what he did but regretted that he was unable to kill all of the people he wanted to kill. He explained that he killed them because his efforts to report the corruption of village cadres had failed. In the preceding four years, he and other villagers had repeatedly reported problems to various departments, but nothing came of their efforts. While on trial, the killer asked, "Where can we find justice? Who can speak for us?" and stated that "the only option is to use violence to deal with injustice." In 2001, he gathered evidence that the village cadres and managers of village enterprises had embezzled more than 5 million yuan. He decided to report the corruption case through regular channels. He collected the signatures of 121 party members, cadres, and villagers and then submitted the reports to pertinent state authorities. However, after eight months, they had yet to receive any response. The report was eventually forwarded to the township DIC and the district's public security bureau. The deputy township party secretary overseeing the township DIC told him, "Even if you send the report to the central DIC, you can do nothing if I do not let you go through the procedures." An official of the public security bureau told him that the bureau did not have enough money to investigate the case. When the villager said he could provide the money, the official said the bureau did not have the personnel.[57]

This case also shows that a lack of intervention from upper-level authorities makes it more possible for local leaders to tolerate their corrupt subordinates. As a result, investigations of important local officials at the city level or even lower must sometimes be carried out by the central agencies to decrease the influence of the targeted officials' local networks.[58]

The cases I collected also reveal the limitations of the party-state's anticorruption efforts. If anticorruption agencies are slow in investigating corrupt Party and government officials, these officials may have more opportunities and time to engage in corruption.[59] For example, of the 165 corrupt government officials, about 43 percent accepted bribes twenty to more than ninety-nine times before they were caught. Moreover, out of the 582 government officials who were accused of taking bribes, about 12.5 percent engaged in corruption for nine or more years before they were caught. If corrupt agents are not caught immediately or disciplined seriously, they serve as encouraging examples to others in power, making others believe that the risk of engaging in corruption is acceptable.

Therefore, dropping even a small number of pursuable tips may have a disproportional effect on the perceptions of state agents and corrupt officials. This practice weakens the deterrent effect of anticorruption when corrupt agents believe that their chances of being investigated and caught are low.[60] Moreover, it discourages those who have provided tips about corrupt agents, as a lack of response from disciplinary agencies leads them to doubt the determination of such agencies or the party-state in eradicating corruption.

Investigation of Corrupt Agents

The state's tolerance of certain corrupt agents notwithstanding, the threat of punishment imposed on convicted agents is not negligible. When the state authority decides to investigate an official who is suspected of corruption, the official will very likely be convicted based on the way the investigation is carried out. In China, corrupt agents are mostly investigated by DICs and the anticorruption bureau of the procuratorate. If a case is first investigated by a DIC, it is forwarded to the procuratorate for the filing of a lawsuit with the court if the evidence is strong and if the state authority has agreed to punish the agent. In theory, the anticorruption bureau is the formal legal organization responsible for the investigation of corrupt agents. DICs and supervision bureaus are the internal state organizations responsible for the investigation and disciplining of party members and state employees. However, in practice, DICs exercise power that is possessed only by legal departments in other societies.

Once the state authority has decided to investigate corrupt agents and especially important officials, it often relies on DICs for the investigation because they have advantages that the legal department does not enjoy. When a DIC decides or is allowed to investigate a person, it forms a team and then adopts the so-called two-regulated approach (*shuang gui*), which means that the detained cadre is required to report his or her problem in a regulated place at a regulated time. This method was initially stated in a 1990 directive promulgated by the State Council. In 1994, the central Party authority issued a document that provided a basis for its use within the Party.

This method essentially amounts to detaining a suspect in the name of the Party organization, thereby removing the constraints imposed by legal procedures at the initial stage of investigation. The procuratorate is responsible for suing suspects, but it requires legal evidence to detain and file a lawsuit against a suspect. The DIC adopts the "two-regulated" method to prevent the suspect from destroying the evidence before the procuratorate can take action. DIC officials believe that this method is very helpful in China's current situation, and they generally detain suspects only when they have some evidence.[61] Thus, this approach is commonly used by DICs at both the central and local levels.

When the central DIC uses this method, a suspected official is usually detained in a hotel, training center, military base, or another place with a quiet environment and convenient food supply. Safety is the primary consideration when a suspect is detained. Houses or low-rise buildings are preferred, and necessary measures are adopted to prevent the suspect from escaping. Further, everything in the room that may be used by the suspect to commit suicide is removed or reinstalled. Personal belongings are likewise removed. At least six to nine people are assigned to monitor each detained suspect, and those on the night shift are not allowed to sleep. If more suspects are involved in a case and are detained, the number of companions sent by the DICs also increases.[62]

During the suspect's detention, the investigation team forms two taskforces. The first—that is, the interrogation group—is responsible for persuading or interrogating the suspect. The other—that is, the investigation group—is responsible for collecting evidence from the organizations or people with whom the suspect has interacted. The investigation of a provincial leader normally requires at least forty or fifty people, with some cases requiring more. For example, the investigation of a smuggling case in Zhanjiang, Guangdong Province, in the late 1990s mobilized about 1,000 people. Given the limited number of employees at the central DIC, provincial DICs send people to provide assistance when necessary. If a local leader is investigated, the DIC in his or her province generally avoids participating in the investigation. For example, DIC officials from Jilin, Jiangsu, Zhejiang, and other provinces conducted the investigation of Chen Liangyu, the former Party secretary of Shanghai.

This method of detaining suspects until they confess places tremendous pressure on the suspects, and very few can stand the interrogations. In some cases, local DICs have abused power and even tortured suspects. The suspects are also generally unable to clear investigations because the disciplinary agency is unlikely to detain a person without at least preliminary evidence.

Not every corrupt agent has been investigated by DICs; many have been investigated by anticorruption bureaus. Table 5.4 reports the investigation of 1,012 corrupt agents in the different sectors included in my data set. Although the majority of the corrupt agents were first investigated by anticorruption bureaus, some variations also existed. Compared with the corrupt agents in the nonadministrative public sector (25 percent) and public firms (14 percent), more officials (39 percent) were first investigated by the Party's disciplinary agencies. The higher proportion of state employees under investigation by DICs may indicate the party-state's caution in dealing with important officials. That many (lower-ranking) corrupt officials are directly investigated by the legal department also suggests that a significant number of corrupt agents are not protected.

TABLE 5.4.
First agencies to investigate cases.

Agencies	Total (percentage)	State sector (percentage)	Nonadministrative public sector (percentage)	Business sector (percentage)
DICs and supervision bureaus	33.4	39.9	25.0	14.2
Anticorruption bureaus	62.7	57.6	71.1	76.5
Police department	2.8	1.5	2.9	7.7
Miscellaneous	1.1	1.0	1.0	1.6
Total[a]	1,012	714	104	183

SOURCE: Author's collection.

[a] Eleven of the 1,012 cases are not included because they do not belong to any of the three categories.

Punishment for Corrupt Agents

Not every official suspected of corruption and investigated is convicted. When a case is accepted by the procuratorate, it is filed for investigation if it passes the initial screening or review of the procuratorate. After the investigation is completed, it may or may not be filed with the court. Whereas some cases are dropped due to a lack of sufficient evidence, others are not seen as severe enough to warrant legal punishment, and party or administrative discipline may be considered suitable.[63] Still others may not be pursued due to cost considerations, as discussed in Chapter Three.

The procuratorates accepted 761,436 cases between 1998 and 2010. Of these cases, 51.7 percent (that is, 393,923) were filed for investigation, and 95.5 percent (that is, 376,392) of the investigations were completed.[64] The provincial procuratorate of Yunnan Province provides more detailed information on the handling of corruption cases in the province. In Yunnan, the categories of corruption cases handled by procuratorates include embezzlement, bribery, misappropriation of public funds, division of collective property, failure to explain large incomes, and others. Between 1998 and 2002, the procuratorates accepted 11,360 cases of corruption, 52.7 percent of which were filed for investigation (see Table 5.5). Of the cases filed for investigation, 93 percent (that is, 5,549) of the cases were completed, 72 percent of which (that is, about 4,000) were eventually pursued for criminal charges. As a whole, about 35 percent (that is, 4,000 out of 11,360) of the cases accepted by the procuratorates were eventually tried in court. Although the reasons why some cases were not pursued are unknown, it is clear that a significant number of cases were dropped during the legal process.

The Chinese party-state is aware of the problem that arises from selective disciplining. If a significant number of corrupt agents are not detected or investigated, the state authority must impose severe punishments on those who have been convicted to show its commitment to anticorruption and to deter corruption if it remains motivated to do so.[65] Compared with local governments, the central party-state is more concerned with regime legitimacy and its governing authority.[66] As discussed in earlier chapters, the central government faces the pressure of preventing "the leakage of authority" at the local level. If the central party-state were to show tolerance toward malfeasant agents, there would be no reason to believe that local leaders would impose due punishments on their erring subordinates. Hence,

TABLE 5.5.
Corruption cases handled by procuratorates in Yunnan Province (1998–2002).

	Cases	Frequency (percentage)
Cases accepted	11,361	100.0
Cases filed for investigation	5,985	52.7
Cases with investigation completed	5,549	100.0
a. Transferred for prosecution	4,002	72.1
b. Transferred but not for prosecution	802	14.5
c. Revoked	745	13.4

SOURCE: Editorial Group of Yunnan Provincial Procuratorate, *Yunnan jiancha nianjian* (Procuratorial Yearbook of Yunnan, 1999–2003) (Kunming: Yunnan Provincial Procuratorate, various years).

concerns over the leakage of authority pressure the central government into imposing due or severe punishments on corrupt agents. Moreover, the exposure of a corrupt high-ranking official can easily attract public attention and become public knowledge. As a result, failing to punish corrupt agents would be interpreted as a lack of commitment to anticorruption on the part of the central authority.

Local leaders who are responsible for monitoring and disciplining lower-ranking officials face a different situation. First, local leaders are not equally worried about the leakage of authority because protecting regime legitimacy is not their primary concern. Local leaders may be more concerned with the costs involved in the disciplining of their subordinates due to their relational proximity. Second, local officials who are investigated by local authorities may not receive equal attention from the public. When cases are handled exclusively by local authorities, local leaders have more discretion to manipulate the discipline process.

AN EMPIRICAL ANALYSIS

If the central authority faces more serious pressure than local authorities in terms of disciplining corrupt agents, the former may be more strongly motivated to mete out severe punishments. An analysis based on the punishment of about 2,500 corrupt officials collected from the *Procuratorial Daily* from 1993 to 2010 reveals this pattern.[67] As the analysis focuses on the punishment of corrupt officials, the data include only civil servants while excluding staff members working in nonadministrative public institutions and state-owned enterprises.[68]

More than 80 percent of the 2,500 cases occurred after 2000. The data seem to suggest that some provinces in the central part of China, such as Anhui, Henan, and Hubei, and a few others in the eastern part, such as Jiangsu and Zhejiang, had seen more corruption cases than provinces in the northwest, such as Tibet, Inner Mongolia, and Qinghai. Certainly, the data are suggestive only of the potential difference in frequency across provinces. These cases are not necessarily representative of the large number of corruption cases ruled by Chinese courts. However, because they were released by the same source and cover a lengthy period, they provide clues related to the punishment of convicted officials in China.

Statistical analyses are conducted to examine the relationship between the likelihood of being severely punished and other factors or explanatory variables. As elsewhere, the punishment for a corrupt official in China is generally determined by the severity of his or her corruption, which is often measured by the amount of money involved. In China, legal punishment for a convicted official ranges from a fixed term of imprisonment to death penalty. The dependent variable in this analysis is the type of punishment that falls into the following categories from less to more severe: (1) a fixed term of imprisonment; (2) life imprisonment; (3) death with reprieve; and (4) death penalty. For analytical purposes, the latter three are treated as severe punishments. Of the 2,430 cases with information on the legal punishment imposed on convicted officials, most officials (that is, 83 percent) were given a fixed term of imprisonment, 8.5 percent were given lifetime in jail, 5.6 percent were sentenced to death penalty with reprieve, and 2.9 percent were sentenced to death penalty with immediate execution.

The data set also shows that fewer higher-ranking officials were given a fixed term of imprisonment, which is seen as less severe punishment. Instead, more high-ranking officials were meted out one of the three modes of severe punishment. Of the seventy-five officials at the administrative rank of "vice governor or higher," 56 percent of them were given severe punishment, as opposed to about 12 percent of those at the administrative rank of "deputy county magistrate" or 8 percent of those at the rank of "township head."

The analysis aims to examine the attitude of the government toward high-ranking corrupt officials; thus, it focuses on the relationship between punishment and the administrative rank of a convicted official. Rank is therefore the independent variable. Government officials are divided into eight groups, ranging from staff or clerk (the lowest) to vice governor (*fu bu ji*) and higher.[69] Of the 2,854 officials with information about their ranks in the data, officials at the administrative rank of township head (*ke ji*) or lower account for approximately 42 percent, whereas officials at the administrative rank of vice governor or higher constitute less than 3 percent.

Four sets of control variables are also included. First, the type and the magnitude of corruption are controlled because the penalty of a corrupt agent is tied to the amount of money involved in his or her corruption.[70] Some officials may have also committed other crimes that can be divided into three types. Type 1 crimes include neglect of duty, abuse of power, and violating laws for personal gains. Type 2 crimes include introducing bribe, dividing public property, and the like. Type 3 crimes include sheltering criminals and illegally keeping guns.

A second set of control variables includes the attitudes and attributes of corrupt officials. They include (1) whether the corrupt official makes concessions and (2) whether the official is the major local leader (that is, the Party secretary or the head of the government). Major local leaders (such as Party secretary and head of the government) are assumed to receive a more severe punishment compared with other officials who have the same administrative rank but do not assume a position as important as that of local leaders, because punishing high-profile leaders can have a stronger deterrent effect.

A third set of variables includes the career information of government officials. One variable involves the career of the secretary of the provincial DIC. A secretary in the first year of his or her term in office is assumed to have a higher level of determination in terms of anticorruption efforts because he or she needs to perform. A person who is locally promoted is likewise assumed to be less willing to severely punish local corrupt officials because of local connections. The final set of variables includes the consumer price index and the time trend.

An ordinal logistic model is employed to examine the relationship between the severity of punishment and the rank of a corrupt official while controlling for the variables discussed earlier (Table 5.6). The rank of corrupt officials is initially treated as a continuous variable while controlling for the magnitude of corruption. Although a positive relationship exists between rank and the severity of penalty, the relationship is not statistically significant. When the rank of corruption officials is treated as a categorical variable, the effect of rank on severity is not shown because the effect is not linear. Therefore, a quadratic term of rank is included to estimate the relationship between the rank of a corrupt official and the severity of penalty (see Table 5.6). The statistical outcomes indicate that both rank and

TABLE 5.6.
Ordinal logistic regression of rank on the severity of punishment.

	Coefficient
Rank	−
Quadratic term of rank	+
Bribe accepted (log)	+
Embezzlement (log)	+
Misused money (log)	
Unexplained income (log)	+
Crime type 1	
Crime type 2	
Crime type 3	+
Confession	
Local leader	
Secretary of a DIC first year in office	
Secretary of a DIC locally promoted	
Consumer price index	
Time trend	−

SOURCE: Data set created by Lin Zhu and Yongshun Cai.
NOTES: "−" means the sign is negative and the coefficient is statistically significant (at 0.01); "+" means the sign is positive and the coefficient is statistically significant (at 0.01).

its quadratic item significantly affect the severity of penalty but in a nonlinear manner. Specifically, the first order of rank is negatively associated with the severity of penalty. Thus, the probability of receiving a more severe punishment decreases first as the rank of the corrupt officials increases. The probability of receiving a more severe penalty becomes the lowest when the administrative rank is county magistrate (that is, *chu ji*, coded as 5). Among the officials whose administrative rank is at the level of county magistrate or higher, the probability of receiving a more severe penalty increases as the rank of corrupt officials becomes higher.

The control variables, except for the severity of crime and Type 3 crimes, have no significant effect on the severity of penalty. The magnitude of corruption increases the probability of being more severely punished. In other words, officials whose corruption involves a larger amount of money are more likely to be severely punished. The effect of the time trend is significantly negative, suggesting that the probability of receiving a severe penalty decreases each year.

In order to better show the nonlinear relationship between the rank of the corrupt official and the severity of the imposed penalty, Figure 5.1 presents the predicted probability of the punishment for officials of different ranks.[71] The probability of receiving a "fixed term of imprisonment," which

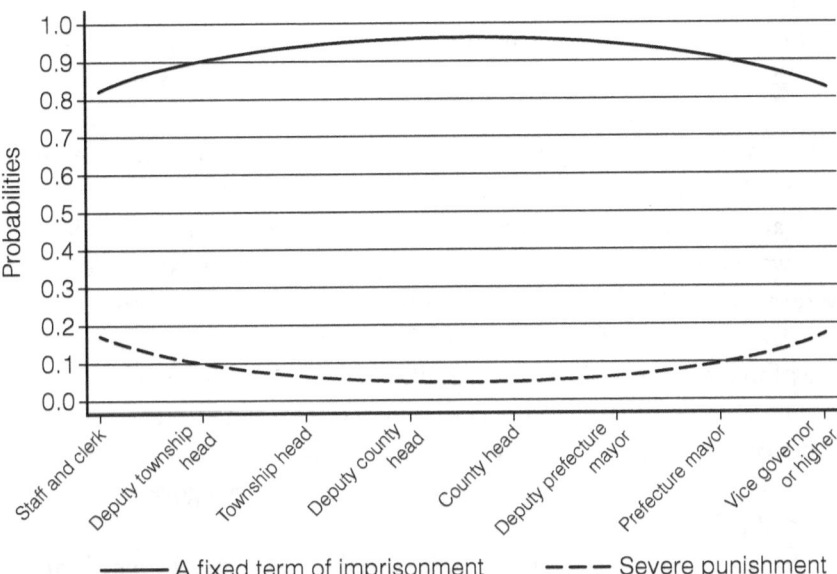

FIGURE 5.1. Predicted probability of imposing different types of penalties on officials of different ranks. *Note:* "Severe punishment" includes lifetime imprisonment, death with reprieve, and death penalty.

SOURCE: Data set created by Lin Zhu and Yongshun Cai.

is the least severe penalty, is relatively low for both staff or clerks and officials at the rank of vice governor or higher. If these officials' likelihood of being given a less severe punishment is lower, their likelihood of being severely punished will be higher (the total probability is 1). Compared to officials at the rank of deputy county head, officials at the lowest and highest ranks are both more likely to receive a severe punishment. This pattern shows that state authority tends to severely punish corrupt higher-level officials, probably to strengthen the deterrent effect. In addition, lowest-ranking officials are likely to be severely punished, perhaps because doing so is less costly.

The finding that high-ranking officials are more likely to be given severe punishment is not limited to corrupt Chinese officials. Crime research has shown that if a person of high status commits a crime that is far from the generally acceptable level, he or she is more likely to be punished more severely compared with low-status officials.[72] The Chinese central authority's tendency to impose severe punishments on higher-ranking officials shows its commitment to anticorruption. Through this measure, it reminds government officials of the potential consequences of engaging in corruption.

A number of corrupt high-ranking officials have been severely punished. During the twenty-five years preceding 2012, the central Party authority disciplined about 100 officials at the administrative level of vice governor or higher. Among the ninety officials who were punished, six were sentenced to death, twenty-six were sentenced to death with reprieve, another sixteen were sentenced to lifetime imprisonment, and the remaining forty-two were jailed for limited terms.[73] For example, Liu Fangren, a former provincial Party secretary of Guizhou, was sentenced to lifetime imprisonment in 2004 for accepting a bribe of 6.77 million yuan. In 2005, Tian Fengshan, a former minister of the Ministry of Land and Resources, received the same sentence for taking a bribe of 4 million yuan. Other officials who were given the same punishment included heads of provincial government agencies and prefecture leaders.

Other officials were given the death penalty with reprieve, which meant they would not be executed. For example, Li Jiating, a former governor of Yunnan, was given this punishment in 2003 for taking 18.1 million yuan in bribes. Gong Fugui, a vice governor of Hebei, was similarly sentenced in 2002 for accepting bribes amounting to 9.36 million yuan. Li Jizhou, a former vice minister of the Ministry of Public Security, was also sentenced to death with reprieve in 2001 for taking 5.03 million yuan in bribes. Many other high-ranking local leaders were also punished in this way.

Still other high-ranking officials have been executed, although the number has declined in recent years. Zheng Xiaoyu, the former head of the National Food and Drug Agency, was executed in 2007 for taking bribes amounting to 6.49 million yuan and also because the corruption in his agency distorted the drug market in the country and angered the central government. Chen Kejie, a former vice chairman of the National People's Congress, was executed in 2000 for taking 41.09 million yuan in bribes. Hu Changqin, a vice governor of Jiangxi, and Wang Huaizhong, a vice governor of Anhui, were executed in 2000 and 2003, respectively, for their corruption.

INCONSISTENCY IN THE PUNISHMENT OF CORRUPT OFFICIALS

Despite the central authority's intention to curb corruption by punishing high-ranking corrupt officials, inconsistencies have been observed in the disciplining of government officials at both the central and local levels. The statistical pattern of corrupt high-ranking officials being more likely to be severely punished can differ from public perception largely due to the inconsistencies in the disciplining of high-ranking officials.

For example, Cheng Weigao, the former provincial Party secretary of Hebei Province, accepted bribes, protected rampantly corrupt subordinates, illegally created business opportunities for his family, and forced the local legal department to put the person who reported his corruption into a labor camp for two years. Officials in the central DIC admitted that while many reports had been submitted about Cheng's malfeasance, the central authority had taken several years to decide to investigate the case. When it finally did, Cheng was exempted from criminal charges and was instead expelled from the Party. Although he was denied the welfare treatment of a minister, he was still treated as a vice minister even after he was proven to be corrupt.[74]

A comparable case is that of Chen Xitong, the former Party secretary of Beijing, who was sentenced to sixteen years in prison in 1998. The charges against him included embezzling expensive gifts, engaging in a self-indulgent lifestyle, reaping benefits through illegal means, and serious dereliction of duty. Although the punishment was serious, the justifications were seen as controversial. Although Chen was charged with embezzling expensive gifts, he did not bring those gifts home but left them in his office. Hence, whether his acts constituted embezzlement became a subject for dispute. Compared with many other seriously corrupt officials, Chen's corruption was not particularly severe. His imprisonment was therefore interpreted as a result of his failure in the power struggle.

Because corruption cases of high-ranking officials are high profile, they naturally catch the attention of both the public and other officials. Such high-profile cases tend to have a disproportionately significant effect on the perceptions of people and officials regarding the state's attitudes toward corruption. Inconsistencies in the punishment of corrupt agents not only undermine the credibility of the punishments but also make people doubt the determination or motivation of the central authority.[75] Moreover, this has led people to believe that anticorruption or the punishment of high-ranking officials is the consequence of a power struggle rather than the central authority's determination to curb corruption. Consequently, the imprisonment of Chen Liangyu was also interpreted by some people, including local officials, as the result of his failure in the power struggle.[76]

These inconsistencies are also reflected in the legal punishments applied to corrupt officials at both the central and local levels. Article 383 of the Chinese Criminal Law stipulates that those who embezzle 100,000 yuan or more or accept bribes of that amount or higher must be sentenced to a prison term of no fewer than ten years. If the case is very serious, a person convicted of this crime may be sentenced to death. To be fair, the legal department considers inflation in making judgments on embezzlement and bribery cases. Nevertheless, the enforcement of this law varies across cases.

According to my collection of forty-one cases in which corrupt officials were seriously punished between 2000 and 2009 (Appendix 5.2), in the ten death penalty cases that arose between 2001 and 2007, the amount of money taken by officials ranged from 2.55 million to 47.44 million yuan. In the twenty cases in which officials were convicted and sentenced to death with reprieve between 2001 and 2009, the amount of money taken ranged from 3.92 million to 190 million yuan. The eleven officials sentenced to life imprisonment between 2000 and 2006 took between 0.5 million and 9 million yuan. Some overlap can be observed in the three ranges. Thus, some corrupt officials may be punished less severely than others despite being convicted of severe corruption, or the former may be more corrupt.

For example, the former governor of Yunnan Province accepted 18.1 million yuan in bribes and was sentenced to death with reprieve. By contrast, Hu Changqing (a vice governor of Jiangxi who accepted a 5.44 million yuan bribe and had an inexplicable 1.8 million yuan income) and Wang Huaizhong (a vice governor of Anhui who accepted a bribe of 5.17 million yuan and had an inexplicable 4.8 yuan income) were executed for their crimes despite taking far fewer bribes.

Corrupt officials may be punished less severely for several reasons. First, some officials are believed to be cooperative in investigations. If a corrupt official shows a cooperative attitude, makes voluntary confessions, reports on the corruption of others, and returns illegal income to the government, he or she may be punished less severely. For example, Chen Tonghai, the former chairman of the board of directors of China Petroleum and Chemical Corporation, accepted 190 million yuan in bribes but was sentenced to death with reprieve rather than the death penalty in 2009. The justifications for his sentence included his "active confessions of his criminal activities" and provision of "information on other people's corruption that was crucial to the investigation of those cases." Furthermore, he "actively turned in all the illegal income." These justifications enabled him to avoid an immediate death penalty.[77]

Second, some seriously corrupt officials are given less-serious punishments due to the way their crimes are defined. According to the Criminal Law, failure to explain the source of a large amount of income (that is, 300,000 yuan or more) is a crime. A person who is convicted of this crime is sentenced to a maximum of five years in prison. Hence, manipulating the calculations of the amount of money embezzled or accepted as bribes and the unexplained income by including more illegal income into the category of "unexplained income" would justify a lighter legal punishment for a seriously corrupt official.[78]

At other times, inconsistencies occur due to political considerations. When the number of corrupt agents is high, the state authority may encounter difficulties in administering serious punishments. In one case in the city of Suihua in Heilongjiang Province, Party secretary Ma De received bribes from 265 party and government officials. When his case was disclosed in 2003, the high-level authorities' concern was that the operation of the city government would be paralyzed if all of the officials were punished. In the end, the disciplinary authorities adopted the policy of punishing seriously corrupt officials and then exempted those who were less seriously corrupt. The officials who received or sent 50,000 yuan or less in bribes were not investigated further. For some important officials, the amount for exemption was raised to 100,000 yuan. This policy was followed despite the acceptance of 100,000 yuan as a bribe being a serious crime according to the Criminal Law. Hence, most officials retained their tenure, and only four government officials were punished.[79] Such cases also point to a highly undesirable scenario faced by the state authority; that is, when the number of corrupt agents becomes too high, curbing corruption becomes too difficult, if not impossible.[80]

Conclusion

Corruption remains a severe problem plaguing the governments of most developing countries. The effectiveness of anticorruption fundamentally depends on a government's political will and ability to detect and punish corrupt agents. This is particularly true for authoritarian governments that face limited or little electoral pressure. Some authoritarian governments have been successful in keeping state agents monitored. Singapore, for example, is one of the least corrupt countries in the world. Lee Kuan Yew, the former prime minister of Singapore, explains his government's commitment to curbing corruption as follows: "We were sickened by the greed, corruption and decadence of many Asian leaders . . . we had a deep sense of mission to establish a clean and effective government. When we took oath of office at the ceremony . . . in June 1959, we all wore white shirts and white slacks to symbolize purity and honesty in our personal behavior and our public life."[81] This determination led to the adoption of serious measures, including the establishment of the disciplinary agency, whose ability to "investigate prominent persons has enhanced its credibility among Singaporeans."[82]

Nevertheless, either not every authoritarian government can have Singapore's determination, or what the Singaporean government has done is not readily feasible in other authoritarian regimes due to the differences in size, resources, and political will among countries. In China over the years, the state authority has claimed its determination to curb corruption. It has also claimed progress on anticorruption, as revealed by the decreasing number of corruption cases and citizen reports.[83] To be fair, a significant number of corrupt officials have been punished. Between 2000 and 2005, more than 200,000 corrupt public employees were disciplined, and some were executed.[84] In addition, China does not seem to be particularly worse off compared with other similar countries in terms of anticorruption. According to the Corruption Perceptions Index released in recent years, China (40 in 2013) scored higher than India (36) and some other transitional economies such as those of Russia (28) and Vietnam (31).

Nevertheless, the public feels that corruption in China remains rampant. The persistence of corruption is tied to the inadequate disciplinary efforts of the party-state. This chapter examines how corruption cases have been handled in China by looking at the investigations and punishments of corrupt officials. Unlike most types of duty-related malfeasance, corruption is a crime that cannot be easily excused once evidence against an agent is undeniable. Hence, the state authority must be cautious in deciding whether to investigate. This caution is reflected in the formal and informal procedures that are instituted to investigate high-ranking officials. These procedures imply that the disciplining of important officials often requires pertinent leaders to build a consensus, which in turn creates veto points and offers protection to some corrupt agents.

However, if the state authority wishes to exempt certain corrupt agents by not investigating their corruption, it must punish some corrupt officials to warn other agents. The state authority is not a unified actor, and the calculations of local authorities may differ from those of the central authority. The central authority tends to impose severe punishments once it decides to investigate a corrupt agent to produce a deterrent effect. However, even the central authority may tolerate some corrupt officials. Local authorities face less pressure to protect regime legitimacy and may exercise leniency in dealing with corrupt local officials. Thus, inconsistencies occur in the investigation and punishment of corrupt agents at both the central and local levels, thereby compromising the credibility of the disciplinary institutions. These inconsistencies are also important factors in the persistence and spread of corruption in China, as they affect the belief of state agents in the likelihood that they will be disciplined.

Given the detrimental consequences that arise from state tolerance, the party-state authority must strike a balance between tolerating and disciplining corrupt agents to protect its authority and legitimacy. Fully aware of the problems with the existing anticorruption measures, the central authority has made new efforts by promulgating new rules and introducing new practices since 2013. For example, to reduce local leaders' discretion in dealing with corruption cases, a new rule specifies that a local DIC needs to report to both the Party committee at the same level *and* the upper-level DIC when the local DIC seeks instructions on whether a corruption case should be investigated. This rule may allow the upper-level DIC to play an important role in determining the investigation of a corruption case.[85]

SIX

The Politics of Blame Avoidance

In discussing the survival strategies of politicians in Latin America, Ames writes, "In their own minds, leaders may seek power in order to assist certain social or ethnic groups, to improve the well-being of all citizens, to enjoy the trappings of office, or to get rich. None of these goals is attainable unless executives can maintain a grip on their offices."[1] Feeling the pressure of (re)election, politicians in democracies extend serious efforts to ensure their political survival. Credit claiming and blame avoidance are two basic methods used by politicians to protect their image and thereby win elections. Politicians tend to pay more attention to blame avoidance. Weaver suggests that, in democracies, "Politicians are motivated primarily by the desire to avoid blame for unpopular actions rather than by seeking to claim credit for popular ones" due to "negativity bias" among voters.[2] Similarly, McGraw points out the importance of blame management: "Success and even survival in politics frequently depends on the ability of politicians and public officials to extricate themselves from various types of predicaments."[3]

Like their counterparts in democracies, Chinese government officials are strongly motivated to avoid blame and ensure their political survival. Staying in power is the only way for officials to pursue their preferred policies or to seek the many social, political, and economic benefits associated with their posts. Although the state authority sometimes exercises tolerance and leniency in disciplining erring agents, agents who commit malfeasance cannot afford to ignore the possibility of punishment. Therefore, Chinese government officials do not remain passive when they have committed malfeasance. Instead, they use various measures to avoid responsibility and protect themselves from (severe) punishment. Such measures are adopted to conceal their malfeasance and/or to seek the tolerance and leniency of the upper-level authorities. Although government officials' attempts to avoid blame are not always effective, they complicate the disciplining.

Political Institutions and Blame-Avoiding Strategies

The survival strategies of politicians are shaped by the political institutions that determine to whom they are held accountable or from whom they need support. For example, Ames finds that, in Latin America, political leaders use public policy, especially public expenditures, as a tool for coalition-building and, consequently, political survival.[4] Politicians in democracies may use other methods, such as winning the support of certain groups of constituents or implementing divide and rule, to ensure their chance of being (re)elected.[5] By offering group-specific benefits, politicians can claim credit from these targets and expect to receive their political support.

At other times, when politicians have to implement unpopular policies and face electoral pressure, they take action to distance themselves from the unpopular policies or lower the salience of controversial issues to avoid public attention. Politicians may also try to complicate the causes and consequences, thus making the task of identifying the person responsible for unwanted policy consequences difficult for the people.[6] Arnold points out that, in the United States, citizens' knowledge of the causal chains that link policy instruments with policy effects allows them to search for a governmental action that may have produced the undesirable outcome. He suggests that an effect is traceable if a citizen can trace an observed effect back to a government action and then back to a representative's (that is, a legislator's) individual contribution.[7] A politician or a government may thus reduce his or her responsibility by complicating what Arnold calls the "traceability chain."[8] Such blame-avoiding strategies are especially important to protecting the image of politicians and helping them win electoral support.

In China, an official's blame avoidance can also be more important than his or her credit claiming, because failing to avoid blame or responsibility may end a political career. Government officials are aware of the need for blame avoidance. For example, as discussed in Chapter Four, agents working in the Party sector are less likely to be held accountable in governance compared with those in the government sector. Thus, government officials may want to transfer their jobs from the government sector to the Party sector. A deputy county magistrate might wish to become a deputy county Party secretary while assuming a position as head of the propaganda department, the organization department, or the discipline inspection committee. In this way, he or she is not subject to responsibility attribution, unlike officials in the government sector.[9] For most officials, however, this method is not feasible simply because such positions are limited.

As Chinese government officials are held accountable to upper-level authorities, lower-level officials have a strong incentive to prevent their malfeasance from being discovered by their superiors. A traditional way of protecting oneself is to block the flow of information relating to one's malfeasance. Government officials are also motivated to hide their malfeasance from the public because the upper-level authorities are likely to discover the malfeasance once the public learns about it. In these circumstances, the discretion of the upper-level authorities in disciplining state agents can be significantly reduced because the former cannot pretend not to know about the malfeasance. For this reason, malfeasant agents commonly cover up or underreport their failures.

Government officials will have to take other blame-avoiding measures when they fail to cover up their malfeasance. One method is the use of justifications or excuses to avoid or shift their responsibility, sometimes by finding scapegoats. The rationale is that well-framed excuses and justifications can better inform the potential blamers about the issues, the difficult tradeoffs, or the particular measures that have or have not been adopted to address the issues. Such efforts may provide the basis for more sophisticated judgments about the blameworthiness of individuals in their handling of a particular issue.[10] However, the effectiveness of justifications and excuses depends on whether they lead the superiors or the public to make new judgments favoring the defenders.[11] At other times, government officials may avoid responsibility through obfuscation or by complicating the causes of unwanted consequences and then preventing potential blamers from linking the consequences to the officials' decision or behavior.[12]

Fundamentally, the effectiveness of Chinese government officials' blame-avoidance efforts is determined by the attitudes of their superiors. Seeking the help and leniency of people with political power or influence is the most effective way of avoiding (severe) punishment. As mentioned in earlier chapters, officials are naturally connected when there is a patron–

client relationship between them. Pye pointed out that "with the erosion of ideology and the lack of clearly defined nationalistic ideals, the personal bonding of the political elite may turn out to be the most critical factor in holding the system together."[13] In facing the threat of punishment, the instant reaction of malfeasant agents is to mobilize their social networks to seek help or protection.[14] Social connections or networks, therefore, are important political resources or assets for Chinese government officials.

Blocking the flow of information, avoiding responsibility, and mobilizing networks are common methods used by Chinese government officials to evade blame and punishment. These measures suggest, to some extent, that disciplining still has some credibility. The blame-avoiding activities of officials also reveal how informal rules or norms influence the operation of political institutions in China.

Blocking Information

Blocking the flow of information is a traditional method used by Chinese local officials, although this may lead to disastrous consequences. The worst consequence arising from the use of this method was seen during the Great Famine in the late 1950s. In the well-known "Xinyang incident" in Henan province, for example, at least one million people starved to death. According to the then district deputy Party secretary, one important reason for the tragedy was that local leaders, including the provincial and the district Party secretaries, prevented local people from reporting the situation to the central authority. In 1958, the total output of grain in the district was reported to be 2.8 billion kilos; in 1959, the district experienced an unprecedented drought, and grain output was reduced to around one billion kilos. Political pressure caused the district authority to report a harvest, and the provincial authority procured grain from the district based on the 1958 quota. As a result, the district turned in 80 percent of the actual amount of grain produced in 1959, leaving a very limited amount for the peasants. When a food shortage occurred very soon after the grain was turned in, some people wrote letters to the provincial Party committee. However, the letters were forwarded back to the district, and those who had written them were seriously punished, as required by the provincial authority. Some were given legal punishment, and others were expelled from the Party. With the support of the provincial authority, the district Party secretary instructed post offices to withhold 12,000 letters that reported on the starvation.[15]

Chinese local officials continue to cover their malfeasance today. Local officials block the flow of information to protect themselves and to create political space for upper-level authorities to manipulate the disciplining. The upper-level authorities sometimes believe that concealing certain malfeasance protects the image and legitimacy of the regime. If this occurs, officials who block information may be tolerated or avoid serious discipline. But if local officials fail to conceal their misdeeds, they run a greater risk of being punished. Upper-level authorities have much less political leeway to manipulate the disciplining when the public knows that the state authority is aware of an agent's malfeasance.

BLOCKING INFORMATION: RATIONALE

Chinese government officials conceal their malfeasance or block information flows in two ways. The first is by attempting completely to conceal their malfeasance to avoid being investigated and punished. The second is to underreport their failures to avoid severe punishment when they believe that a complete cover-up is not feasible. These rationales are reflected in local officials' reporting of death tolls in coal mining accidents.

The coal mining industry in China has been notorious for the frequent and persistent fatal accidents.[16] Between 2001 and 2004, there were at least 188 coal mining accidents, each causing ten or more deaths.[17] Production safety is particularly worrisome in small coal mines. In China, the death ratio is 1.1 per ton of coal in large state-owned enterprises, as opposed to 7.6 for township enterprises.[18] The reasons for the frequent mining accidents were complex, including outdated technology and mismanagement or ineffective monitoring.[19] The strong nexus between government officials and mine contactors was another important reason. Protection from local officials tended to invalidate the numerous stipulations issued by the central government.

Local governments and their officials became involved in coal mining in several ways: (1) government employees or cadres of state-owned enterprises invested in coal mines; (2) government employees or their relatives ran coal mines; (3) government officials took bribes and granted production licenses to private businesses; and (4) government officials permitted illegal coal mining (for example, mining without a business license).[20] In 2005, a provincial official in Shaanxi province reported that there were 4,600 mines with business licenses in Shaanxi, yet there were at least 4,000 without licenses. Township cadres thus complained that they were unable to prevent illegal mining operations because these were operated by local officials whose power enabled them to invalidate the many efforts of the government.[21] Some illegal mines survived because of the support of local governments that collected fees from these firms.[22]

Due to the close connections between the government and coal mines, together with the party-state's decreasing tolerance of mining accidents, local governments and officials have a strong incentive to cover up such accidents. According to government regulations, an accident that causes between three and nine deaths is categorized as a serious incident (*zhong da*), and one that causes ten or more deaths is categorized as an especially serious accident (*te da*). If an accident causes more than thirty deaths, it will be directly investigated by the State Council or its designated agencies. Once an incident occurs, the local authority that is directly in charge of the mine needs to rescue the people and report the case to the higher-level authorities.

The responsibilities of local officials vary according to the severity of an incident. To avoid (severe) punishment, local officials commonly allow or help mine contractors to conceal accidents. Table 6.1 reports a number of cases in which local governments tried to underreport or conceal an accident by covering up the incident and preventing any media investigation. In July 2005, for example, a local government in Henan province paid off journalists in an attempt to cover up a coal mining accident. The payoffs were as follows: 500 to 1,000 yuan for journalists of a central media agency; 200 to 500 yuan for journalists of a provincial-level media agency; and 200 yuan for journalists of a city-level media agency. As a result, 480 journalists

TABLE 6.1.
Examples of covering up coal mine accidents.

Location	Year	Deaths	Reported deaths
Hejin city, Shanxi	2000	38	4
Nandan county, Guangxi	2001	81	Not reported
Fanshi county, Shanxi	2002	38	2
Linfen city, Shanxi	2002	30	7
Lenshuijiang city, Hunan	2003	5	2
Yongdeng county, Gansu	2003	19	5
Handan county, Hebei	2004	12	1
Wu'an city, Hebei	2004	29	5
Ningwu county, Shanxi	2005	36	19
Huangling county, Shaanxi	2005	12	Not reported
Zuoyun county, Shanxi	2005	11	Not reported

SOURCE: Author's collection.

or self-proclaimed journalists had received 200,000 yuan within a day of the incident.[23]

A case that occurred in Nandan County in Guangxi autonomous region illustrates local officials' reluctance to report coal mining accidents. In the early morning of July 17, 2001, water flooded a coal mine in the county, claiming eighty-one lives. The contractor of the mine reported the incident to the deputy county Party secretary and the deputy county magistrate in charge of the mining industry in the late afternoon, requesting them not to report it to higher-level authorities. When the county Party secretary and the magistrate learned the news, they both felt that failure to handle the case properly could end their political careers. Nevertheless, closing the coal mine would seriously affect the revenue of the county because the mine was a major source of income. This county relied heavily on the revenues from the mines; revenue and taxes contributed by this mine, together with those of a few others, constituted one-third of the revenue of the county.

Against this background, the local officials decided to cover up the accident. The county Party secretary, the magistrate, the deputy Party secretary, and the deputy magistrate held a meeting the next day. The Party secretary eventually decided that (1) the case would be handled by the mine, and the county authority would not report it to higher-level authorities; (2) the deputy county Party secretary and the deputy magistrate would work with the mine contractor to prevent the release of the news and monitor public reaction; and (3) if the higher-level authorities learned of the news, the county authority would report that it had not received a formal report from the mine, attributing the responsibility to the mine contractor.

From late July to early August, the county authority repeatedly reported to higher-level authorities that no one was drowned in the accident. Meanwhile, the mine contractor allocated 4 million yuan to pay for the silence of the victims' families. The mine also paid each of the remaining miners 30,000 yuan on the condition that they would not say anything about the accident. These efforts enabled the local authority and the mine to conceal the incident for seventeen days. The case was eventually disclosed because a few journalists from central media agencies, including the Xinhua News Agency and the *People's Daily*, carried out serious investigations at great risk and then reported the case directly to the central government, which sent a working team to investigate the case.

At the trial, the county Party secretary explained why he had decided to conceal the incident. In October 2000, another accident had occurred in the county, killing twenty-nine people, and he did not want to report another case within such a short time. He was also worried that closing the mines due to the accident would seriously affect the local economy. Another important reason was the corruption among local officials: The Party secretary had accepted 3.2 million yuan in bribes within three years, and the county magistrate, 440,000 yuan. Eventually, the Party secretary was given the death penalty, and three other county officials and the contractor were jailed for up to twenty years.[24]

The reporting of mining accidents reflects the political logic behind the behavior of local officials. Despite the many problems with the disciplinary institutions and the party-state's tolerance, local officials face serious uncertainty or risk when committing severe malfeasance. As revealed by the Nandan case and other cases discussed in Chapter Four, local officials are motivated to conceal their failure in governance because they risk being investigated not only for duty-related malfeasance but also for corruption. Such investigations could therefore seriously jeopardize their political careers. In today's China, local officials find it increasingly difficult to hide their malfeasance because of a better flow of information, but these difficulties do not discourage them from attempting to do it.

DEALING WITH THE MEDIA

As the Nandan case shows, media exposure may trigger an investigation by upper-level authorities and significantly reduce the discretion they enjoy in dealing with exposed officials. Media exposure makes it difficult for the upper-level authorities to pretend not to know or to tolerate agent malfeasance. Government officials, therefore, make extensive efforts to prevent media coverage of their problems.

Local officials' methods for dealing with the media largely depend on the administrative level of a news agency. Normally, local governments adopt a "soft" approach when dealing with news agencies under higher-level authorities. To prevent media exposure, local officials may offer gifts or money to journalists or editors; they may also mobilize their networks for this purpose.[25] Another method is noncooperation, which aims to prevent journalists from collecting information using both violent and nonviolent measures. For instance, some local cadres accompany correspondents to prevent the locals from telling the truth. Others order the police to trail journalists to discourage people from reporting the truth.[26]

Persuasion is another way to prevent investigative activities or the publication of findings. As local officials have no authority over higher-level news agencies, they can only hope to persuade the latter not to publish negative reports on their localities. For example, a journalist from the *People's Daily* once wrote a report on the misuse of farmland in a city in Henan Province. After she returned to Beijing, a few of the city leaders went to the *People's Daily* in an attempt to prevent the publication of the report. One told the correspondent that he had traveled to Beijing twice for the sake of the report. If the report was published, he would not be able to face the leaders in his city who were being reviewed for promotion and whose careers might be adversely affected.[27]

In another case, in a city in Shanxi Province, the Party secretary and the mayor were both blatantly corrupt. A journalist planned to write a report on their corruption for internal circulation. When the city cadres heard the news, they searched for the journalist, knowing that their careers would be ruined if the corruption was uncovered. The city leaders rushed to a hotel on learning that the journalist was there to see a friend. In a secret meeting, the Party secretary went on his knees to beg the journalist to abandon his report. At the same time, the journalist's father was brought to persuade him on behalf of the cadres. The following day, the Party secretary and his staff went to the capital city of the province to invite the journalist's superiors to a feast. The report was eventually abandoned.[28]

Local authorities are most reluctant to see their malfeasance exposed by influential national media. As major media agencies in China are controlled by and serve as mouthpieces of the Party, government officials are strongly motivated to establish connections with such media agencies. As a result, important media agencies face great pressure in deciding whether to cover negative reports on local governments. Reportedly, a majority of the cases reported on the Chinese Central Television (CCTV) program *Focus* are eventually broadcast after surviving the attempts of local governments to stop the disclosure.[29] When Premier Wen Jiabao inspected CCTV in 2003, a correspondent from *Focus* complained to him that such disturbance significantly reduced the number of critical reports the program was able to broadcast.[30] As another example, a survey of 660 media workers found that 37 percent of them believed that critical reports could not be published on time because of persuasion by various parties.[31]

In dealing with media workers from other provinces, local governments do not need to use the soft approach. For example, to conduct interviews and other investigative activities, journalists who are not from upper-level state authorities need to obtain the permission of the propaganda department in a locality. Such approval is often difficult to obtain when the case is believed to damage the image of the locality or its officials. Some local governments make it clear that "we only welcome those who report positive news about us or those who project a positive image of us."[32]

When handling news agencies under their jurisdiction, local governments face fewer constraints and can threaten punishment at will. Local media journalists have been criticized, disciplined, fired, and even imprisoned for exposing the misconduct of local governments and officials.[33] In 1995, some peasants in a city in Shanxi province invented a new water-saving method for irrigation. The provincial leaders held a meeting in the city to promote the frugal use of water and arranged for delegates from other provinces, who happened to be attending a national meeting in Shanxi, to visit the water-saving project. This was a political opportunity for the city government to demonstrate its achievement. The city government decided to build the water-saving irrigation project for one million *mu* of land. But when it received notice of the visit, the irrigation project was still on paper.

In August and September, the provincial leaders accompanied the delegates visiting the irrigation projects. Local people reported that only those projects that were visited by the delegates were functional, whereas the rest were not. Some local people were very upset and proceeded to destroy the fake structures. The visit continued without disruption only after the government dispatched the police. In May 1998, a news reporter from a local newspaper published an article disclosing the truth in the internal circulation of the *People's Daily*. When both national and other local media reported the journalist's findings, the city leaders had to admit their wrongdoing. However, the local authorities, including the provincial authority, presented false charges and put the journalist in jail for twelve years.[34]

Nevertheless, with the emergence of new information technologies, especially the Internet, local governments face unprecedented difficulties in controlling the flow of information. Depending on the type of information, local governments may receive help from websites where messages are posted or from the central government agencies responsible for monitoring the Internet. Therefore, it is not unusual for reports on certain issues to be quickly deleted from websites, although the websites are beyond the control of local governments that are exposed by online reports.

DEALING WITH PETITIONERS

Petitions from citizens to upper-level authorities, including the central and provincial authorities, are another source of information on officials' malfeasance because they reveal local problems.[35] However, petitioners can be seen as troublemakers by local governments. Anxious that petitions made by local residents could damage their image and affect their performance evaluations, local governments are reluctant to see local residents approach upper-level authorities.[36] The relationship between petitioners and local governments can turn seriously sour because of the pressure faced by local officials. The negative attitude of some local governments toward petitions is reflected in propaganda, through the posting of slogans such as "Strike hard against unreasonable petitions" or "Strike hard against direct petitions to higher-level authorities."[37]

A county Party secretary complained that some of the issues raised by petitioners are very difficult to address because of historical reasons. Even the provincial authority may be unable to solve them, not to mention the county authority:

> The upper-level authorities stress only social stability, regardless of the causes of petitions. We have to cover up the problems. On the one hand, we try to make friends with petitioners and have drinks with them, in the hope that they will not make petitions. On the other hand, we are ready to stop petitioners at all times. We will use hard approaches if soft ones do not work. We often hold "study sessions" for petitioners. Petition leaders whose actions threaten social stability or cause bad influence are detained, fined, or put into labor camps. The provincial government adopts the "one-item-veto" system to evaluate city governments' maintaining of social stability, and the city government uses the same method to evaluate county governments.[38]

Therefore, local governments commonly stop local petitioners from traveling to the provincial capital or Beijing. If local officials know that local residents are likely to present petitions to upper-level authorities, they can detain the petitioners under various pretexts. While some petitioners have been arrested or detained, as the county Party secretary admitted, others have been put into mental hospitals by local officials who falsely claimed that these petitioners had mental problems.[39]

When local governments fail to prevent petitioners from leaving their place of residence, they often send officials or police officers to stop them before they reach the upper-level authorities and bring them back.[40] One local official reported that each year approximately 600 government officials from his province were sent to Beijing in rotation to stop petitioners.[41] Although this practice is costly, local governments in both developed and less developed areas see it as important in protecting their images. An official from Sichuan Province admitted that bringing back a petitioner from Beijing cost 10,000 yuan. Another local official from a poverty-stricken county in Henan Province reported that preventing petitions cost his county 2 million yuan in 2004. However, the county was praised by the provincial government for its success in preventing 146 petitions from being recorded by the National Complaints Bureau.[42]

Local governments' attempts to stop petitioners from presenting their grievances have even led to the outsourcing of state power. In 2010, an influential newspaper in Guangdong province, *Southern Metropolis News*, published an investigation detailing how local governments had signed contracts with safety services companies in Beijing and allowed the latter to act as a state agency to detain and return petitioners to their residences. Although local governments have representative offices (*zhu jing ban*) in Beijing that are responsible for handling petitioners who go there, these offices have limited staffing and resources. As a result, local governments "outsource" the handling of petitioners to private safety services firms in Beijing. When local petitioners present petitions in Beijing, the representative offices will send them to a safety services company for detention. The company will then send the petitioners back to their residences at a predetermined price.[43]

The most high-profile private safety company, Anyuanding, used to dominate this market in the national capital. At Anyuanding, which once hired more than 3,000 security guards, hundreds of detained petitioners were treated as prisoners, and some were beaten and extorted. Some female petitioners were subjected to sexual harassment. A local government might need to pay the company 200 to 300 yuan for every day that a petitioner was detained. Local governments might also ask the company to send the petitioners back to their localities, with the charge largely determined by the distance. For example, driving one petitioner back to her county in the Guangxi took two days, and the company charged the county government 30,000 yuan. In another case, the company charged Guizhou Province 300,000 yuan to send two busloads of petitioners back to the province.

In 2010, more than seventy such firms reportedly dealt with petitioners in Beijing. This practice was common knowledge among police officers in Beijing and local governments, but none had the incentive to stop it. Petitioners had repeatedly reported the criminal activities of the companies to the police department in Beijing, yet it failed to take any serious measures to stop such practices. Indeed, some companies had connections with officials in state agencies in Beijing, including the police department. These companies could be seen as sharing the burden of maintaining stability with the local state. Hence, the police department took action and detained the chief executive and the manager of Anyuanding only after the media exposed this case.

Efforts by local governments to prevent local residents from presenting petitions have bred strong resentment among the people. In March 2012, a group of citizens displayed a silk banner printed with "Advanced Work Unit for Stopping Petitions" (*jiefang xianjin danwei*) in front of the city petition bureau of Changsha to embarrass the bureau after the latter had stopped petitioners from approaching upper-level authorities.[44] However, given the need to protect their images, local governments are unlikely to cease the practice of stopping petitioners.

When local officials fail to prevent petitioners from approaching upper-level authorities, they still have one last resort—they can approach officials in petition management agencies and request that they delete the recorded petitions by offering gifts or money. However, it may be too late or too difficult to delete the record if a petition has already been accepted, so a more effective way is to prevent petition management agencies from accepting petitions in the first place. This is possible if local officials are well connected to those working in the agencies. With such connections, local officials can receive the information in a timely manner and take action to stop the petitioners. For this purpose, local officials need to establish connections with officials in petition management agencies by offering gifts or throwing banquets. One official of a city's representative office in Beijing admitted that they spent hundreds of thousands of yuan on gifts sent to upper-level petition management agencies in 2008. Some of these agencies or their officials see deleting petition records as a good opportunity to reap benefits.[45]

DEALING WITH INSPECTIONS

To gain accurate information about policy implementation or local governance, higher-level governments, including the central government, sometimes send investigative teams to carry out direct inspections. This method is more reliable than relying on the reporting of local officials, but it is too costly to be used frequently. On the other hand, local officials are not passive in dealing with direct investigations. They may take creative and effective measures in dealing with inspection teams to hide their malfeasance.

A common method used by local officials is influencing or even manipulating the agenda of the investigation teams. For example, inspectors sent by higher-level authorities may spend most of their time feasting on banquets and other entertainment activities rather than on inspection work. Depending on the administrative ranks of the inspectors, top local party and government leaders will meet with important inspectors in person and exert all efforts to receive the inspectors with absolute respect and politeness. The respect and hospitality accorded by lower-level officials often force inspectors to forgive their malfeasance and "give face" to them.[46] Even inspection teams sent by the central authorities are sometimes prevented from carrying out their investigation by local governments.[47]

The way local governments deal with the higher-level authorities who oversee the implementation of family planning is an illuminating example of how local officials protect themselves against scrutiny and blame. The family planning policy in China has been repeatedly violated by the people, especially peasants, with or without the tolerance of local cadres. In some places, village cadres encourage peasants to have extra children so that they can collect fines from them.[48] However, the implementation of the family planning policy directly affects the performance of local officials. The one-item-veto system has commonly been used by upper-level authorities, under which the performance of local officials is seen as a failure if there is a violation of the family planning policy in the place under their jurisdiction. This pressure leads local officials to hide the truth from higher-level authorities.[49]

The aggregate effect of such practices distorts the statistics. For example, in 2000, the census in Shaanxi province showed that the population declined by 2 million compared with that of the previous year, which was impossible given that the birth rate was higher than the death rate. In some places, the gap between the actual population and the reported population is surprisingly large. An important reason is that local authorities are reluctant to report the truth for fear of punishment.[50] According to a report by *Beijing Youth News* on November 12, 2000, 10 million people were not counted in the census in Hunan province. A report in the *People's Daily* published on November 19, 2000, claimed that the report by *Beijing Youth News* was false. The *People's Daily* gave two main reasons for the discrepancy in the population numbers: First, 6 million migrant workers were excluded from the census based on the census rules; and second, some grassroots cadres were reluctant to report the actual number, suggesting that the news published by *Beijing Youth News* may not have been far from the truth. In Sichuan province, between 1991 and 1998, 407,000 people were not counted.[51]

Aware that local officials may cover up true population, higher-level authorities regularly organize inspections to ensure the strict implementation of the policy. But these inspections do not always present insurmountable problems for local officials, who can often prepare for the inspection by asking those families who have violated the policy to leave the village for a while. In addition, local officials entertain the inspectors by throwing banquets and giving them cash and other gifts.[52]

To avoid being influenced by the diversions orchestrated by local governments, higher-level authorities sometimes organize sudden checks. Unlike regular inspections, sudden checks are beyond the knowledge of local governments, and inspectors go directly to the villages they have chosen. But local officials may still be able to protect themselves. The following case, reported by a research officer from the State Council, reveals the creative countermeasures that local officials may use to deal with inspectors.[53]

To check whether the family planning policy is enforced, provincial authorities in some places organize checks without even telling the team members the places they will be visiting beforehand. The head of the team is given three sealed envelopes that contain information about the villages to be inspected. The head of the team is allowed to open the first envelope when the team is inside the vehicle on the day of the inspection. After entering the county, the head of the team can open a second envelope to find out which township is to be checked. On arrival at the township, a third envelope is opened to find the names of the villages to be checked, after which the officials conduct a thorough check of all households in these villages.

In theory, such sudden checks are difficult for lower-level officials to prepare for, but in practice, lower-level officials can still make preparations to invalidate them. Lower-level officials may have information providers within the provincial authority. Local governments can then begin to make preparations as soon as they are told the inspection team has left the provincial capital and the license plate of the car. Once the car enters the city, concerned authorities at the city, county, and township levels cooperate closely to monitor the inspection team. Although the team does not interact directly with the local governments, local officials know the team's activities (for example, where they are and even what they eat).

Local authorities assign people to monitor the whereabouts of the inspection team along the roads so that they can estimate the team's destination based on the direction the car takes. With such information, local authorities can warn the villages that are likely to be checked to make preparations. Although these preventive measures are not always flawless, they are largely sufficient to deal with sudden inspections. This practice shows that local authorities at all levels cooperate with one another to protect themselves. When the inspection is conducted by provincial officials, authorities at the city, county, township, and village levels are all mobilized. The city authority tries to obtain information in advance and releases it to lower-level authorities as part of their duty to give "free public service." When the inspection is carried out by the city authority, the county officials do the same for township governments. The inspection team is thus always isolated, like "a small boat sailing into an ocean."[54] Whether such methods are commonly used by local officials is hard to assess, but these strategies reveal the creativity and efforts exerted by local officials to ensure their performance and political survival.

Responsibility Avoidance

If local officials are unable to avoid responsibility or unwanted events *ex ante*, they will try to avoid the blame *ex post*. One way to evade blame is to find scapegoats—a tactic that has been used by both the central and local governments in China. For example, although the Great Famine between 1958 and 1962 largely resulted from the flawed political system and government policies at that time, the central authority, especially Mao, did not take the blame.[55] Instead, the blame was passed on to the grassroots officials, and punishment was meted out accordingly. The central authority punished local officials by claiming that the grassroots cadres were the "surviving supporters of the KMT." By putting the blame on those officials, the central authority appeased the peasants, mediated the tension, and made the peasants feel that "the Center is good, but local cadres are bad." Given that these people were surviving supporters of the KMT, this mode of blame attribution shifted the responsibility of the Great Famine from the CCP to the KMT.[56]

Against this background, the previously mentioned Xinyang case in Henan was depicted as an antirevolutionary restoration of KMT rule. Considering the antirevolutionary nature of this case, the people sent by the central government and upper-level local leaders prepared an execution plan of 800 cadres from each large county and 400 cadres from each small county. From each brigade, three to five people were to be executed. Based on this plan, more than 10,000 people should have been executed in this district. Fortunately, the plan was rejected by the central government. Nevertheless, a large number of local officials were arrested, their homes were searched, and some of their family members were apprehended and humiliated.[57]

High-ranking local officials also tried to find scapegoats. In Henan Province, which was among the provinces with the highest death rates, the provincial Party secretary, Wu Zhipu, chaired a mass meeting in one of the counties. He announced that the county Party secretary was an antirevolutionary element and needed to be arrested immediately. In truth, when dropsy occurred among the local population in 1959, this county Party secretary wrote a letter to the provincial authority to report the situation and request a grain allocation to address the people's needs. Wu wanted to punish the county Party secretary to cover up his own wrongdoing. The county Party secretary was then jailed for a few years after Mao disapproved his death penalty. As the central authority attributed the famine to factors other than government policies, none of the provincial party secretaries in the provinces that had the greatest number of deaths was punished.[58]

Forcing lower-ranking officials to shoulder the blame continues to be used by government officials today. For example, in the fake milk powder incident in Fuyang city in Anhui Province in 2003, some 190 babies suffered malnutrition and twelve died. Media exposure caused anger among the public across the entire country, and the central government had no choice but to respond. A total of thirty-one business people were arrested, and about twenty local cadres were given party discipline, administrative discipline, or legal punishment. The mayor was punished with "misconduct highlighted," and a vice mayor and the head of the commercial and industrial bureau were required to resign. A subdivision of the county commercial and industrial bureau was believed to be partly responsible. Hence, the county bureau decided to remove the head and a deputy head of the subdivision and fired two other employees. The decision on this punishment was reported to the investigation team sent by the State Council. However, it was later revealed that those four people were not actually disciplined. When the leaders of the county decided to discipline the four employees, the former explained to the latter that the discipline was for "dealing with upper-level authorities," otherwise "county leaders would be disciplined." The bureau promised that this decision would be submitted to the investigation team of the State Council only and it would not be distributed to other agencies for record keeping. The bureau also told the four employees that they could continue working at the bureau as usual.[59]

There are other ways of shifting blame or responsibilities. The case of conflict management reveals the various methods that government officials use to avoid responsibility. When someone has to take responsibility for a conflict, local officials can attribute the blame to the citizens involved in the disputes. In this way, the officials can justify their decision to punish the citizens and evade responsibility. This method is possible because collective action is generally illegal in China, and citizens' actions are subject to the interpretation of the government, which can file criminal charges against protesters.

Table 4.3 in Chapter Four illustrates that officials have been exempted from a majority of the cases of social conflict. One reason is that large-scale protests did not result in serious consequences, such as heavy losses or casualties. Another reason is that local authorities impose criminal charges on participants as a preemptive move. In some cases, citizens violate the law and are duly punished. At other times, citizens take action to defend their rights, but they may still be punished. Hence, it is much more common for participants to be punished by local governments than for local officials to be disciplined by upper-level authorities.

Some conflicts are associated with or caused by the behavior of state agencies, such as the legal departments in law enforcement. Yet, when citizens rally behind a cause, they can be accused of obstructing the performance of duties, disrupting social order, attacking state agencies, or staging illegal gatherings.[60] For example, in a county in Guangxi, a suspect allegedly committed suicide by drinking poison while detained in the police station. The family could not accept the police department's conclusion simply because the detained suspect was not supposed to have access to poison. Dozens of villagers stormed the county seat to protest and confronted police officers in the office compound of the city government. Eight of the participants were arrested and were accused of attacking state agencies and holding illegal demonstrations.[61] A similar case occurred in a county in

Zhejiang province in 2005. Again, a suspect died while detained in the police station, and the police officers claimed that the suspect had died from a disease. The suspect's mother, together with at least twenty people, confronted the police and demanded an explanation. The woman ended up being accused of injuring police officers and was sentenced to five years in jail.[62]

Although the suspects in these cases could possibly have died due to the reasons cited by the police department, their family members had legitimate reasons for seeking clarification and explanation. However, when citizens take actions that could be interpreted as illegal, the police department and the local government have more discretion in dealing with protestors. As a result, the participants place themselves at the mercy of the state authority. In the two cases in the preceding paragraph, although the state agency might have been responsible, or partly responsible, for the death of the suspects, it was in a better position to avoid responsibility after imposing criminal charges on the family members who sought justice. In these cases, local officials use repression as a preemptive measure to avoid responsibility.

Politicizing citizens' actions is another way of avoiding responsibility. Local officials may claim that certain demonstrators, particularly leaders or activists, protest because they have political goals such as subverting the government. Some protesters are accused of receiving the support of antagonistic forces overseas. By politicizing people's actions, the local government can attribute social conflict to the dissatisfaction of certain groups with the political system, instead of local governance. Hence, while Chinese protesters tend to depoliticize their actions and claims, the government sometimes politicizes the protesters' actions to avoid responsibility. In a high-profile workers' protest in Liaoyang in Liaoning province in 2002, workers from a ferroalloy factory staged protests to demand allowances and were joined by workers from other factories. Local governments negotiated with the workers by offering financial aid and sending the corrupt former manager to jail. However, the local government also imprisoned two of the leaders (one was jailed for four years, the other for seven) based on the charge of "subverting the government," although the charges were unfounded.[63]

Finally, local officials may also attempt to defend themselves by obscuring the causes of their failures or by offering justifications and excuses. Justifications or excuses provided by local officials serve two functions. One, effective justifications can reduce the officials' responsibilities and help them to avoid serious punishment. Two, local officials' justifications may reduce the pressure faced by the upper-level authority, should the latter decide not to punish the officials. McGraw points out that certain types of justifications and excuses are less effective than others. For example, "the excuses involving diffusion of responsibility . . . are consistently poor accounts."[64] However, in the Chinese context, what is important to erring agents is the superiors' interpretation and acceptance of the account. When upper-level authorities are reluctant to punish certain officials, they accept the officials' justifications as valid and then prohibit the media from covering the case.

For example, a conflict arising from land use in a village in Guangdong Province in 2005 escalated into a bloody confrontation between villagers and police officers. Three villagers were shot dead, and eight were wounded. Opening fire on unarmed people in nonpolitical disputes is uncommon in China, thus the incident caught the attention of the provincial and central authorities. The local authority explained as follows: "In this very emergent situation, police officers opened fire as a warning. But as it was already dark, the police officers accidentally shot some people in the chaotic situation. Three people died, and another eight were wounded, three of them seriously."[65] The report did not attribute the shooting to the police officers. In China, strict procedures for opening fire must be followed, and police officers are not supposed to take action without the approval of their superiors. Despite the dubious explanation, no single official was held legally liable for the shooting. Five city officials were subjected to Party discipline, but only a deputy head of the city public security bureau was removed from office.

Networks as Political Buffers

The state authority or pertinent leaders assume discretion in disciplining agents, and connections with these leaders can serve as protection. The use of social networks is an important way of seeking leniency. Social networks or *guanxi* traditionally play an important role in people's daily life in China, creating a moral binding effect on people's interactions. Yang writes, "*Guanxi* places much more emphasis on *renqing* (human relations) and the long-term obligations and bond of the relationship than the material interest exchanged, whereas in bribery and corruption, the social relationship is a means, not an end, of the exchange."[66] People who are socially connected may have a moral obligation to help one another. Social networks, therefore, are the social and political assets of individuals.

Social networks in China affect the operation of state agencies. For example, social connections can be an important obstacle in achieving justice. Legal agents are repeatedly criticized for handling legal cases on the basis of money–power exchanges, social connections, and personal relations.[67] In 2001, the president of the Supreme Court acknowledged that "if we cannot eliminate factors such as 'social connections,' 'personal relations,' and 'money-justice exchange' in legal practice, we will never be able to prevent legal workers from sacrificing laws for personal benefits. The fairness and authority of the law will be severely damaged or may even disappear completely."[68]

In the political arena, networking is seen as one of the basic conditions for government officials to retain their power and obtain promotions.[69] Burns explained how the *nomenklatura* system operated in China about two decades ago as follows: "Because officials are almost completely dependent on their official sinecures for their livelihood, they need patrons at higher levels of the bureaucracy, particularly those who are well connected to party committees and core groups, to further their careers."[70] This remains true today in that networks are crucial to officials' political careers and political survival.[71]

Against this background, government officials are strongly motivated to establish connections with upper-level leaders, their family members, and those who have political influence. There are different ways of networking. Government officials from the same place of birth or who used to be classmates or colleagues have natural connections. Those who used to be colleagues can therefore form patron–client relations when one of them is promoted. Such connections may also become the base of factions within the state authority.[72] Connections with upper-level leaders benefit lower-level officials' personal careers and local development because the superiors can help to obtain resources or favorable policies for their subordinates.

Networking has directly contributed to the persistence of the "gift-sending" culture in China. On important dates (for example, the spring festival), local officials send gifts to upper-level officials and important government agencies, including central government agencies. Gift giving by local governments or officials can be covered by public expenditures. Major local leaders earmark funds for networking for both individual and local interests. For example, a county Party secretary can be allocated 1 million yuan or more for networking (*huo dong jingfei*).⁷³ The use of public funds for such purposes understandably creates ample opportunities for corrupt officials.

The disciplining of malfeasant agents is complicated when officials of different levels are embedded in social networks. Higher-level officials who are connected with malfeasant lower-level officials may be reluctant to see them punished, because punishment would not only imply that they had promoted the wrong person, it would also weaken their power base.

A former secretary of the DIC of Hunan province acknowledged that an official who reaches the administrative rank of city mayor or higher is very likely to have close connections with even higher-ranking officials. The disciplinary department must take into account an official's social networks.⁷⁴ Therefore, when local authorities decide to discipline an important official and are unclear about the official's networks with upper-level authorities, they may need to take cautious measures to avoid offending upper-level officials who are connected to the malfeasant official. The local authority may intentionally leak information about the possible disciplining of a local leader and then wait to see whether the upper-level authorities provide hints of disagreement. For example, if the media or upper-level authorities publish a report praising the achievements of a particular locality, it may be interpreted as a signal that the upper-level leaders do not want to see the local leader disciplined. A visit to the locality by upper-level leaders may also be interpreted as support for that leader. In these circumstances, it is highly likely that the lower-level authority will drop its plan to impose discipline.⁷⁵

Agents who face the threat of punishment may directly approach people in their networks. Sun affirms that "as soon as an official learns of an impending investigation or summoning, his first instinct is always to *zhao ren*, or look for people in the right political position to influence investigators."⁷⁶ A leader of a county DIC admitted that the networks are the most difficult issue faced by the DIC in investigating cadres. In one case, just before the standing committee of the DIC was about to hold a meeting to discuss the sanctioning of a cadre, the secretary of the DIC received a phone call from a city leader.⁷⁷ Such networking can help some people to avoid punishment.

For example, one manager of a state-owned firm was able to avoid being investigated and punished because of his networks. His problem was revealed by another case under investigation by the local anticorruption bureau. In 2011, officials from the local anticorruption bureau went to his office to arrest him. He managed to obtain permission to go to the bathroom, where he made a phone call to his wife. While he was detained, his wife sought help through their networks. They eventually received help from a senior provincial leader who said that arresting or jailing this person would affect the operation of the company, which hired tens of thousands of people. In the end, the manager was released after being detained for two weeks.[78]

Networks may also help convicted agents to avoid severe punishment. For example, in 2005, Liu Zhixiang, the former head of the Hankou Railway Station in Wuhan, was jailed after he was found to have murdered a person who had reported his corruption and to have made an illegal income of about 40 million yuan. He was initially sentenced to the death penalty with reprieve. A few years later, his death sentence was changed to lifetime imprisonment, and then later reduced to fifteen years in jail. In 2011, Liu was released on probation under the pretext of receiving medical treatment. In the Chinese legal system, an official who has been seriously corrupt and has committed murder is unlikely to receive such lenient treatment. The reason Liu was not executed was that his brother was the minister of the Ministry of Railways at the time. Ironically, Liu's probation was withdrawn and he was returned to jail after his brother, the minister, was also arrested for corruption in 2011.[79]

Social networks can no longer offer protection if a case is not exclusively handled by officials within the network or if there is intervention from higher-level authorities. For example, in a county in Shanxi Province, a poorly trained person, Yao, became a vice president of the county court.[80] He had worked as a driver for the public security bureau of the county but was fired. He was then hired by the county court and eventually became a vice president, although he was very poorly educated (*wen mang*), abusive (*liu mang*), and ignorant of the law (*fa mang*). During his term as vice president, he was not only corrupt but also ruthless. He illegally detained hundreds of people. However, his networks with higher-level cadres in legal departments and government and Party organs enabled him to survive a series of investigations by the discipline departments. His case was not properly investigated until the then Party secretary, Jiang Zemin, read the report in the internal reference of the Xinhua News Agency. At Jiang's instruction, the central DIC sent an investigation team to the county in 1999. The next day, the team decided to detain Yao. But within twenty-four hours of the team's arrival in the county, Yao had received more than 200 phone calls tipping him off, and he escaped before the team could take action. He went to Beijing to approach someone working in a bureau at the State Council who promised to send his petition to a central leader's secretary. Yao also sought help from journalists of the *People's Daily* and the Xinhua News Agency. But his efforts failed, and he was sentenced to twenty years in jail.

Conclusion

Politicians everywhere tend to avoid blame and responsibility. Machiavelli's dictum, "The prince should delegate to others the enactment of unpopular measures and keep in his own hands the distribution of favours," is still commonly practiced by government and politicians.[81] This chapter has discussed the tactics and measures that Chinese government officials adopt to avoid blame and responsibility. Similar to politicians or state agents elsewhere, Chinese government officials have a strong incentive to distance themselves from undesirable incidents. State agents' blame-avoidance measures are partly shaped by political institutions. In democracies, politicians are accountable to their constituents, and they need to avoid displeasing their constituents to stay in power. When carrying out unpopular policies, politicians may resort to methods such as obfuscation or lowering the salience of certain issues to protect themselves.[82] In China, local officials are accountable to their superiors, and their blame-avoidance strategies revolve around seeking the tolerance of their superiors. The preventive measures that local officials use include covering up their malfeasance or preventing their malfeasance from being disclosed by the media. When they fail to cover up their malfeasance, government officials seek tolerance from upper-level authorities, often by mobilizing their social connections. Therefore, the Chinese political system, which holds state agents accountable to upper-level authorities, not only shapes the ways the agents commit malfeasance but also dictates the strategies they use to protect themselves.

Understandably, the effectiveness of government officials' blame-avoiding efforts depends not only on the tactics they use but also on the upper-level authorities' perception of the nature and severity of the agents' malfeasance. The state authority is more likely to tolerate duty-related malfeasance than the illegal pursuit of personal interests. Traditionally, the CCP tolerates erring agents if they are politically correct, even when their malfeasance has severe consequences, as in the Great Famine. Some malfeasant agents may be protected by individual leaders or the party organization because of the leaders' personal or other calculations.

Nevertheless, local officials' use of blame-avoiding measures suggests that the state authority's discipline is still credible. This is reflected in local officials' attitudes toward journalists from the central media agencies. As previously discussed, local governments tend not to use violence to deal with journalists from media agencies owned by central authorities. However, there have been cases in which journalists from Chinese Central Television (CCTV), the *People's Daily*, and the Xinhua News Agency have been ignored or even assaulted by local authorities. For example, between 1999 and 2013, there were at least ten cases in which CCTV journalists were beaten while carrying out investigations.[83] It would seem to be irrational to risk offending these most powerful media agencies in China. Such practices can suggest only that the local authorities have too much at stake in covering up their problems or that disclosure of their problems would threaten their careers. Therefore, although disciplinary institutions have limitations, errant agents cannot afford to ignore the threat of punishment, which prompts them to take blame-avoiding measures.

SEVEN

Reform-Minded Officials, State Tolerance, and Institutional Change

Chinese government officials have exhibited conflicting behavioral patterns. On the one hand, as earlier chapters have shown, they can be abusive, irresponsible, irresponsive, and corrupt. On the other hand, they have played pivotal roles in the country's economic development.[1] Chinese local officials have also contributed to socioeconomic and political changes by undertaking institutional initiatives or reforms.[2] Local officials sometimes initiate important reforms by violating rules, or even the law, because the rules do not appear to be functional or reasonable in a changing environment. However, breaking even obsolete rules carries political risks. Politicians everywhere tend to be conservative in initiating controversial reforms because to do so can be career threatening.[3] Chinese government officials' great stakes in their posts should make them conservative or risk averse, offering them little incentive to carry out reforms that contradict existing government policies or law. If this is true, why are Chinese government officials, especially those at the local level, willing to risk their careers and initiate reforms?

This chapter explores how rule-breaking reform is possible and why reformers can be exempted from legal or political responsibility. It shows that relaxed disciplining of rule-breaking officials is crucial to both the success of reform and the political survival of reformers. Relaxed disciplining implies upper-level leaders' tolerance of, permissiveness toward, or even support for the initiatives of reform-minded and sometimes self-sacrificing local leaders. Therefore, local officials carry out reforms not only because they have a sense of responsibility or moral obligation but also because they are tolerated or supported by upper-level authorities. Such tolerance creates flexibility in the political system and allows reform-minded officials to become driving forces for economic and even political development in China. Locally initiated reform contributes to regime resilience by presenting solutions to some of the challenging issues faced by the party-state.

Nevertheless, in the Chinese political system, reform that has important political implications is doomed to be incremental. Local officials' reform measures that carry risks do not diffuse automatically because the political system prevents what can be called "flabby flexibility."[4] Important reforms need the consensus of central leaders, and their consensus building determines whether a reform will be advocated, extended, or speeded up. The process of consensus building signals to local officials a lack of central endorsement of the reform. The lack of consensus implies uncertainty and discourages imitations, or at least prevents widespread diffusion of the reform, because some local officials are unwilling to follow suit unless they receive clear positive signals from the central authority.

Authoritarian governments tend to face severe uncertainty when undertaking reforms with political repercussions; hence, they need to be adept at managing social forces and controlling social change through the adoption of appropriate strategies.[5] The experience of reform in China suggests that this uncertainty can be reduced if local governments initiate trial initiatives in a limited number of places. Although such pockets of reform tend to be limited because of the political risks faced by reformers, the exploratory efforts of reform-minded officials are likely to continue as long as the state or pertinent leaders are tolerant of some of the initiatives.

Reform and Risks

Reform is often necessary when existing institutions or practices worsen the current situation or fail to achieve intended goals. However, reform is an undertaking replete with uncertainty and risk. Huntington maintains that reformers may face more difficulties than revolutionaries because the latter do not need to confront the constraints of the existing institutions, but destroy them instead.[6] Politicians are reluctant to take reform measures if they anticipate that such measures will trigger opposition and threaten their careers. In other words, politicians will be motivated to carry out reform only when they believe that the proposed reform does not harm, or even benefits, their careers. In her study of administrative reform in Latin

America, Geddes discusses politicians' risk-averse behavior, concluding that reform will take place "only if the individual aspirations for power, status, wealth, or policy change on the part of political activists and politicians can be furthered by the provision of reforms will they be provided."[7]

Although politicians everywhere face risks when carrying out reform involving opposition, the sources of risk vary across political systems. In democracies, elected politicians need to avoid being blamed by voters if they take reform measures that threaten the voters' interests. Pierson points out that in democracies reform can be treacherous, "requiring the imposition of concrete losses on a concentrated group of voters in return for diffuse and uncertain gains."[8]

Given the uncertainty and risks arising from reform, reformers need to act strategically by adopting appropriate strategies to avoid blame and reduce the risk of carrying out the reform. For example, when possible, reformers can provide compensation to those who suffer losses due to the reform. Reformers can also use the strategy of "divide and rule" to minimize the potential opposition to proposed reforms or can target politically weak groups to reduce the opposition and thereby political risk.[9] Moreover, politicians can dissociate their reform measures from the unwanted consequences by lowering the salience of negative consequences, blurring the connections between policy and adverse consequences, shifting blame to others, or finding scapegoats.[10]

Although politicians or government officials in nondemocracies are equally motivated to avoid risk when carrying out reform that may cause opposition, their concern is to avoid being blamed not by the people but by their superiors who decide their tenure and promotion. In China, where the political hierarchy dictates that lower-level officials are held accountable to their superiors, the former's rule-violating reforms must be accepted or tolerated by the latter. Given that the most important goal of Party cadres and government officials is to stay in power and be promoted,[11] they are unlikely to carry out reform if they believe that it will threaten their careers.

RISKS OF REFORM IN CHINA

Analyses of the incentive structure for local officials in China assume two dimensions: (1) personal interests, including personal career goals and other personal or family welfare benefits, and (2) community interests. Most local officials are motivated to carry out reforms that serve both their personal and community interests, but such scenarios are rare because reforms often cause opposition and thereby imply uncertainties and risks. Local officials may also have the incentive to implement a reform if it benefits the community without threatening their own interests. Perhaps more commonly, local leaders face the situation whereby reform measures, if adopted, will benefit community interests but threaten their own interests or even careers.

Chinese reformers face several types of obstacles: (1) existing laws or regulations that prohibit reform measures; (2) opposition from those whose interests are threatened, including other officials; and (3) the objections of higher-level authorities. Depending on the reform consequences and the upper-level authority's interpretation, unacceptable reformers may be accused of violating Party rules, government regulations, or the state law. The penalty also varies in light of the accusations against the reformers, ranging from criticism, job transfer, demotion, dismissal, to expulsion from the Party or the government.

Given the risks, reformers often place themselves in a difficult situation. As a Chinese scholar points out, some reforms in China inevitably start with violations of the law or even the constitution because some laws may be outdated or unreasonable.[12] Yet violation of the law or regulations, even unreasonable ones, carries political risks. In the 1950s and 1960s, some central and local officials proposed to reform the collective farming system, but their suggestions were used as evidence of their political errors.[13] In the late 1970s, when Anhui Province was reforming the incentive-dampening collective farming system, local officials, including the supportive provincial Party secretary, Wan Li, faced serious pressure from other local officials and some national leaders.[14] Reformers still face significant pressure today. A county Party secretary in Sichuan Province, Li, who in 2003 carried out one of the earliest direct elections of township Party secretary, admitted that "the notion of a direct election was a revolution for the Party's organization department; the same is true for us because we were launching a revolution against ourselves . . . When carrying out that election, I was under tremendous psychological pressure because it was against Party rules. For me, the political risk was direct."[15]

The potential risk of reform becomes a deterrent to most officials who believe that "a big innovation implies a big risk, a small innovation implies a small risk, and no innovation implies no risk."[16] Some officials who have implemented reforms have fared poorly in their careers. It is difficult to trace all of the reformers in China, but the available reported cases suggest the different career paths followed by reform-minded officials, including promotion, staying in power, transfer, resignation, and dismissal. My collection of fifteen cases shows that the Chinese authorities do not seem to have seriously punished reform initiators.[17] Among these cases, two city-level officials were eventually promoted. At the county level, two were promoted, four were transferred, one stayed in power, and another was removed. At the township level, two resigned, and two were transferred. In the Chinese political context, however, promotion may not always be a reward. Some higher-level positions do not accrue power to the holders. Such a promotion may be a sign of the higher-level authority's rejection of reform measures and thereby the end of a reformer's political career. This is all the more true for some job transfers.[18]

When reform measures violate existing rules, threaten other officials' interests, or violate the will of higher-level authorities, reformers tend to suffer setbacks in their careers. For example, Dong Yang was appointed Party secretary of a poor township in Hubei Province in 1996. When he tried to streamline redundant employees in the township government, eighteen cadres, including six leaders of the township authority, collectively requested that the higher-level authority transfer Dong, and they succeeded in their request. The upper-level Party secretary commented that "Dong ignored the organizational rules when carrying out the reform. Some of the cadres had been appointed by the district authority and Dong disciplined them without our permission." The head of the upper-level government said that "he was transferred because he could not control the situation and failed to achieve solidarity in his leadership."[19] Hence, violation of the norms among officials is an important reason for the failures of some reformers. Some officials were transferred because they introduced transparency into the government, such as open bidding for public construction projects, while others were blamed simply because they refused to accept bribes from those who wished to purchase posts or promotions. In Anhui, one cadre was transferred because he thought that the government's misconduct provoked resistance to tax collection among the peasants, for which he apologized to the peasants.[20]

Frustrated reform-minded officials may also resign. Dong rejected the job transfer and became the manager of a firm. In another case, Li Changping, the Party secretary of a township in Hubei Province, wrote a letter to Premier Zhu Ronji in 2000, disclosing that "peasants are really suffering, the countryside is very poor, and agriculture is in real danger." His action was seen as norm violating because Chinese local officials tend to cover up undesirable situations in their localities instead of reporting them to higher-level authorities. After his letter was widely reported in the media, Li remained in the county for about six months. Initially, the city-level leaders planned to transfer him to another county, believing that he had jeopardized the stability of the leadership in his own county. Li explained that if he accepted the transfer, he would not have real power and would be wasting his life. Consequently, he chose to quit.[21]

Local Officials and the Initiation of Reform in China

Initiating political or socioeconomic change entails political resources or power on the part of the individuals concerned. In the Chinese political context, major local leaders, mainly the Party secretary and the head of the government at each level, assume the most power. This concentration of power in top leaders enables reform-minded officials to overcome resistance toward reform and push for political and economic initiatives. For example, as will be detailed later, there have been a few cases where local authorities introduced the election of township head. In almost all the cases reported, the reform was initiated by the Party secretary at the county or township level.[22] Bureaucracies in China tend to be assertive, and bureaucrats often departmentalize and institutionalize their power on the basis of regulations issued by higher-level counterparts and themselves.[23] Major local leaders, given their political power, are the only persons to overcome bureaucratic hurdles in forging initiatives. For example, research on the reform of small state-owned enterprises across China before the mid 1990s finds:

> Based on the experience of the reform of small state-owned enterprises across different places, it was in those prefectures and counties where the Party secretary was in charge of the reform that people had a unified opinion, the plan was well-conceived, and the coordination among departments was more effective. It was in those places that the reform was more thorough and the pace was faster. If it was not the Party secretary orchestrating the reform, it was difficult to have people adopt the same attitude and the resistance from the departments involved was stronger. The reform was neither fast nor thorough.[24]

Nevertheless, given the risks discussed in the preceding paragraphs, why are some officials willing to take the initiative to make changes? One reason may be that reform initiatives are the result of the (mis)calculations of career-driven officials.[25] Some officials initiate reform because they believe that it may increase their likelihood of being promoted. But still others initiate innovations despite the foreseeable risks, and they do so because of their strong motivation to pursue certain policy goals. At other times, important rule- or law-violating reforms become possible when reformers and their reform measures are tolerated by their superiors, who do not impose a penalty on the reformers and even support their reform initiatives, despite their illegality. Reformers are also willing to implement changes when they believe that their reform initiatives will not threaten their careers, especially when their career prospects are foreseeable (for example, the chance of promotion is negligibly slim).

RISK-TAKING REFORMERS

Politicians sometimes face a collective action problem whereby certain changes, if made, would benefit the majority of society, but taking such action could be costly.[26] Under such circumstances, some politicians may be willing to act as political entrepreneurs and make collective action possible at high risk to themselves. Research on regime transition shows that the emergence of soft-liners or revolution from above in authoritarian regimes is possible because those political actors believe that revolutionary changes are in their best interest, or because those changes benefit their countries or governments.[27] In other words, the emergence of such actors may not be motivated by personal gains. Literature on social movements attributes the rise of political entrepreneurs to their strong sense of moral responsibility.[28] Although such people are inevitably limited in number, the reform experience in China suggests that they do exist.

For example, a city Party secretary commented, "It is the public interests that motivate officials to carry out reform. If the priority is to achieve personal gains, nobody wants to carry out reform."[29] Another city Party secretary, who had initiated reform measures in his city and was then transferred elsewhere, acknowledged the difficulty in initiating reform and the rationale:

> Introducing innovations and carrying out reform is likely to make the reformer confront upper-level authorities, contradict the system, and turn against his colleagues. The reformer's subordinates may not understand him either. People who introduce innovations are lonely, and those who carry out reform suffer. To choose reform is to choose suffering, but if the current leaders do not suffer, the pain will be left to future generations. So, we must choose suffering for the well-being of the people.[30]

Such motivation for reform can certainly be strengthened when reformers believe that reform will have a limited negative effect on their careers. Understandably, if government officials are divided into climbers and conservers (cf. Chapter Two), it is the climbers who are reluctant to undertake risky reform. In contrast, officials with lower expectations of their careers may behave differently from those with higher expectations, in terms of their attitude toward risk-carrying reform. It is reasonable to assume that government officials are motivated to seek promotion, but the chance of promotion is limited.[31] When officials realize that their chance of promotion is slim, perhaps due to old age or lack of connections, they may be willing to carry out reforms that they would not conduct if they were still driven by promotion. Yet, reform without the blessing of upper-level leaders carries risks. One case in point is the initiation of the medical reform in a county in Shaanxi Province. In this case, the reformer suffered a setback, although he had low expectations of his career prospects.

THE MEDICAL REFORM IN SHENMU COUNTY

The 2009 medical reform in Shenmu County in Shaanxi Province reveals how local leaders who are no longer motivated by promotion may embrace the possibility of reform.[32] With a population of about 400,000, this county was once poverty stricken and in receipt of aid from the national government. However, by the early 2000s, its financial situation had drastically improved because of the discovery and subsequent mining of coal. With the increase in financial resources, the county Party secretary, Guo Baocheng, hoped to improve the welfare of local residents by introducing a series of important welfare policies. Guo believed that "Chinese politics is still characterized by the top leader's preferences. Many issues cannot be pursued without the agreement of the top leader." With his power as the top leader, Guo then began to push through a series of reform measures in his county.

The first important policy involved providing twelve-year free education to local residents. Introduced in 2005, this policy exempted students from tuition, textbook, boarding, and other fees, and each student was offered a subsidy of 600 yuan per year. The county government also subsidized poor students who had been admitted into universities. The county government built a school for disabled children, teaching them marketable skills. Needless to say, these policy measures significantly reduced the financial burdens of local residents, especially the poor.

What brought the public's attention to this county and the county Party secretary was the medical care scheme introduced in 2009. After thorough investigations led by Guo, the county authority was able to estimate the budget for providing almost-free medical care to all registered residents in the county. This scheme was formally introduced in March 2009 without notifying the upper-level state authorities. In taking such a "low-profile" approach, Guo took political considerations into account because he was concerned about opposition from upper-level authorities. Guo and his associates believed that, in the Chinese political arena, if a county government suddenly announced a free medical care scheme for the people, their upper-level leaders could face a dilemma: If the leaders agreed, people in other counties might raise the same demands to their governments; if they did not agree, the efforts of lower-level officials would be thwarted.

Although the county intended to keep the reform low profile, the free medical care scheme was widely covered by the media. What puzzled Guo was that some of the media, including Chinese Central Television (CCTV), expressed doubt or even criticism of this policy. He complained, "These are Chinese people. Government officials drive luxury cars, live in five-star hotels, and have expensive food, but nobody criticizes all this. Why is providing free medical care to the people seen as unacceptable?" Guo's complaints were widely echoed by Internet users who strongly supported the scheme. Indeed, in a society where only government officials enjoy the best medical care, most people would be glad to enjoy such free medical care.

However, the controversial views of the media, especially CCTV, put pressure on local leaders at the city and provincial levels. Some provincial leaders believed that Guo had caused trouble for the local authority and disgraced them. Although the policy was warmly received by the local people, given the amount of attention it had attracted from the media and the public, local leaders became cautious. In 2010, the provincial Party committee decided to transfer Guo as deputy chairman of the people's congress of the upper-level city. In the Chinese political system, as Guo himself acknowledged, this job transfer meant at least partial demotion, although his administrative rank remained unchanged.

Guo anticipated the possible consequences of his reform measures. In 2004, at the age of fifty-four, Guo realized that his chance of promotion was slim, as age is an important factor in determining promotion. A county leader of Guo's age is unlikely to be promoted as a major leader of an upper-level Party committee or government. In 2009, Guo said in a media interview, "I become bolder as I get older. As I get closer to retirement age, I think that I should deliver concrete benefits to the people."[33] Although the provincial authority transferred Guo, it did not stop the reform.

LOCAL LEADERS' TOLERANCE AND REFORM

Although officials like Guo do exist, it is unrealistic to expect the emergence of a large number of "irrational" or self-sacrificing officials to introduce reforms that carry political risks. Reformers in China may take other measures to reduce the risk of reform. One is self-discipline. Some reform-minded officials have been accused of being corrupt (for example, taking bribes or having extramarital affairs) by those who oppose the reform or by their rivals. Therefore, reform-minded officials must be self-disciplined to avoid being attacked.[34] Second, reformers may also assign legitimacy or legal status to reform measures by having the leadership group or the local people's congress pass the measures, thereby turning them into a decision of the collective leadership or a legal resolution. They can reduce the risk, therefore, by seeking support within or outside the political system.

Unlike reformers in democracies, who must answer to their constituencies,[35] reform-minded local officials in China must face their leaders who decide their tenure and promotion. Hence, a third and safer way to initiate change is to obtain permission or support from higher-level leaders. For example, Qiu He, who used to be a city Party secretary in Jiangsu province, adopted an iron-handed mode of development, and became the "most controversial city secretary in China."[36] In 1996, Qiu became the Party secretary of a county and vice mayor of the city that had jurisdiction over his county (and was later promoted to Party secretary of the city). Qiu strongly believed that he must use iron methods in carrying out reforms to address the problems in less-developed areas such as his county.

To discipline local officials, he appointed a new secretary of the county DIC and a new head of the county procuratorate. In 1996, the county punished 243 cadres for corruption. To improve local public security, in 1997 he removed the head of the public security bureau and rotated the heads of forty-one police stations overnight. To clean up the county, he required the more than 5,000 cadres to do cleaning for one week. To speed up local development, he told public employees to donate part of their salaries to the construction of the local infrastructure. Within three years, the transportation system in the county had dramatically improved. A provincial leader said the construction would have taken more than fifty years had the county adopted the regular mode of development. To speed up economic development, Qiu required one-third of the officials in public agencies to concentrate fully on seeking external investments and linked their tenure and promotion to their fund-raising performance. Nevertheless, Qiu was strategic in taking these dramatic measures. He was able to seek permission from the provincial authority to take these unusual measures to speed up local development, and he posted the permission on the city's bulletin boards as justification for his measures.

The tolerance and support of upper-level leaders are crucial to both reformers and their reforms. This is reflected in the introduction of the Household Responsibility System (HRS), which dismantled the collective farming system. This reform was first initiated in a very poor village in Anhui in 1978 and then received support or protection from Party secretaries at the county, city, and provincial levels. Upper-level local leaders were alarmed by the peasants' poverty. When the township Party secretary reported the village's "capitalist" approach to the county Party secretary, the latter replied, "The village could not be poorer. How can it develop capitalism?" The city Party secretary said, "Does socialism mean poverty? . . . If anyone wants to assign responsibility for this reform, I will take it. There is no reason to depress the peasants any longer." The provincial Party secretary, Wan Li, had a clear picture of poverty in the province. In 1977, Wan inspected some of the villages and was astonished to find some of the adults half-naked during the winter because they could not afford to wear trousers. Moreover, the peasants commonly faced food shortages. With tears in his eyes, Wan said, "Without the support of these people, how could we come to power? Yet after so many years of development, the people still have no clothes to wear and no food to eat. Even eighteen-year-old girls do not have trousers to wear . . . How can we face these people? We are guilty." Thus, Wan Li, like his reform-minded subordinates, was a strong supporter of the reform.[37]

The introduction of the election of township heads serves as another illuminating example of how the attitude of higher-level authorities or leaders affects the careers of reform-minded officials.[38] According to the Chinese constitution, the township head is not directly elected by residents (mainly peasants) but by the people's congress. Hence, introducing direct elections, which has profound implications for the political development of China, carries political risks. The support of higher-level authorities or leaders for such elections is thereby deemed crucial. In 1998, Zhang, a district Party secretary (that is, at the county level) in Sichuan Province, organized one of the earliest direct township head elections in China. She faced serious pressure because of the potential political consequences. One week after the election, the secretary of the provincial organization department visited the district. Zhang apologized to the secretary, saying "I am sorry that I stepped on the bottom line." The secretary replied, "You did not step on the line; you crossed the line." However, the secretary still gave Zhang his support by publicly claiming that introducing more democracy in the selection of cadres was an inevitable tendency.[39] Although Zhang was later promoted, she said that her promotion would have been faster had she not introduced the reform.[40]

In contrast, Wei fared much worse, although he conducted the election reform five years later than Zhang. In 2001, Wei was appointed Party secretary of a township in Chongqing municipality. In 2003, he decided to hold direct elections of both the Party secretary and head of the township. However, he was removed from his position because the reform was seen as having violated laws and regulations. Although Wei had a bottom line of "no imprisonment" when he decided to carry out the reform, he did not expect to be investigated by a joint group formed by the municipal (that is, provincial-level) discipline inspection committee, the organization department, the people's congress, the procuratorate, and even the national security bureau (which is responsible for investigating cases that are seen as threatening national security). Impressed by his integrity, a municipal official on the investigation team said to him, "If you are one step ahead of others, you are seen as advanced; if you are two steps ahead, you are a martyr; but if you are three or four steps ahead of others, nobody dares to defend you."[41]

To some extent, Wei's experience serves as a lesson to local officials elsewhere. Since the early 2000s, direct elections of township heads have been tried in a number of places, but they are often supported or initiated by higher-level authorities. For example, in Yunnan Province in 2004, a county decided to adopt direct elections of all township heads in the county. The local authority tried to keep this initiative low profile. The reform decision was passed in a vote by the city Party committee and was formally issued as a local Party document. The city and county Party committees respectively formed election leadership groups. The city leadership group was headed by a deputy Party secretary and the chairperson of the city people's congress.[42] Subsequent trials of direct elections of township heads in other places have commonly been initiated, coordinated, and organized by upper-level authorities.[43]

Why are some higher-level leaders more supportive of institutional innovations than others? Possible reasons include their ideological orientations and their perceptions of the risks involved. High-level politicians may support their subordinates' reform initiatives because their support will strengthen their respective political powers.[44] Some reforms are tolerated because they solve practical issues while posing only limited political risks for upper-level leaders. Qiu He was promoted as vice governor of Jiangsu province in 2006, in recognition of his achievement as city Party secretary. He was promoted partly because he had implemented a new way of developing areas that were lagging behind. Over the years, the provincial government in Jiangsu had invested quite large amounts of personnel and funds to help the northern area develop quickly, but these poverty-alleviation efforts were not very effective. In contrast, Qiu's developmental strategies indicated to both the provincial government and other local governments in the northern area that certain development strategies may prove to be effective in less developed areas.[45]

Therefore, reform or innovation is more likely when there is a strong consensus between lower-level officials and higher-level leaders, probably brought about by their shared policy preferences based on their similar work and/or life experiences. This is reflected in the case of the HRS reform in Anhui. Upper-level leaders' tolerance or support may also be based on their close personal connections with their reform-minded subordinates. When upper-level leaders allow reform initiatives, they can defend or justify the reformers' actions by stressing the latter's non–self-interested motivation and the reasonableness of the reform measures. They may offer protection by covering up the reform measures, pretending they do not know about the reform, providing justifications, and/or imposing symbolic punishment.

The following section presents the case of tax-for-fee reform in rural China in the late 1990s and early 2000s to demonstrate how the protection offered by supportive leaders makes rule- or law-violating reform possible.

The Case of the Tax Reform in Rural China

The tax reform, which sought to reduce peasants' financial burdens, was perhaps the most important reform in rural China since the 1980s. Although an economic reform, it started with a political decision at the local and central levels and produced significant political influence on state–peasant relations in China. The initiation of this reform and its eventual endorsement by the central authority demonstrate the flexibility and constraints faced by reform-minded officials in China. The case suggests that decentralization and the resulting autonomy of local officials allow China to take a unique approach to economic and political development in a single-party regime.

INITIATION OF THE TAX-FOR-FEE REFORM

From the early 1990s to the early 2000s, peasants' financial burdens, in the form of taxes and many unauthorized fees, were a predominant source of widespread grievances and resistance in rural China.[46] The National Complaints Bureau received 460,000 appeals in the form of letters and visits in 1998, and two-thirds of these appeals concerned rural issues, of which peasants' financial burdens were the most frequent complaints.[47] Between 1992 and 1996, at least sixty-four peasants died due to confrontations over tax and fee collection.[48] The fundamental reason for peasants' financial burdens was the fiscal arrangements that left local officials in agricultural areas with little choice but to extract money from peasants. Rural China was in large part economically segregated from urban areas, in the sense that peasants in rural areas were mostly responsible for financing public institutions such as education. When rural governments lacked adequate funding to fulfill these responsibilities, they often turned to peasants.

Michelson's survey of 2,970 peasant households in seven counties in China found that "peasants' burdens exert a dramatic and detrimental effect on overall life satisfaction." He elaborated that "burdens not only produce grievances, but, together with these grievances, they also erode the general happiness of those who are subjected to them."[49] Although the central authority seemed to know that peasants' financial burdens not only threatened social stability but also damaged regime legitimacy, the process of adopting reform measures to address this issue was far from smooth. At the local level, the initiation of the reform was made difficult because of the opposition from some higher-level authorities; at the central level, the lack of sufficient attention from major leaders prolonged the acceptance of the reform measure initiated by local governments.[50] It was not until 2000 that the Chinese government formally endorsed the tax-for-fee reform that had been initiated in Anhui eight years earlier.

The tax-for-fee reform was initially proposed by Chinese research officers in Anhui and Hebei as early as 1990 and was first tried in a township in Anhui in 1992.[51] The plan was to reform the grain procurement system by making peasants pay just one tax with grain instead of cash; all other fee collections would be abolished. When He Kaiyin, a research officer from Anhui Province, made this suggestion to a city Party secretary in Anhui, the Party secretary showed strong interest in the idea and introduced the proposed reform in two counties, Yingshang and Woyang, in his city in 1992. However, there were difficulties from the beginning. Although the county Party secretaries and the magistrates in both counties supported the proposed reform, the attitude of the political consultative conferences was ambiguous, and the people's congresses opposed it, claiming that it violated the existing laws or regulations.

The proposed reform was thus abandoned in Yingshang County, but not in Woyang County. Despite the opposition of the county people's congress in Woyang, the county Party secretary and the magistrate gave their support to Xinxin township, where the peasants had been heavily taxed and the township Party secretary and head wished to implement the reform. Between 1990 and 1992, the average annual per capita income among peasants in Xinxin township was less than 600 yuan, while the amount of fees and taxes they were required to pay was 170 yuan, or more than 28 percent of their total income. The two major township leaders decided to adopt the reform mainly because they hoped to redress peasants' financial burdens.[52] For that purpose, the township authority conducted a survey of peasants' views of the proposed reform in five villages and found that 95 percent of the peasants supported it.[53]

Yet, when the township cadres learned about the disagreement among the county leaders, they realized the risk. The county leaders told them that, although they supported the trial of the reform, they could not sign a formal document to endorse it. To reduce the risk, the township leaders submitted the reform proposal to the township people's congress for formal endorsement. In November 1992, the township held its people's congress, and all of the 109 deputies present voted in favor of the proposal.[54] In 1993, when the supportive county Party secretary and the magistrate wished to extend the reform measures to the whole county, they again met strong resistance from the people's congress. In the Chinese political system, it is unusual for the county people's congress to openly oppose the county

Party secretary and the magistrate. It was later discovered that the county people's congress conveyed the message of the provincial people's congress, which claimed that the reform violated existing laws and regulations.[55]

In this circumstance, the township cadres decided to carry on even though the supportive county leaders could not show their support explicitly. The county people's congress and the financial bureau then conducted an inspection of the township with a plan to stop the reform.[56] The township Party secretary was transferred after the inspection. The township head was promoted to Party secretary, and a deputy township head, another strong supporter of the reform, was promoted to township head. When the township leaders decided to continue with the reform, the provincial people's congress issued a formal document to the county people's congress, requiring it to pass a resolution to invalidate the resolution of the township people's congress on the tax-for-fee reform.[57]

The intervention by the provincial people's congress put serious pressure on local leaders. The township Party secretary sought the support of the county Party secretary, who replied, "If you insist on the reform, you will be removed." A county leader later implied to him, "If you are removed, it is still possible to be rehabilitated."[58] With this implicit support, the township continued with the reform. The effect of the reform was immediate. In rural China, it was common for local governments to organize work teams to collect taxes and fees from peasant households by force, because some peasants refused to pay. In this township in the year the reform was adopted, it took only ten days for the township government to collect all of the taxes and fees, without the use of the militia or the police. Nevertheless, considering the political constraint, local officials at both the township and county levels tried to keep a low profile in the reform to avoid risk. Whenever the township leaders were asked about the reform, they would reply that it had ceased.

Given the political constraints, in 1993 another county in the same district, Taihe County, adopted a safer approach to carrying out the tax reform by submitting a reform plan to the provincial government for approval. At a meeting convened to discuss the plan, the provincial government agencies and the leaders of the county were opposed by the provincial financial bureau, which was concerned that the reform would decrease revenues. However, the county Party secretary and the county magistrate both supported the reform. The revised plan was eventually approved by the provincial government. The reform plan, which fixed the fees and taxes paid by the peasants, was put into effect in the county in 1994. However, the provincial governor then intervened and ordered that the reform be stopped, perhaps because it contradicted some of the existing regulations on taxes and fees. The governor was soon removed for unknown reasons. Following the intervention of the provincial Party secretary, the reform continued. Again, the effect of the reform was immediate. Peasants' financial burdens were reduced by half, and it took the local government only five days to collect all of the taxes and fees from the 353,495 peasant households in the county—a speed of collection that would have been impossible in the past. In previous years, about 15 percent of the taxes could not be collected, but after the reform, not a single peasant household refused to pay the tax.[59] In 1993, the year before the reform, about 500 peasants had made ninety-three petitions regarding their financial burdens to Party committees at different levels; in 1994, after the tax reform, not a single peasant made such a petition.[60]

While the initiation of the reform encountered opposition, the lack of consensus among major central leaders delayed the central endorsement and thereby the promotion of the reform. Although Zhu Rongji, a vice premier in charge of economic affairs, was not enthusiastic about the tax reform at first, other leaders were supportive. Li Lanqing and Jiang Chunyun were both vice premiers at that time and were supporters of the reform, as was Wen Jiabao, secretary of the Central Party Secretariat between 1993 and 1997 and vice premier between 1998 and 2002. With Jiang Zemin's direct involvement, the central leaders eventually reached a consensus.[61] The central government decided to try the reform in Anhui Province in 2000, extended it to twenty provinces in 2002 and then the whole country. The effect of the reform in reducing peasant burdens and improving peasant–cadre relations was immediate and significant. After the tax reform, peasants' financial burdens in different provinces decreased by between 24 and 60 percent.[62] In 2004, the central government further decided to abolish the agricultural tax within five years.

The initiation and promotion of the tax reform in rural China demonstrates the serious constraints faced by reform-minded local officials and the importance of the support of major leaders at different levels. Given the opposition of the people's congresses at both the county and provincial levels, the risk faced by the leaders in Xinxin township was clear. Hence, although the people's congress in a neighboring township had also passed a resolution on the tax reform at that time, the township Party secretary gave up the reform plan after learning about the disagreement among the county's authorities. In contrast, the township leaders in Xinxin were willing to face the worst scenario, that is, being removed or transferred.[63] Their risk was reduced because they had the support of some county leaders. Hence, as in the case of the HRS, the initiation of the tax reform would have been less possible without the support of the major county leaders, and it would have been unlikely to survive without the support of the city and provincial leaders. At the central level, supportive leaders enabled the tax reform to reach the agendas of the top leaders.

As in the case of the HRS, some like-minded officials supported the tax reform, partly because of their work or life experiences. At the local level, the major leaders at the township and county levels understood the rural situation and thus were willing to carry out the reform. At the provincial level, the previous governor and the people's congress were not supportive (ironically, the people's congress was supposed to represent the people's interests). The new governor supported the reform because he understood the rural situation. In fact, he was a graduate of an agriculture school and had worked in areas related to agriculture for thirty years.[64] At the central level, in addition to the pressure generated by widespread resistance to fee collection, the reform received support from leaders who were familiar with the rural situation. Such leaders included Jiang Chunyun, a vice premier in charge of agriculture; Li Lanqing; and Wen Jiabao, who became the premier in 2003. Wen had inspected numerous rural areas in China and had been a supporter of the tax reform over the years. However, while Zhu was the premier, Wen had limited power to support the reform although he had the intention to do so. Not surprisingly, in 2004, Wen announced the revoking of the agricultural tax within five years. This case suggests that the existence of supportive leaders creates possibilities for reform-minded officials to initiate reforms and sustain their reform efforts.

Local Officials and the Diffusion of Reform

Local and central leaders' tolerance of local officials' reform initiatives allows the emergence of pockets of innovation, which may then serve as a crack that enables "a tree to grow out of the rock" in China.[65] This, however, is premised on the condition that the reform can be extended beyond the place where it originates and thus lead to systematic change. New institutions may be diffused because of the promotion of a power center or because other actors find that the new institutions are more effective or can bring legitimacy, thus giving them an incentive to adopt similar reform measures.[66]

In China, the diffusion of reform measures initiated by local governments is also conditional. Consensus building among central leaders implies a lack of agreement among them and thereby a lack of decision. This lack of decision is subject to different interpretations by local officials. Those who interpret the central government's lack of action as an acceptance of reform will adopt similar measures to address similar issues in their own areas. In contrast, local officials who interpret the central government's hesitation as uncertainty are more likely to wait and see. As a result, local rule-violating initiatives may be adopted in some other places, but they are unlikely to diffuse automatically across the country without the promotion of the central authority.

One example is the dismantling of the commune system. In the first village that adopted the HRS in Anhui, agricultural output increased dramatically in the year following the reform. In the twenty-three years prior to the reform, the village had failed to turn any grain in to the state; rather, it had received grain subsidies. After the reform, the village had an unprecedented harvest and, for the first time, presented agricultural products to the state. The success of this village encouraged other neighboring villages to implement the same measures.[67] However, given the political environment at that time, most local governments did not take action until the central government made the HRS a national policy and strongly promoted it.

Risk-averse officials are unlikely to take the same reform measure if they do not believe that the central government is supportive of the reform. This is why few local governments have adopted the medical reform in Shenmu County, despite having the financial resources to do so. Moreover, when the central government makes it explicit that it does not accept certain reform practices, local officials tend to react accordingly.

For example, although some local governments have tried the direct election of township head, this practice is still uncommon because the central authority is either uncertain or concerned about the potential political repercussions. It has therefore discouraged local governments from conducting such elections. In 2006, a vice chairman of the National People's Congress published an article in the magazine *Qiushi* (Seeking the Truth), which is published by the central Party committee, criticizing the direct election of township heads. He said that in the previous two rounds of the selection of township heads, a few places had adopted direct elections and even saw such elections as a trial of expanding grassroots democracy and of electing cadres: "This practice is not in accordance with the constitution and pertinent laws. Those places [that have implemented direct elections] have corrected this practice. In this round of elections, the selection of township heads must strictly follow the procedures regulated by the Constitution and the Local Organization Law. Direct elections of township heads must be prevented."[68]

Another example is the discontinuation of the tax-for-fee reform. After the reform was started in Anhui, some 100 counties in other provinces took similar measures before 1998. Yet in March 1998, when Zhu Rongji became the premier, the State Council issued a directive entitled "Regulations on Grain Procurement." This directive stipulated a series of measures that were intended to protect peasants' interests, but some of these measures contradicted the tax-for-fee reform measures carried out in a number of places. In particular, the directive suggested that grain procurement could only be carried out by the state grain system, not by nonstate agencies. In many of those areas that had adopted the tax-for-fee reform, however, the grain procurement quota had been abolished, which implied that peasants could choose to sell grain to other parties as long as they had paid their taxes.[69]

When local governments in those areas received this directive, they were puzzled and disappointed. In Hebei, provincial leaders instructed that the directive should be enforced. The tax reform that had been extended to thirty-seven counties in the province was stopped, as it was in more than sixty counties in seven other provinces. But the reform in Anhui was not entirely stopped. The new governor of the province wrote a report to the State Council requesting that the reform continue in the district where it originated. Because of his efforts, the tax-for-fee reform continued in some parts of this province.[70] This case shows the political constraints that prevent the diffusion of reform measures in China.

Understandably, local officials are strongly motivated when a reform initiative is strongly promoted by the central government, especially when the reform initiative also serves local or their personal interests. The privatization of public enterprises in China is a good example. Although a number of local governments tried privatization in the early 1990s, this reform proceeded slowly until 1997. In twenty-nine provinces between 1993 and 1997, the number of state-owned enterprises decreased by 6 percent, but it dropped by 38 percent between 1997 and 1998. Similarly, the number of collective enterprises decreased by only 16 percent between 1994 and 1997, but by 62 percent between 1997 and 1998.[71] The dramatic change between 1997 and 1998 was due to the relaxation of political constraints by the central authority. At the 15th party Congress in 1997, the central authority issued a formal party document that encouraged local governments to develop the private economy and adopt multiple modes to reform small- and medium-sized public enterprises. Local governments saw the promulgation of the directive as an encouragement of privatization and also believed it to be a golden opportunity to evade the debts owed by local public firms, thus contributing to the wave of privatization across the country.[72]

The coexistence of the tolerance of reform-minded officials and the checks on the diffusion of reforms points to the flexibility of the political system and the state's capacity in cadre management. The tolerance of upper-level local leaders creates political space for reforms that can be used to address the practical issues faced by both the central and local governments. Such tolerance is crucial to the success of reforms and the reformers' careers. Nevertheless, local officials' awareness of risks dictates that reform initiatives are not diffused automatically. If the central authority does not explicitly prohibit certain local initiatives, this lack of action may be interpreted by some local officials as tolerance, but as a risk-ridden move by others.

Certainly, if local innovations or reforms serve local interests while carrying limited political risks, local officials tend to be more willing to take the initiative or follow suit. In recent years, Chinese local governments have initiated various reforms to improve local governance, alleviate social tensions, and encourage citizens' participation in public affairs.[73] The motivations behind local officials' adoption of the reform measures can be complex. Some officials initiate such reforms to increase their chance of promotion, whereas others do so to solve practical issues. Regardless of the motivation, such initiations may contribute to the flexibility of the Chinese political system.

Conclusion

Reform is often difficult because reform without losers is rare; most reforms involve losers and thereby invoke resistance. Given the uncertainty and risks involved, politicians generally lack the incentive to carry out reform. Consequently, reform becomes possible when reformers discount or fail to anticipate the risks involved, or when they are able to shore up sufficient support or adopt effective strategies to avoid or reduce the risks. Politicians' risk-reducing strategies are affected by the political system. In democracies, politicians are subjected to elections and thus need to take into account the reactions of voters when considering reform measures that affect them.[74] In nondemocracies, where government officials are held accountable to their superiors, reformers need to gain their superiors' tolerance when carrying out controversial reforms.

In China, local officials have high stakes in their posts, which undermines their incentive to carry out reforms that contradict existing rules or regulations. Yet a series of important reforms in China have been initiated by local officials, sometimes at the risk of their careers. Local officials may undertake reform initiatives because they underestimate the risks. More often than not, however, reform without the blessing of upper-level leaders is unlikely to succeed, and the reformers' careers are also endangered. Some important reforms become possible and successful because reformers and their reform measures are tolerated or even supported by their superiors, who share the same policy preferences or are closely connected to their subordinates. Such tolerance or support implies that reform-minded officials can be exempted from the (severe) responsibilities associated with their rule violation. Consequently, tolerance makes it possible for pockets of innovation to emerge, thereby creating flexibility in the political system. Yet the flexibility is limited because the central authority's attitude toward reform serves as a check on the diffusion of innovation.

China's experience extends our understanding of political and socioeconomic changes in authoritarian regimes. This local initiation-central endorsement path may help an authoritarian government to address the dilemma it faces—introducing political or even socioeconomic changes may trigger the collapse of the regime, but a lack of change prevents the regime from addressing the serious problems it faces.[75] In China, local initiatives present a set of choices to the central authority because the implementation of such initiatives provides a chance for the central authority to examine their effectiveness and potential consequences. There is no guarantee that such a local initiation-central endorsement path will help the authoritarian government to endure. However, this practice can contribute to regime resilience by helping the central authority to address certain challenging issues. In addition, the gradual changes introduced may become political assets that reduce the chaos arising from the eventual regime transitions, because such changes lay the foundation for future political and socioeconomic development in new regimes.

EIGHT

Conclusion

Huntington suggests that "the primary problem of politics is the lag in the development of political institutions behind social and economic change,"[1] because institution building and strengthening are crucial to governance. The Chinese party-state faces daunting challenges arising from social, economic, and political changes during this transitional period. To surpass these challenges, the party-state needs strong state power embodied by capable, loyal, and disciplined agents who are responsible for the operation of state institutions, in addition to financial resources.[2] Inevitably, the state has to deal with the crucial issue of agent management. Individuals have different motivations to work for the government, whether these concern self-interests or public interests. In reference to government officials in the United States, Downs points out that "purely self-interested officials" are motivated almost entirely by goals that benefit themselves rather than society as a whole, whereas "mixed motive officials" have goals that combine self-interest with altruistic loyalty to values beyond themselves.[3] Similarly, Solnick holds that in the former Soviet Union, "individual bureaucrats were primarily self-interested and highly opportunistic in pursuit of that self-interest."[4] Given agents' mixed motivations, the state cannot rely on their good intentions to ensure accountability. Instead, the state has to manage the agents through institutionalized procedures that reward those who perform well and punish those who fail to perform. However, managing agents is not an easy undertaking in most societies, especially in authoritarian regimes where a free press and an independent legal system are often lacking.

This book addresses the management of state agents in China by focusing on the state authority's use of sanctions. As in other authoritarian regimes, the party-state in China faces a dilemma in dealing with malfeasant agents because neither unprincipled tolerance of agents nor rigid rule-following discipline serves the multiple interests of the state authority and its leaders. As a result, the state authority resorts to selective or differentiated discipline, often meting out punishments based on the severity of the consequences of an agent's malfeasance and his or her responsibility for the malfeasance. The influence of consequence severity and responsibility attribution may also be mediated by cost considerations. Differentiated discipline implies that the threat of sanction does not lie in the state's punishment of each erring agent, but in the potentially severe consequences the agents would receive if the state authority decides to carry out the discipline. Differentiated discipline compromises the credibility of discipline and contributes to the persistence of officials' malfeasance. However, selective or differentiated discipline also suggests that the state's tolerance is selective, which means the state authority is still able to achieve its important policy goals when it is determined to do so. An examination of the politics of disciplining state agents promotes understanding of state capacity, governance, and the regime's legitimacy and resilience in China.

Tolerating and Disciplining State Agents in China

This book has shown that the salient characteristic of the disciplinary scheme for government officials in China involves the coexistence of tolerance and punishment. Some malfeasant agents are not duly disciplined because of the leniency or other considerations of the decision makers. Such tolerance has resulted in the persistence of local officials' malfeasance, including corruption, abuse of power, dereliction of duty, and irresponsiveness. For example, recurring social conflict can be attributed, to a large extent, to the state's tolerance of agents' abuse of power.

One example is housing demolition, which has caused numerous conflicts in China since the 1990s.[5] Despite the central authority's repeated warnings, forced evictions continue to recur. In a housing demolition in Tianjin, a primary school teacher refused to move, and local leaders talked to her a number of times from 2009 to 2010. The school president told her that the county Party secretary said that as long as the school did not violate the law, the county authority would support whatever measures the school adopted to convince her to move. He said, "Many of the central government policies have been distorted at the provincial and city levels, not to mention the county level. Now the county leader is the emperor." The head of the county education bureau told her, "In Britain, if you do not agree to relocation, nobody dares to force you to move. But in China, if you do not agree to eviction, the eviction will be carried out." The Party secretary of the education bureau was also frank in saying:

> Do you believe that the county Party secretary or the magistrate will be removed if you douse yourself with gasoline [and commit self-immolation]? If you conduct self-immolation, your son will lose his mother. Have you considered this? This is true in the whole country now. Who has been disciplined [for forced evictions]? Even if some officials are disciplined, they are transferred to other places, and they are still officials.[6]

What this bureau Party secretary said is largely true. In Chengdu, Sichuan province, a deadly confrontation occurred between the district government and a household in November 2009, when the former sent people to demolish the family's house. As the family was unable to stop the forced eviction, the wife set herself on fire and died sixteen days later. The local government viewed the family's resistance as a violent obstruction to the enforcement of the law and thus detained her husband. None of the district leaders was punished, and only the head of the city management bureau in the district was suspended from his post, but only for a few months. This official, who led the team in demolishing the house, showed little remorse over the woman's death, claiming that the latter was ignorant of the law.[7] This incident is not an isolated case of abusive officials being pardoned. A review of eight similar cases of residents committing suicide because of forced eviction from 2008 to 2010 shows that none of the county Party secretaries or magistrates in the eight localities had been disciplined.[8]

The case of housing demolition highlights the reasons for local authorities' tolerance of abusive agents. In the Jiahe case (see Chapter Four), the disciplined township Party secretary admitted that when he was assigned the responsibility for conducting housing demolition, he never thought about whether the project was legal and "did not even dare to doubt it."[9] In other words, the pressure faced by local officials may force them to abuse power to accomplish assigned responsibilities. Such was the case in the enforcement of the family planning policy and in tax and fee collection in rural China before 2004. Similar to the high-ranking officials in the Great

Famine who were tolerated because they were seen as politically correct, some abusive local officials in today's China have also been exempted when they abused their power in performing their duties.

Tolerance or leniency is also used to deal with corrupt officials. Rampant corruption damages regime legitimacy and the people's confidence in the political system. Corruption indicates that government officials themselves have lost faith in the official ideology or the political system. MacFarquhar wrote, "Why has ownership of wealth become so important for the Chinese elite? And why have so many Chinese leaders sent their children abroad for education? One answer surely is that they lack confidence about China's future."[10] Determining whether senior leaders themselves have lost faith in the regime is a difficult task; however, as cases like that of Bo Xilai reveal, high-level leaders or their families are eager to amass wealth by abusing their political power and resources.

Given the complex causes of corruption, it is unlikely to be wiped out, at least in the near future. Connections among officials from different levels can serve as an important "protective umbrella" for corrupt agents. As a result, corrupt officials may remain at large despite repeated reports on their corruption. Worse, corrupt officials may still be promoted at both the central and local levels.[11] For example, in Guangdong province in 2012, when a city authority decided to promote an official, it received tips about his corruption. It was found that this official had an illegal income totaling 170 million yuan, and his family lived overseas.[12] Similarly, despite his corruption and abuse of power, Bo Xilai might have become a national leader had accidental events not revealed his problems and forced the central authority to respond. Zhou Yongkang did become a national leader (that is, a member of the Standing Committee of the Politburo) regardless of his corruption and his family's illegal amassing of wealth.

Nevertheless, to conclude that Chinese officials face little risk when they commit malfeasance can be misleading. Both high-ranking and lower-level officials have been punished because of their abuse of power in governance, failures in duty, and corruption. Indeed, if Politburo members, such as Chen Xitong, Chen Liangyu, Bo Xilai, and Zhou Yongkang, can be disciplined, albeit sometimes because of power struggles, there is no guarantee that lower-ranking erring officials will be tolerated. If the central authority decides to investigate a high-ranking official suspected of corruption, the punishment will be harsh if the person is convicted (see Chapter Five). Harsh punishment is used to reduce the leakage of authority at the local level and to build the central state's reputation, which is crucial to deterring deviations in the political hierarchy.

The threat of punishment is also the reason for corrupt officials to take possible measures to avoid punishment. When suspected or investigated, corrupt agents generally mobilize their networks to avoid (severe) punishment. As a preventive measure, corrupt officials may also use various occasions, especially festivals, to send gifts not only to party and government leaders but also to the leaders of disciplinary agencies who have important or decisive influence over the disciplining of corrupt agents. For an uncaught official to expose him- or herself by sending gifts to leaders of disciplinary agencies is rather puzzling, but exposing oneself to some leaders rather than being exposed by the disciplinary agencies can be deemed rational.[13]

The blame-avoiding efforts of erring agents, including corrupt officials, suggest that discipline in China is still credible. The credibility of punishment is associated with the fact that government officials have too much at stake in their positions. The benefits associated with working for the party-state are the reason many state agents go to great lengths to keep their positions and others seek such positions. In this transitional period when few officials, including high-ranking ones, have faith in communism or the doctrine of serving the people, nepotism has become common at both the central and local levels. But nepotism has caused public dissent and damaged the party's image.

For example, in April 2012, a district government in a city in Hunan Province publicized the candidates for promotion in the district government. One of the candidates attracted public attention and was widely questioned. This candidate was born in 1991 and received a degree from a Singaporean school that is not acknowledged by the Ministry of Education in China. She became a public servant at the age of twenty without going through the stipulated recruitment procedures. Just one year later, in 2012, she became a candidate for the position of deputy head of a bureau in the district government. After the case received wide attention, the local authorities were under pressure to intervene in the case. Eventually, it was revealed that this candidate's father was the director of a provincial government agency. Consequently, her father was removed, and six other local officials were also disciplined. Three of these officials were removed, and the district Party secretary was investigated.[14]

This incident is only one of the many cases in which irregularities occur during the selection and promotion of officials. Children of senior party and government officials, including Politburo members, have been given important positions in government agencies or state-owned enterprises. Others have set up companies and generated profits by using political power and connections. Relatives of current and former senior officials "have amassed vast wealth, often playing central roles in businesses closely entwined with the state, including those involved in finance, energy, domestic security, telecommunications and entertainment. Many of those so-called princelings also serve as middle men to a host of global companies and wealthy tycoons eager to do business."[15] Such cases set detrimental examples for both lower-level officials and the people, weakening the Party's moral authority and legitimacy. However, these cases also reveal that holding onto power in China brings various benefits to power-holders and their family members. Precisely because government officials value their positions, discipline remains a non-negligible threat to them.

This book also finds that the state's tolerance varies, depending on the type of malfeasance. The state authority is more likely to tolerate duty-related malfeasance, especially cases with less severe consequences or cases that are not directly caused by government officials. In dealing with such cases, the state authority can exercise leniency by exempting agents, imposing less severe punishment, or reinstating previously dismissed officials. Officials in disciplinary agencies also admit that they have to exercise more caution in dealing with agents who commit duty-related malfeasance, as opposed to corruption. Officials who are disciplined for duty-related malfeasance may be reappointed or even promoted later, whereas those who are convicted of corruption often come to the end of their careers.[16]

State Tolerance and Local Governance

Differentiated discipline makes government officials aware of the types of malfeasance that are forgivable and those that are not. As a result, officials are selectively accountable; that is, they devote more attention to issues that are on the top of the agenda of the upper-level authorities and pay less attention to those that are not. Government officials' selective accountability may also be true in other societies. What complicates this issue in China is that local officials face multiple principals from different levels, and they pay more attention to the biddings of those who directly affect their tenure and promotion. The priorities of the national government can be different from those of local governments, but local agents are directly answerable to their local leaders rather than the central leaders. Considering their personal or local interests, local leaders can be tolerant toward their subordinates who take unusual or rule-violating measures to address local issues.

The central authority may also tolerate local governments' varying practices in local governance, and this tolerance allows local governments to take different measures to deal with similar issues. This is reflected in the manner in which local governments deal with popular resistance in China. The case of Chen Guangcheng points to some local governments' abuse of power in dealing with citizens seeking justice. Chen, a self-taught blind lawyer, helped local residents to defend their rights against local governments. Upset by Chen's rights-protection activities, the local government in Shandong used controversial charges and evidence to put him in jail from 2008 to 2010. Indeed, Chen's actions cannot even be classified as political dissidence because what he did was largely rule-based resistance, rather than regime-challenging contention. After he was released in 2010, the local government put him under house arrest, denying him of freedom and access to people outside his home. At great expense, the local government hired people to monitor Chen around the clock. Ironically, despite the heavy guard, Chen managed to escape from his home in April 2012, which exposed the local government's malpractice and caused great embarrassment to the state authorities at both the central and local levels.[17]

On the other hand, as the Wukan case shows, other local governments can be more responsive to citizens' needs. After the conflict in Wukan village was settled, the provincial authority took further measures to strengthen village governance and improve the welfare of the villagers. In February and March 2012, with the monitoring of the local authority, villagers in Wukan held elections to select village representatives and committee members. Approximately 100 outsiders, including journalists, scholars, volunteers, and people from foreign consulates in Guangzhou, observed the elections.[18] Interestingly, the protest leader was elected director of the village committee, and another activist in the protest was elected deputy director. The provincial Party secretary cautiously admitted that there was no innovation in terms of the village election. Instead, what the government did was to strengthen the enforcement of the election law. In April, the county authority announced the punishment of eight former village cadres for their corruption. Furthermore, the provincial government also helped with village construction projects to improve the villagers' welfare, although the land issue remained unsolved.[19]

Such cases suggest that both abuse of power and interest-accommodating practices are possible and acceptable to the central authority. Given the decentralized power structure, Chinese local officials assume considerable autonomy in local governance. Certainly, such autonomy has to be conditional because autonomy also allows some officials to abuse power for personal gains. The worst scenario of officials' abuse of power is when they pursue personal or local interests with impunity, creating so-called independent kingdoms beyond the reach of the central authority.[20]

As discussed in Chapter Seven, not all local governments and their officials abuse their power and autonomy for personal interests. Some local governments' innovative practices in addressing local issues have proven to be meaningful options for other local governments or the central government to address similar issues. In recent years, local governments have extended efforts to develop innovations that do not seriously violate rules or laws. For example, local governments have introduced new institutions or granted more power to social associations to improve the management of social conflict. Some local governments have also made budgeting more transparent by assigning more power to the people's congress or introducing more democracy in the budgeting process.[21]

The longevity of China's communist regime has given rise to a debate on the reasons for its resilience. For example, Nathan points out that the CCP has adopted a number of measures, including the establishment of institutions for political participation, to increase the degree of institutionalization within the CCP, which in turn enhances its resilience and ensures its political survival.[22] However, opinions may differ. According to Pei, institutionalization is not the major reason behind the regime's resilience. "Instead, the principal reasons for the CCP's survival since Tiananmen have been robust economic performance and consistent political repression. Although it is true that the CCP may have improved its political tactics, its survival for the last two decades would have been unthinkable without these two critical factors."[23]

Economic development enables the party-state to acquire resources to address many social and economic problems. Repression may also continue to be crucial to the CCP's survival. Fundamentally, however, a regime's resilience relies on its ability to address the problems in ways that do not threaten the political system. Local governments' social, economic, and political initiatives may serve as practical solutions to some of the pressing issues faced by the party-state. For example, some practices of the local people's congresses, such as inspection of law enforcement, have been adopted by the National People's Congress and have been promoted nationwide. Therefore, local initiatives can contribute to regime resilience by helping the central party-state to address certain important issues.

Managing Agents in an Authoritarian Regime

This book suggests that although Chinese local governments and officials have achieved fast economic development over the past few decades, they have also caused a variety of problems. The central government has long faced the issue that national policies are ignored or distorted as they reach local governments. However, as Yang points out, "For many countries with per capita income levels similar to China's, the existence of an effective state that can maintain order and provide basic public goods remains a forlorn dream."[24] In other words, the Chinese party-state is still able to ensure the accountability of its agents, although the accountability tends to vary across issues.

Compared to the former Soviet Union, the collapse of which was tied to its failure in managing its agents, the Chinese state authority seems better able to keep its agents in check. To some Soviet watchers, "The remarkable feature of Chinese reforms is that the center has held as long as it has."[25] The Chinese state authority is motivated to discipline agents and is better able to do it for several reasons. One is the central authority's need to protect its authority. The central authority has to maintain its reputation to deter deviations and to rule the country. Local agents are responsible for the enforcement of the central government's policies, and the latter's unprincipled tolerance of local agents' deviations undermines its authority and ability to achieve policy goals. In a political hierarchy, the determination of the top authority is a crucial factor that prevents the leakage of authority at lower levels. To some extent, compared with the Soviet government, "Chinese leaders were more prepared to take decisive actions to preserve their reputation for discipline."[26]

Another reason is the legitimacy constraint, which means that the central authority that represents the political system is under pressure to maintain or enhance its legitimacy. As discussed in Chapter One, an authoritarian government aspires to shore up its legitimacy because a high level of legitimacy promotes state agents' confidence in the regime and improves its chance of surviving crises. It also reduces the costs arising from constant repression.[27] Understandably, an authoritarian government that already has high legitimacy is strongly motivated to maintain it. It has been found that Chinese governments, especially the central government, enjoy a rather high level of political trust among the people.[28] As a result, the central authority is under the pressure to maintain the trust. This legitimacy constraint accounts for the state's responsiveness when its agents' malfeasance causes popular resentment.

The concern over authority and the legitimacy constraint constitute pressure on the party-state to monitor and discipline state agents. This pressure is also the reason the party-state uses or accepts different monitoring mechanisms. In the Chinese political system, to hold local officials accountable simply by relying on the monitoring of the central or provincial authorities is essentially impossible because the number of agents to be monitored is too large. Ideally, a more effective way to ensure agents' accountability is "to develop some means of assuring compliance other than correction of errors after they are observed."[29] Although the operation of state agencies in China has become increasingly institutionalized,[30] it is still not rare for local officials to ignore rules or procedures specified by the central authorities. Therefore, other mechanisms, such as third-party monitoring, can help reduce the agency problem. Social forces, such as media and popular contention, can lend help to achieving accountability or monitoring state agents.[31]

The media plays an increasingly influential role in monitoring and disciplining state agents in China because of the state's legitimacy constraint. The Chinese government is facing an unprecedented situation in which information flows more easily than in the past. A better flow of information is not only effective in exposing local agents' malpractices but also in generating pressure on the state authority to discipline such agents. Despite the Party's tight control over the media, "Every day an article appears that the propaganda ministry doesn't like,"[32] which can be largely attributed to the emergence of new information technologies. The state authority has apparently felt the pressure because an improved flow of information makes it difficult to pretend not to know about the problem. The deputy provincial Party secretary of Guangdong, who headed the team dealing with the Wukan case, admitted the pressure:

We are in the era of the Internet. Everybody has a "microphone," everybody is a spokesman, everybody has the right to engage in discourse, and everybody is a journalist. Rights protection through the Internet has become one of the most convenient and effective weapons of the people. At the peak of the Wuhan case, about 100 media agencies came to the village and they sent reports overseas.[33]

Once media exposure makes certain issues public knowledge, the state authority is under pressure to show accountability. Failing to respond leads to the loss of legitimacy. This pressure to respond will remain or even increase as long as the flow of information continues.

A common way for the state authority to protect itself when dealing with cases exposed by the media is to show its accountability through resentment-appeasing interventions. In recent years, the central government has intervened to address the governance failures of local governments, including mass protests, food safety, production safety, and other local governance crises such as pollution. Intervention from the central government generally resolves the issues and sometimes results in the punishment of errant local officials. For example, the fake milk powder incident in the city of Fuyang in Anhui Province in 2003 was largely attributed to the city authorities' failure to inspect products being sold in markets. Disclosure of the case by the Chinese Central Television prompted the State Council to send a team to investigate, and a number of city officials were eventually penalized.[34] In the case of child labor in Shanxi Province, where children were forced to work in brick kilns in 2007, both the central and provincial authorities intervened after the media exposé. A total of ninety-five public employees were given Party or administrative sanctions, and thirty-one others faced criminal charges.[35] Other high-profile cases include the death of Sun Zhigang, which resulted in the abolition of the custody and repatriation system in 2003, and the punishment of officials responsible for the melamine-tainted milk in Hebei province in 2008.

In 2012 and early 2013, a number of government officials were dismissed, removed, and/or investigated after their malfeasance was disclosed. In 2012, the director of the safety supervision bureau of Shaanxi province was removed and investigated for corruption after the pictures of his expensive watches were posted online. Another official in Guangdong was removed and investigated by the local DIC after the media disclosed his ownership of a surprisingly large number of apartments.[36] Several officials were removed or investigated after their sex scandals were posted online. In

January 2013, the head of the National Bureau of Compilation and Translation was sacked after a woman who claimed to have had an affair with this head posted a long article online, detailing their relationship. Again in early 2013, about ten high-ranking officials in Chongqing were dismissed because of sex scandals.

Regardless of whether the party-state is willing to see the media's exposure of its agents' malfeasance, it feels the pressure of responding. Clearly, the Chinese government and society now operate in a new environment that was not encountered by any communist government in former socialist regimes. Israel's former foreign minister, Shimon Peres, suggested that communism fell in Russia without the participation of the Russian army, without the emergence of a new political party against the Communists, or without intervention from other countries; rather, the fall was accomplished by the communists themselves. As he stated, "Authoritarian governments became weak the minute they could no longer blind their people or control information."[37]

In China, a better flow of information has not resulted in the collapse of the regime but has generated unprecedented pressure of responsiveness on the state authority. Certainly, the state authority still retains effective control over the media and new information communication technologies and has time and again punished people whose information dissemination offended the state authority, but the difficulties in doing so are obvious. State agencies responsible for media management feel pressure from both society and the media industry. Even state-owned media have shown their resentment, though often in subtle ways. On May 4, 2012, *The New Beijing Post* published an article criticizing the United States for its involvement in the case of Chen Guangcheng, claiming that diplomats should not do what they were not supposed to do. In the early morning of May 5, the newspaper posted a message on its Sino Weibo account in the form of a one-line statement accompanied by a large black-and-white picture of a withered, old-fashioned clown taking a lonely drag of his cigarette. The message reads, "In the still of the deep night, removing that mask of insincerity, we say to our true selves, 'I am sorry.'"[38] The protests over censorship at *Southern Weekend*, one of China's most liberal newspapers, in early 2013 also signaled the resentment of the state-controlled media.[39]

Another important source of pressure faced by the central government is popular contention. Social movements are "an important source of countervailing group power" in democracies "when movement espouses goals that attract large segments of the middle class."[40] Social protests can also cause non-negligible pressure on authoritarian governments. Acemoglu and Robinson suggest that nondemocracies face "revolution constraints"; that is, "an important issue in nondemocracies is to ensure that no group is unhappy enough to attempt to overthrow the regime or take other political or economic actions detrimental to the utility of the group in power."[41]

In China, popular contention has contributed to policy implementation and policy adjustment and has also led the party-state to view "building a harmonious society" as a top priority.[42] The party-state has disciplined agents who have caused or mishandled popular protests because of the need to protect its legitimacy and authority. Numerous conflicts indicate that if the state agencies or government officials do not observe the rules or laws, the people may simply do the same, although they often face risks when doing so. Except in the case of village elections, Chinese citizens cannot pose a credible threat to abusive officials through election; instead, they have to take other measures to deter or resist these officials. Although citizens' actions may not always be successful, these can cause uncertainty for the officials responsible for such conflicts.

These different sources of pressure on the central and local authorities can enhance the accountability of state agents. Nevertheless, improving the institutionalization of discipline in terms of rule specification and rule enforcement is fundamental. This book has argued that differentiated and selective discipline has helped the Chinese party-state to address the dilemma it faces in dealing with malfeasant agents. Although selective tolerance has created uncertainty among state agents, the challenge faced by the state authority in cadre management remains.

To prevent serious leakage of authority in cadre management, the central authority needs to have a clear consensus regarding the bottom line of state tolerance and must mete out due punishment to ensure that officials are aware of that bottom line. Consensus building will certainly be difficult when it involves faction politics or other cost considerations.[43] The worst scenario of ineffective management of state agents involves a lack of consensus among central leaders on what can and cannot be tolerated. The credibility of discipline will be undermined if the leaders' positional responsibilities are overshadowed by cost considerations. Needless to say, the credibility will also be weakened if the leaders themselves engage in immoral or illegal conduct. When such problems occur, government officials' abuse of power will be prevalent, and state power and other political and economic resources will be monopolized and abused by officials for personal gains. If the number of malfeasant agents becomes so large that the central authority loses its authority of control, the regime's survival will be endangered.[44] In these circumstances, the state will be unable to enforce its policies, and its agents will either directly cause social grievances and unrest or will refuse to support the regime that is believed to lack legitimacy or a future. In spite of the fact that a regime's legitimacy and resilience can be tested only in crises, the Chinese party-state is certainly unwilling to witness the occurrence of such crises. Concern over the ineffective management of agents and the resulting consequences can be a constant pressure on the party-state, prompting it to continue to extend efforts to discipline its erring agents as long as it hopes to continue its rule. This explains why the new administration under the leadership of Xi Jinping has taken extensive and intensive measures to regulate government officials since it assumed power. But it remains to be seen whether such measures will be sustained and institutionalized.

Appendix

Data Collection

Appendix 3.1: Collection of 111 Cases of Media Exposure

The 111 cases of media exposure were collected with the criterion that they contain the following information: causes of a problem, outcome of the exposed issue, and officials involved and disciplined. They were collected from the following sources.

BOOKS (7)

Dong Zhe and Xiao Yuan, *Difang renda jiandu anli xuan* (Beijing: Renmin ribao chubanshe, 2001)

Ling Fei, *Zhongguo meiti jizhe diaocha* (Beijing: Guangming ribao chubanshe, 2004)

Liu Jianming, *Tianli minxin* (Beijing: Jinri zhongguo chubanshe, 1998).

Ren Yanfang, *Minyuan* (Beijing: Zhongguo wenlian chubanshe, 1999).

Yang Zhenjiang, *Anjian cong zheli tupo* (Beijing: Zhongguo jiancha chubanshe, 2002).

Yuan Yulai, *Min gao guan shouji* (Beijing: Zhongguo jiancha chubanshe, 2004).

Zhan Jiang, *Yulun jiandu lanpishu* (Guangzhou: Nanfang ribao chubanshe, 2004).

MAGAZINES (16)

Baixin; *Dadi*; *Falu yu shenghuo*; *Fazhi yu xinwen*; *Jiancha fengyun*; *Jinri minliu*; *Lvshi yu fazhi*; *Minzhu yu fazhi*; *Tuoling*; *Waitan huabao*; *Xinwen daxue; Xinwen chuanbo; Xinwen jizhe; Xinwen tongxun; Xinwen zhanxian; Zhongguo xinwen zhoukan*

NEWSPAPERS (15)

Beijing qingnian bao; Chengdu shangbao; Dahe ribao; Fuzhou gongan bao; Gongren ribao; Huaxi dushibao; Minzhu yu fazhi shibao; Nanfang dushi bao; Nanfang zhoumo; Qilu wanbao; Renmin ribao; Shidai shangbao; Xinwen zhoubao; Yunnan ribao; Zhongguo jingji shibao

WEBSITES (7)

http://law.big5.auhuinews.com; http://news.sina.com.cn; http://news.sohu.com; http://www.bandao.cn/news; http://www.feelor.com; http://www.folkchina.org; http://www.rfa.org

Appendix 3.2: Collection of 133 Cases of Officials' Duty-Related Malfeasance

The criterion for the collection of the 133 cases is that there is information about the causes of a problem, the consequences of the problem, the administrative posts of the officials disciplined, and the mode of discipline. The 133 cases occurred in twenty-six provinces, including Henan (16), Shanxi (15), Sichuan (14), Guangdong (11), Hebei (9), Hunan (8), Hubei (5), Jiangsu (5), Shaanxi (5), Anhui (4), Heilongjiang (4), Jilin (4), Shandong (4), Gansu (3), Guangxi (3), Jiangxi (3), Liaoning (3), Beijing (2), Chongqing (2), Fujian (2), Inner Mongolia (2), Xinjiang (2), Yunnan (2), Zhejiang (2), Guizhou (1), Ningxia (1), Shanghai (1).

The 133 cases were collected from the following sources.

MAGAZINES (10)

Banyue tan; Chuanmei; Dongfang zhoukan; Fenghuang zhoukan; Jiancha; Liaowang dongfang; Sanlian shenghuo zhoukan; Zhongguo jiancha; Zhongguo lushi; Zhongguo xinwen zhoukan

NEWSPAPERS (26)

Chengdu shangbao; Chongqing chenbao; Diyi caijing ribao; Dongfang zaobao; Fazhi ribao; Fazhi wanbao; Fazhi zhoubao; Guangxi ribao; Huaxi dushibao; Hua shangbao; Jiancha ribao; Nanfang dushibao; Nanfang zhoumo; Nong-

min ribao; Renmin ribao; Shanxi qingnian bao; Shanxi ribao; Shaanxi ribao: South China Morning Post; Takungpao; Xiandai nongcun bao; Xinjing bao; Xinwen chenbao; Zhongguo huanjing bao; Zhongguo jingji shibao; Zhongguo qingnian bao

WEBSITES (24)

chinasafety.gov.cn; news.163.com; news.sina.com; news.xinhuanet.com; www.asjj.gov.cn; www.chiancoal.org.cn; www.china.com.cn; www.china.court.org; www.enorth.com.cn; www.enorth.com.cn; www.esafety.cn; www.findlaw.cn; www.gov.cn; www.jlmj.gov.cn; www.js119.com; www.jxmkaqjc.gov.cn; www.1kagri.gov.cn; www.people.com.cn; www.safety.com.cn; www.singtaonet.com; www.ycaii.gov.cn; www.ytsafety.gov.cn; www.zhejiang.gov.cn; yzdsb.hebnews.cn

Appendix 4.1: Cases of the Disciplining of Cadres in Conflict Management

The 228 cases of popular contention (190 + 38) were collected from the following sources, in addition to the author's fieldwork.

NEWSPAPERS (49)

Beijing wanbao; Beijing yule xinbao; Chengde ribao; China Daily; Chuzhou wanbao; Chongqing chenbao; Chutian dushi bao; Dahe bao; Dongfang ribao; Fazhi kuaibao; Fazhi ribao; Financial Times; Gongren ribao; Hainan jingji bao; Huhehaote wanbao; Huashang bao; Huasheng bao; Jiancha ribao; Jiangnan shibao; Jieyang ribao; Jinhua shibao; Lanzhou chenbao; Mingpao; Nanfan dushi bao; Nanfang zhoumo; Nanfang ribao; Nanyang ribao; New York times; Ningbo wanbao; Pingguo ribao; Qingyuan ribao; Shantou ribao; Shanxi fazhi bao; Shidai shangbao; South China Morning Post; Washington Post; Wenzhou ribao; Wuhan wanbao; Xindao ribao; Xinkuai bao; Xinwenhua bao; Xibu shangbao; Xuchang ribao; Ya'an ribao; Yangzi wanbao; Zhejiang xinshengbao; Zhejiang laonian bao; Zhongguo qingnianbao; Zhongguo shibao;

BOOKS AND PERIODICALS (9)

The Research Group, *Zhongguo zhuanxingqi quntixing tufashijian duice yanjiu* (Beijing: Xueyuan chubanshe, 2003); *Far Eastern Economic Review;*

Fenghuang zhoukan; *Minzhu yu fazhi*; *Minqing yu xinfang*; *Xinmin zhoukan*; *Ying zhoukan*; *Zhanlue yu guanli*; *Zhongguo xinwen zhoukan*

WEBSITES (52)

en.epochtimes. com; finance.people.com.cn; fy.putuo.gov.cn; ga.hainan.gov.cn; hnfy.chinacourt.org; lyzy.chinacourt.org; news. anhuinews.com; news. boxun.com; news.creaders.net; news.mlr.gov.cn; news.qianlong.com; news.sdinfo.net; news.sina.com.cn; www.66wz.com; www.aboluowang.com; www.bbzy.org; www.cctv.com; www.chinanews.com.cn; www.chinesenewsnet.com; www.cn-doc.com; www.cnradio.com; www.cq.chinanews.com.cn; www.crd-net.org; www.dffy.com; www.fhnews.com.cn; www.fsou.net.cn; www.gd. xinhuanet.com; www.gscn.com.cn; www.gsfzb.gov.cn; www.gx.xinhuanet.com; www.hnby.com.cn; www.jcrb.com; www.jxnews.com.cn; www.lawon.cn; www.lirun. pdx.cn; www.longhui.gov.cn; www.lz160.net; www.new.bbc.co.uk; www.pxepb.gov.cn; www.qtfy.gov.cn; www.rfa.org; www.shm.com.cn; www.sociology.cass.cn; www.szls.gov.cn; www.washington post.com; www.wyzxwyzx. com; www.xinhuanet.com; www.xs.gd.cn; www.yinzi.cn; www.zhinong.cn; www.zjol.com.cn; ycjc.gov.cn

Appendix 5.1: Cases of the Disciplining of 1,012 Officials

The 1,012 corruption cases occurred mostly between 1995 and 2010, and they were collected from the following sources.

BOOKS (8)

Chen Weiwei *Jingtian da'an bao tanhun* (Beijing: Renmin ribao chubanshe, 2009).

Ju Bin (ed.), *Fantan gonggao* (Beijing: Jingji ribao chubanshe, 1999).

Shao Daosheng, *Zhongguo: Juji fubai* (Beijing: Shehui kexue chubanshe, 2009).

The Writing Group, *Fubai minmie qinqing* (Beijing: Zhongguo fangzheng chubanshe, 2011).

Xiao Chong (ed.), *Zhonggong haiguan heimo* (Hong Kong: Shafer International Publishing Company, 2001).

Ye Feng (ed.), *59 shui xianxiang* (Beijing: Dazhong wenyi chubanshe, 2000).

Yu Jiyang, *Tianhen—zhongyang jiwei jianchabu zai xingdong* (Beijing: Zhonghua gongshang lianhe chubanshe, 1998).

Zhang Zhanbin (ed.), *Gongheguo fanfu zhilu* (Beijing: Zhongguo jingji chubanshe, 1999).

MAGAZINES (16)

Banyue tan; Caijing; Dadi; Datequ dangfeng; Falv yu shenghuo; Fangyuan fazhi; Fazhi yu xinwen; Jiancha fengyun; Jiating; Jijian yu jiancha; Lianzheng liaowang; Liaowang dongfang zhoukan; Minzhu yu fazhi; Nanfang renwu zhoukan; Zhiyin; Zhongguo jiancha

NEWSPAPERS (81)

21 shiji jingji baodao; Beijing Chenbao; Beijing qingnian bao; Beijing wanbao; Beijing yule xingbao; Caijing shibao; Changjiang ribao; Changsha wanbao; Chongqing chenbao; Chongqing ribao; Chongqing wanbao; Dahe bao; Dazhong ribao; Diyi caijing ribao; Dongfang zaobao; Falv fuwu shibao; Fazhi ribao; Fazhi wanbao; Fazhi zhoubao; Fazhi zhoumo; Fujian ribao; Fuzhou wanbao; Gansu fazhibao Yanzhao dushi bao; Gansu ribao; Guangming ribao; Guangzhou ribao; Guizhou dushi bao; Guizhou shangbao; Hainan ribao; Haixia dushi bao; Hangzhou ribao; Huaxi dushi bao; Jiancha ribao; Jianghuai chenbao; Jiangnan shibao; Jiangsu fazhi bao; Jinan ribao; Jinghua shibao; Jinghua wanbao; Lanzhou chenbao; Liaoning ribao; Liaosheng wanbao; Liaoning fazhi bao; Minzhu yu fazhi shibao; Nanfang dushi bao; Nanfang ribao; Nanfang zhoumo; Neimenggu ribao; Qilu wanbao; Qingdao ribao; Quanzhou wanbao; Renmin fayuan bao; Renmin ribao; Sanqin dushi bao; Shanghai zhengquan bao; Shanxi wanbao; Shenzhen tequbao; Shichuan ribao; Sichuan fazhi bao; Wenzhou ribao; Wuhan wanbao; Xi'an ribao; Xiangfan ribao; Xiaoxiang chenbao; Xin fazhi bao; Xinhua meiri dianxun bao; Xinhua ribao; Xinjing bao; Xinkuai bao; Xinmin wanbao; Xinwen wanbao; Xinwen zhoubao; Xinxi shibao; Yangcheng wanbao; Yangzi wanbao; Yunnan ribao; Zhejiang fazhi bao; Zhejiang ribao; Zhengzhou wanbao; Zhongguo jijian jiancha bao; Zhongguo qingnianbao

WEBSITES (106)

http://baike.baidu.com; http://data.jxwmw.cn; http://digest.icxo.com; http://fzb.zjol.com.cn; http://gxjc.gov.cn; http://gzdsb.gog.com.cn; http://gzsb.gog.com.cn; http://hongjian.fyfz.cn; http://jsc.jseti.edu.cn; http://jw.cqu.edu.cn; http://mba.ce.cn; http://news.cnnb.com.cn; http://news

.eastday.com; http://news.qq.com; http://news.qqhru.edu.cn; http://tieba.baidu.com; http://web.peopledaily.com.cn; http://wgb.zhenjiang.gov.cn; http://www.10yan.com; http://www.163.com; http://www.21cn.com; http://www.anhuinews.com; http://www.asjj.gov.cn; http://www.benxi.ln.cn; http://www.cctv.com; http://www.china.com.cn; http://www.chinacourt.org; http://www.chinaelections.org; http://www.china-fantan.net; http://www.chinafzgc.cn; http://www.chinanews.com.cn; http://www.cnfamily.com; http://www.cnhan.com; http://www.cnhubei.com; http://www.cnnb.com.cn; http://www.cnnb.com.cn; http://www.ctnews.com.cn; http://www.dflz.gov.cn; http://www.dzwww.com; http://www.eastday.com; http://www.enorth.com.cn; http://www.fiet.gov.cn; http://www.foshan.net; http://www.gov.cn/jrzg; http://www.gutian.gov.cn; http://www.gxjjw.gov.cn; http://www.gxjjw.gov.cn; http://www.gxnews.com.cn; http://www.gylq.com; http://www.hainan.gov.cn; http://www.hebzx.cn; http://www.hefei.gov.cn; http://www.hicourt.gov.cn; http://www.hicourt.gov.cn; http://www.hl.jcy.gov.cn; http://www.hnsc.com.cn; http://www.hudong.com; http://www.hzdx.gov.cn; http://www.ifeng.com; http://www.jcj.dl.gov.cn; http://www.jcrb.com; http://www.jiaodong.net; http://www.jnds.gov.cn; http://www.jrj.com.cn; http://www.lawtime.cn; http://www.lawtime.cn; http://www.lqzx.com; http://www.mos.gov.cn; http://www.nbcp.gov.cn; http://www.nen.com.cn; http://www.neweralaw.com; http://www.people.com.cn; http://www.qingdaonews.com; http://www.qzwb.com; http://www.sdtvu.com.cn; http://www.shm.com.cn; http://www.sina.com.cn; http://www.smxlz.gov.cn; http://www.sohu.com; http://www.southcn.com; http://www.southcn.com; http://www.sxdaily.com.cn; http://www.sy-dj.gov.cn; http://www.sznews.com; http://www.taiants.jcy.gov.cn; http://www.taihainet.com; http://www.wellrunlaw.com; http://www.wenweipo.com; http://www.xici.net; http://www.xinhuanet.com; http://www.xtgc.com.cn; http://www.xxcb.com.cn; http://www.xxcb.com.cn; http://www.yahoo.com; http://www.ycwb.com; http://www.yfw.com.cn; http://www.zfwlxt.com; http://www.zjol.com.cn; http://www.zjsjw.gov.cn; http://www.zjsjw.gov.cn; http://www.zsdsb.gov.cn; http://www.zsdsb.gov.cn; http://www.zslz.com; http://www.zzyu.cn; http://ysjj.qyjj.gov.cn; http://zjdaily.zjol.com.cn

APPENDIX 5.2
Cases of high-ranking officials given serious legal punishment (N = 41).

	Positions held when arrested	Amount[a]	Year[c]
Death penalty (10)			
Li Youcan	Deputy head, provincial foreign trade bureau, Hebei	47.44	2004
Chen Kejie	Vice chairman, National People's Congress	41.09	2000
Li Zhen	Head, National Tax Bureau, Hebei	10.84	2003
Ma Xiangdong	Vice mayor, Shenyang, Liaoning	9.76 + 10.7[2b]	2001
Zheng Xiaoyu	Head, National Food and Drug Agency	6.49	2007
Hu Changqing	Vice governor, Jiangxi	5.44 + 1.8[b]	2000
Wang Huaizhong	Vice governor, Anhui	5.17 + 4.8[b]	2003
Lin Longfei	Party secretary, Zhouning County, Fujian	2.36 + 2.1[b]	2004
Guo Jiusi	Deputy head, Financial Bureau, Shenyang,	3.02	2001
Yu Ding	Secretary, political-legal committee, Guilin	2.55	2001
Death with a reprieve (20)			
Chen Tonghai	Director and chairman, Sinopec Corporation	195.7	2009
Wang Shouye	Deputy navy command-in-chief	160.0	2006
Shi Faliang	Head, Transportation Bureau, Henan Province	19.0	2006
Tian Yufei	Party secretary, Jianwei county, Sichuan	18.04 + 13.3[b]	2006
Li Jiating	Governor, Yunnan	18.1	2003
Huang Yihui	Head, Civil Affairs Bureau, Shenzhen, Guangdong	15.9 + 19[b]	2004
Bi Yuxi	Deputy head, Transportation Bureau, Beijing	10.04	2005
Gao Yong	Head, city propaganda department, Chengdu, Sichuan	9.55 + 6.66[b]	2005
Cong Fukui	Vice governor, Hebei	9.36	2002
Zhao Gengxiao	Vice mayor, Loudi city, Hunan	8.0	2003
Wang Zhaoyao	Vice chairman, Political Consultative Conference, Anhui	7.04 + 6.5[b]	2007
Wang Wulong	Vice chairman, people's congress of Jiangsu	6.83	2007
Mu Suixin	Mayor, Shenyang, Liaoning	6.61 + 2.7[b]	2001
Han Guizhi	Chairperson, Political Consultative Conference, Heilongjiang	7.02	2005
Xu Guojian	Head, Organization Department, Jiangsu	6.4	2005
Ding Naijin	Party secretary, Jixi city, Heilongjiang	6.2 + 8.8[b]	2006
Ma De	Party secretary, Shuihua city, Heilonjiang	6.03	2005
Li Jizhou	Vice minister, Ministry of Public Security	5.03	2001
Zhang Xinyuan	Head, Local Tax Bureau, Heilongjiang	4.94	2006
Xu Qiyao	Head, Construction Bureau, Jiangsu	3.92	2001
Life in prison (11)			
Zhao Yucun	Head, Customs, Shenzhen	9.0	2002
Liu Fangren	Party secretary, Guizhou	6.77	2004
Xiao Zuowu	Head, National Tax Bureau, Inner Mongolia	4.8 + 3.9[b]	2004
Tian Fengshan	Minister, Ministry of Land Resources	4.0	2005
Cao Zhongjun	Division head, Construction Bureau, Shaanxi	3.71	2006
Tian Fengqi	President, High Court, Liaoning	3.3	2003
Chen Zhaofeng	Party secretary, Dingyuan County, Anhui	2.89 + 5.5[b]	2006
Yang Zhida	Head, highway management bureau, Hunan	2.95 + 2.6[b]	2005
Sun Yanbiao	Mayor, Taizhou, Zhejiang	1.18	2001
Zhang Kuntong	Head, Transportation Bureau, Henan	1.0	2001
Ding Yangning	Party secretary, Zhenghe County, Fujian	0.52	2000

SOURCE: Author's collection.

[a] Amount of bribes accepted (million yuan).
[b] The sources of the income could not be explained.
[c] The year when the ruling was made.

Notes

Notes to Chapter One

1. Michael Wines, "A Village in Revolt Could Be a Harbinger for China," *New York Times*, December 25, 2011; *Nanfang ribao*, November 22, 2011; *Ming Pao*, December 12, 2011.

2. Yongshun Cai, "Local Governments and the Suppression of Popular Resistance in China," *China Quarterly* 193 (2008): 24–42.

3. *Nanfang dushi bao*, December 26, 2011. Later, the provincial government agreed to pay a large amount of compensation to the villager's family, and the family gave up the request for further investigation. Interviews, Guangdong, 2012.

4. *Nanfang dushi bao*, December 26, 2011.

5. *Nanfang ribao*, December 20, 2011.

6. Susan Whiting, "The Cadre Evaluation System at the Grassroots: The Paradox of Party Rule," in Barry Naughton and Dali Yang, eds., *Holding China Together: Diversity and National Integration in the Post-Deng Era* (New York: Cambridge University Press, 2004), 101–109; Maria Edin, "State Capacity and Local Agent Control in China: CCP Cadre Management from a Township Perspective," *China Quarterly* 173 (2003): 35–52; Kevin O'Brien and Lianjiang Li, "Selective Policy Implementation in Rural China," *Comparative Politics* 31, 2 (1999): 167–186.

7. Jae Ho Chung, "Managing Political Crises in China: The Cases of Collective Protests," in Jae Ho Chung, ed., *China's Crisis Management* (London: Routledge, 2011), 25–42.

8. Dong Xueqin, Zhang Heping, and Zhang Zeyuan, "Women shishui? Xianweishuji caifang lu" (Who Are We? Interviews with County Party Secretaries), *Liaowang xinwen zhoukan* (Outlook Weekly), November 10, 2005.

9. Ibid.

10. As discussed in Chapter Four, a vice governor in Anhui was jailed largely because of his failure in managing a large-scale protest. *Nanfang dushi bao*, July 2, 2005.

11. Steven Solnick, *Stealing the State: Control and Collapse in Soviet Institutions* (Cambridge, MA: Harvard University Press, 1998), 15.

12. Ibid., 241.

13. Theda Skocpol, "Bringing the State Back In: The Strategies of Analysis in Current Research," in Peter Evans, Dietrich Rueschemeyer, and Theda Skocpol, eds., *Bringing the State Back In* (New York: Cambridge University Press, 1985), 3–43.

14. Ruth Grant and Robert Keohane, "Accountability and Abuses of Power in World Politics," *American Political Science Review* 99, 1 (2005): 29–43.

15. Terry Moe, "The New Economics of Organization," *American Journal of Political Science* 28, 4 (1984): 739–777.

16. Roderick Kiewiet and Mathew McCubbins, *The Logic of Delegation: Congressional Parties and the Appropriations Process* (Chicago: University of Chicago Press, 1991).

17. Mathew McCubbins and Thomas Schwartz, "Congressional Oversight Overlooked: Police Patrols versus Fire Alarms," *American Journal of Political Science* 28, 1 (1984): 165–179.

18. Gerald Caiden, "The Problem of Ensuring the Public Accountability of Public Officials," in Joseph Jabbra and O. P. Dwivedi, eds, *Public Service Accountability* (West Hartford, CT: Kumarian Press, 1988), 17–38.

19. Brendan O'Flaherty, "Why Are There Democracies? A Principal Agent Answer," *Economics and Politics* 2 (1990): 133–155.

20. Delmer Dunn, "Mixed Elected and Nonelected Officials in Democratic Policy Making: Fundamentals of Accountability and Responsibility," in Adam Przeworski, Susan Stokes, and Bernard Manin, eds., *Democracy, Accountability, and Representation* (New York: Cambridge University Press, 1999), 297–325.

21. Carl Friedrich, *Constitutional Government and Democracy* (Boston: Ginn and Company, 1950), 398.

22. Guy Peters, *The Politics of Bureaucracy* (New York: Longman, 1978), 207–229.

23. Veron Key, *Politics, Parties, and Pressure Groups* (New York: Vintage Books, 1996), 76.

24. Anthony Downs, *An Economic Theory of Democracy* (New York: Harper and Row, 1956).

25. Paul Pierson, *Dismantling the Welfare State: Reagan, Thatcher, and the Politics of Retrenchment* (New York: Cambridge University Press, 1994), 21.

26. Jose Maria Maravall, "Accountability and Manipulation," in Adam Przeworski, Susan Stokes, and Bernard Manin, eds., *Democracy, Accountability, and Representation*, 154–196.

27. Sunil Sondhi, "Combating Corruption in India: The Role of Civil Society," paper prepared for the XVIII World Congress of International Political Science Association, August 2000, Québec, PQ, Canada.

28. Madhu Limaye, *Decline of a Political System* (New Delhi: Wheeler Publishing, 1992), 156.

29. Bernard Manin, Adam Przeworski, and Susan Stokes, "Elections and Representations," in Przeworski, Stokes, and Manin, eds., *Democracy, Accountability, and Representation*, 29–54.

30. See, for example, McCubbins and Schwarts, "Congressional Oversight Overlooked"; Matthew McCubbins, Roger Noll, and Barry Weingast, "Structure and Process, Politics and Policy: Administrative Arrangements and the Political Control of Agencies," *Virginia Law Review* 75 (1989): 431–482.

31. Anthony Oberschall, "Opportunities and Framing in the Eastern Europe Revolts of 1989," in Doug McAdam, John D. McCarthy, and Mayer N. Zald, eds., *Comparative Perspectives on Social Movements* (Cambridge, UK: Cambridge University Press, 1996), 172–99.

32. David Easton, *A Systems Analysis of Political Life* (Chicago: University of Chicago Press, 1979), 288.

33. William Gamson, *Power and Discontent* (Homewood, IL: Dosey Press, 1968), 180.

34. Steven Saxonberg, *The Fall: A Comparative Study of the End of Communism in Czechoslovakia, East Germany, Hungary and Poland* (Amsterdam: Harwood Academic, 2001), 147.

35. In the long run, the lack of discipline may lead to the rampant misconduct of state agents, as was the case in some former socialist regimes. Steven Solnick, "The Breakdown of Hierarchies in the Soviet Union and China," *World Politics* 48, 2 (1996): 209–238; Konstantin Simis, *USSR: The Corrupt Society: The Secret World of Soviet Capitalism* (New York: Simon and Schuster, 1982), 64.

36. Peter Evans, *Embedded Autonomy: States and Industrial Transformations* (Princeton, NJ: Princeton University Press, 1995).

37. William Zartman, "Introduction: Posing the Problem of State Collapse," in William Zartman (ed.), *Collapsed States: The Disintegration and Restoration of Legitimate Authority* (Boulder, CO: Lynne Rienner Publisher, 1995), 1–11.

38. Simis, *USSR: The Corrupt Society*, 64.
39. Solnick, *Stealing the State*, 3.
40. Ibid., 7.
41. Dali Yang, *Remaking the Chinese Leviathan: Market Transition and the Politics of Governance in China* (Stanford, CA: Stanford University Press, 2004).
42. Melanie Manion, "The Cadre Management System, Post-Mao: The Appointment, Promotion, Transfer, and Removal of Party and State Leaders," *China Quarterly* 102 (1985): 203–233; John Burns, "Strengthening CCP Control of Leadership Selection: The 1990 Nomenklatura," *China Quarterly* 138 (1994): 458–491; Yasheng Huang, "Administrative Monitoring in China," *China Quarterly* 143 (1995): 828–844.
43. James Kai-sing Kung and Shuo Chen, "The Tragedy of the Nomenklatura: Career Incentives and Political Radicalism during China's Great Leap Famine," *American Political Science Review* 105, 1 (2011): 27–45.
44. Pierre Landry, *Decentralized Authoritarianism in China: The Communist Party's Control of Local Elites in the Post-Mao China* (New York: Cambridge University Press, 2008); Hongbin Li and Li-an Zhou, "Political Turnover and Economic Performance: The Incentive Role of Personnel Control in China," *Journal of Public Economics* 89, 9–10 (2005): 1743–1762; Zhiyue Bo, *Chinese Provincial Leaders: Economic Performance and Political Mobility since 1949* (Armonk, NY: M. E. Sharpe, 2002).
45. Susan Whiting, "The Cadre Evaluation System at the Grass Roots: The Paradox of Party Rule," in Barry Naughton and Dali Yang, ed., *Holding China Together: Diversity and National Integration in the Post-Deng Era* (New York: Cambridge University Press, 2004), 101–119.
46. Whiting, "The Cadre Evaluation System at the Grass Roots"; Maria Edin, "State Capacity and Local Agent Control in China: CCP Cadre Management from a Township Perspective," *China Quarterly* 173 (2003), 35–72; Susan Whiting, *Power and Wealth in Rural China: The Political Economy of Institutional Change* (New York: Cambridge University Press, 2000); Kevin O'Brien and Lianjiang Li, "Selective Policy Implementation in Rural China," *Comparative Politics* 31, 2 (1999): 167–186; Samuel Ho, *Rural China in Transition: Non-Agricultural Development in Rural Jiangsu, 1978–1990* (Oxford, UK: Clarendon Press, 1994), 212–215.
47. Whiting, *Power and Wealth in Rural China*.
48. Edin, "State Capacity and Local Agent Control in China."
49. Landry, *Decentralized Authoritarianism in China*, 114.
50. John Burns and Xiaoqi Wang, "Civil Service Reform in China: Impacts on Civil Servants' Behavior," *China Quarterly* 201 (2010), 58–78.

51. Thomas Heberer and Rene Trappel, "Evaluation Processes, Local Cadres' Behavior and Local Development Processes," *Journal of Contemporary China* 22, 84 (2013): 1048–1066.

52. McCubbins, Noll, and Weingast, "Structure and Process, Politics and Policy," 439–440.

53. O'Brien and Li, "Selective Policy Implementation in Rural China."

54. *Zhongguo qingnian bao*, November 14, 2005.

55. Edin, "State Capacity and Local Agent Control in China"; Yasheng Huang, *Inflation and Investment Controls in China: The Political Economy of Central-Local Relations during the Reform Era* (New York: Cambridge University Press, 1996).

56. Wengfang Tang, *Public Opinion and Political Change in China* (Stanford, CA: Stanford University Press, 2005), 55–78; Zhengxu Wang, "Before the Emergence of Critical Citizens: Economic and Political Trust in China," *International Review of Sociology* 15 (2005): 155–171; Jie Chen, *Popular Political Support in Urban China* (Stanford, CA: Stanford University Press, 2004), 21–53.

57. Lianjiang Li, "Political Trust and Petitioning in the Chinese Countryside," *Comparative Politics* 40, 2 (2008): 209–226.

58. Solnick, *Stealing the State*.

59. Downs, *Inside Bureaucracy*, 134–135.

60. Gordon Tullock, *The Politics of Bureaucracy* (Lanham, MD: University Press of America, 1987), chapters 15–19.

61. Manion, "The Cadre Management System, Post-Mao."

62. See Manion, *Corruption by Design*; Sun, *Corruption and Market in Contemporary China*; Ting Gong, "The CCP's Discipline Inspection in China: Its Evolving Trajectory and Embedded Dilemmas," *Crime, Law and Social Change* 49, 2 (2008): 139–152; Stephen Ma, "The Dual Nature of Anticorruption Agencies in China," *Crime, Law, and Social Change* 49, 2 (2008): 153–165.

63. Manion, "The Cadre Management System, Post-Mao."

64. Tang Jun, "'Min guan bi' zhenxiang" (The truth about the ratio between the population and the number of officials), *Nanfengchuang* (South Reviews) 9 (2005): 26–27.

65. See, for example, Jean Oi, *State and Peasant in Contemporary China: The Political Economy of Village Government* (Berkeley: University of California Press, 1989).

66. O'Brien and Li, "Selective Policy Implementation in Rural China."

67. Anthony Downs, *Inside Bureaucracy* (Glenview, IL: Scott, Foresman and Company, 1967), 134–135.

68. Sherwin Rosen, "Prizes and Incentives in Elimination Tournaments," *American Economic Review* 76, 4 (1986): 701–715.

69. Yongshun Cai, "Between State and Peasants: Local Cadres and Statistical Reporting in Rural China," *China Quarterly* 163 (2000): 783–805.

70. Kung and Chen, "The Tragedy of the *Nomenklatura*."

71. Yongshun Cai, "Power Structure and Regime Resilience: Contentious Politics in China," *British Journal of Political Science* 38, 3 (2008): 411–432.

72. O'Brien and Li, "Selective Policy Implementation in Rural China."

73. One recent example is the trial of the tax-for-fee reform. See Chen Guidi and Chun Tao, *Zhongguo nongmin diaocha* (Survey of Chinese Peasants) (Beijing: Renmin wenxue chubanshe, 2003).

74. *Nomenklatura* means "(1) the list of key positions, appointments to which are made by the higher authorities in the Party, and (2) lists of persons appointed to those positions or held in reserve for them." Michel Voslensky, *Nomenklatura: The Soviet Ruling Class* (New York: Doubleday & Company), 75.

75. John Keep, *Last of the Empires: A History of the Soviet Union 1945–1991* (Oxford, UK: Oxford University Press, 1995), 208.

76. Manion, "The Cadre Management System, Post-Mao"; John Burns, "Strengthening Central CCP Control of Leadership Selection"; John Burns, ed., *The Chinese Communist Party's Nomenklatura System* (Armonk, NY: M. E. Sharpe, 1989); John Burns, "China's Nomenklatura System," *Problems of Communism* xxxvi, 5 (1987): 36–51.

77. Zhu Guanglei, *Dangdai zhongguo shehui gejieceng fenxi* (An analysis of social strata in China) (Tianjin: Tianjin renmin chubanshe, 1998), 139.

78. In 1987, among the 29.03 million cadres, those working for Party and government agencies accounted for 19 percent, whereas those working for public firms accounted for 37.1 percent. The remainder worked in nonadministrative public agencies and schools. In 1991, 9.2 million employees of state agencies accounted for 27.1 percent of the 33.86 million people who were on the government payroll, whereas those in nonadministrative agencies (such as teachers and doctors) accounted for about 73 percent. In 1996, employees in state agencies accounted for 30 percent of the 36.73 million people covered by the government budget, whereas the remaining 70 percent were employed in nonadministrative public agencies. Ren Jie and Liang Ling, eds., *Gonghe guo jigou gaige yu bianqian* (Organizational reform and evolution of the republic) (Beijing: Huawen chubanshe, 1999), 142.

Notes to Chapter Two

1. Max Weber, *Politics as a Vocation*. H. H. Gerth and C. Wright Mills, trans. (Philadelphia: Fortress Press, 1965).

2. Anthony Downs, *Inside Bureaucracy* (Glenview, IL: Scott, Foresman and Company, 1967), 83.

3. Barry Ames, *Political Survival: Politicians and Public Policy in Latin America* (Berkeley: University of California Press, 1987), 211.

4. Susan Whiting, "The Cadre Evaluation System at the Grass Roots: The Paradox of Party Rule," in Barry Naughton and Dali Yang, eds., *Holding China Together: Diversity and National Integration in the Post-Deng Era* (New York: Cambridge University Press, 2004), 101–119; Maria Edin, "State Capacity and Local Agent Control in China: CCP Cadre Management from a Township Perspective," *China Quarterly* 173 (2003): 35–72; Susan Whiting, *Power and Wealth in Rural China: The Political Economy of Institutional Change* (New York: Cambridge University Press, 2000).

5. Xiaobo Lü, *Cadres and Corruption: The Organizational Involution of the Chinese Communist Party* (Stanford, CA: Stanford University Press, 2000).

6. Ye Yangbin, "1956–1957 nian hezuohua gaochao hou de nongmin tuishe fengbao" (The wave of peasants exiting from rural cooperatives between 1956–1957), *Nanjing daxue xuebao* (Journal of Nanjing University) 6 (2003): 51–59.

7. Yongshun Cai, "Managed Participation in China," *Political Science Quarterly* 119, 3 (2004): 425–451.

8. *Guangzhou ribao*, June 22, 2011.

9. Downs, *Inside Bureaucracy*, 88.

10. The Discipline Inspection Committee and the Supervision Bureau of Guangdong Province (ed.), *Guangdong jijian jiancha zhi* (A record of discipline inspection in Guangdong) (Guangzhou: Guangdong renmin chubanshe, 1999), 105.

11. Ibid., 104.

12. Kevin O'Brien and Lianjiang Li, "Selective Policy Implementation in Rural China," *Comparative Politics* 31, 2 (1999): 167–186.

13. Wang Xinhai, "Jihua shengyu zai henduo difang yijing tuibian cheng 'hefa shanghai quan" (Family planning has enabled the government to legally harm people's rights in many places). Retrieved on February 20, 2011, from http://wangxinhaipku.bokee.com.

14. *Huashang bao*, June 14, 2012.

15. Thomas Bernstein and Xiaobo Lü, *Taxation without Representation in Contemporary Rural China* (New York: Cambridge University Press, 2003).

16. Yongshun Cai, *Collective Resistance in China: Why Popular Protests Succeed or Fail* (Stanford, CA: Stanford University Press, 2010), 77.

17. Bernstein and Lü, *Taxation without Representation in Contemporary China*.

18. Yongshun Cai, "Between State and Peasants: Local Cadres and Statistical Reporting in Rural China," *China Quarterly* 163 (2000): 783–805.

19. Zhao Shukai, "Xiangzhen zhengfu de wenze tixi" (Township cadres' responsibility system), *Sannong zhongguo* (Rural China) 1 (2005): 3–6.

20. See the website of *Guoji caijing shibao* (International Business Times). Retrieved on June 20, 2011, from www.ibtimes.com.cn/ articles/ 20110929/040401.htm.

21. Han Jia, "Tudi caizheng yu xinfang" (Land finance and petitions), unpublished manuscript, 2011.

22. Yongshun Cai, "Collective Ownership or Cadres' Ownership? The Nonagricultural Use of Farmland in China," *China Quarterly* 175 (2003): 662–680; Xiaolin Guo, "Land Expropriation and Rural Conflicts in China," *The China Quarterly* 166 (2001): 422–439; David Zweig, "The 'Externalities of Development': Can New Political Institutions Manage rural Conflict?" in Elizabeth Perry and Mark Selden, eds., *Chinese Society: Change, Conflict and Resistance* (London: Routledge, 2000): 120–142.

23. *Xinjingbao*, November 5, 2011.

24. Elizabeth Economy, *The River Runs Black: The Environmental Challenge to China's Future* (Ithaca, NY: Cornell University Press, 2004).

25. *Nanfang zhoumo*, February 5, 2004.

26. "Ganbu ligang zhaoshang shushishufei" (About cadres focusing on attracting external investment), *Liaowang* (Perspective) 18 (2006): 10–11.

27. *Zhongguo qingnian bao*, November 12, 2006.

28. *Zhongguo jingji shibao*, November 20, 2005.

29. Wolfgang Streeck and Kathleen Thelen, "Introduction: Institutional Change in Advanced Political Economies," in Wolfgang Streeck and Kathleen Thelen, eds., *Beyond Continuity: Institutional Change in Advanced Political Economies* (Oxford, UK: Oxford University Press, 2005), 3–39.

30. Ouyang Bing, "Dalu jihua shengyu zhengce bianju muhou" (Behind the changes in the family planning policies in the Chinese mainland). Retrieved on May 21, 2011, from www. phoenixtv.com.cn/home/ phoenixweekly/155/1581page.html.

31. Liu Feixiao, "Guojia caifu zai'yinshui' heidong zhong liushi" (State revenue losses in the black hole of tax borrowing), *Liaowang* (Perspective), 12 (2005): 23–25.

32. *Dazhong ribao*, September 25, 2006.

33. *Zhongguo zhengquan bao*, September 21, 2006.

34. *Xinjingbao*, September 21, 2006.

35. *Zhongguo zhengquan bao*, September 21, 2006.

36. Jean Oi, *Rural China Takes Off: Institutional Foundations of Economic Development* (Berkeley: University of California Press, 1999).

37. Peter Evans, *Embedded Autonomy: States and Industrial Transformation* (Princeton, NJ: Princeton University Press, 1995), 10.

38. Interviews, China, 2000, 2004.

39. Dong Yuyu and Si Binhai, *Zhengzhi zhongguo* (Political China) (Beijing: Jinri zhongguo chubanshe, 1998), 334.

40. *Renmin ribao*, July 21, 2000.

41. Gu Huizhong, "Difang zhengfu: Zhaiwu fengxian you duoda?" (Local governments: How serious is the debt?), *Nanfeng chuang* (South Reviews) 5 (2001): 21–3.

42. *Fazhi ribao*, August 19, 2000.

43. Interview, China, 1999.

44. *Beijing chenbao*, June 1, 2001; *Jiefang ribao*, June 13, 2001; Zhu Kun, "Chaoqian duoshao cai suan gou" (How early is enough?), *Xinzhoukan* (New Weekly), July 19, 2001.

45. *Renmin ribao*, December 25, 2000.

46. *Renmin ribao*, July 7, 2001.

47. "Zhonggong zhongyang guanyu jiaqiang he gaijin dang de zuofeng jianshe de jueding" (The CCP's decision on the strengthening and improving of the Party's discipline), *Qiushi* (Seeking the Truth) 19 (2001): 3–13.

48. The Document Research Office of the CCP Central Committee, *Shisanda yilai zhongyao wenxian xuanbian* (Selections of important documents after the 13th Party Congress) (Beijing: Renmin chubanshe, 1993), 931.

49. Ibid., 1705.

50. Li Jinyu, "Quanli cuisheng chengshi fuhua bin" (Power leads to problems in city construction), *Xinwen zhoukan* (Newsweekly), March 8, 2004.

51. *Chengde ribao*, September 27, 2004.

52. *Zhongguo jijian jiancha bao*, April 13, 2012.

53. *Guangzhou ribao*, June 22, 2011.

54. *Zhongguo qingnian bao*, June 22, 2004.

55. *Lianhe zaobao*, December 28, 2008.

56. Shaoguang Wang, "The Problems of State Weakness," *Journal of Democracy* 14, 1 (2003): 36–42.

57. *Guangzhou Ribao*, June 22, 2011.

58. Fan Xiaochun, "Nongcun jiceng ganbu yu 'siqing' yundong de qiyuan" (Rural cadres and the origin of the 'Four Cleaning' movement), paper presented at the 2nd Annual Graduate Seminar on China, Chinese University of Hong Kong, January 5–9, 2006.

59. Wang Yongqian, "Pojie qunzhong xinfang ba da redian" (Addressing eight hot issues raised in people's petitions), *Ban yue tan* (Bimonthly forum) 11 (2003): 23–26.

60. *China Law Yearbook* (1996–2001).

61. Li Xiuping and Lu Juan, "Shangfang, bieyang de ziwei" (Petitions: A unique experience), *Falu yu shenghuo* (Law and Life) 8 (2002): 4–8.

62. *Gongren ribao*, October 8, 1998.

63. James Fearon, "Electoral Accountability and the Control of Politicians: Selecting Good Types versus Sanctioning Poor Performance," in Adam Przeworski, Susan Stokes, and Bernard Manin, eds., *Democracy, Accountability, and Representation* (New York: Cambridge University Press, 1999), 55–97.

64. Scott Shane, *Dismantling Utopia: How Information Ended the Soviet Union* (Chicago: Ivan R. Dee, 1991), 184–185.

65. Michael Voslensky, *Nomenklatura: The Soviet Ruling Class* (New York: Doubleday & Company, 1984), 296.

66. George Kennan, "Witness," *New York Review of Books*, March 1, 1990. Cited in Anthony Oberschall, "Opportunities and Framing in the Eastern European Revolts of 1989," in Doug McAdam, John McCarthy, and Mayer Zald, eds., *Comparative Perspectives on Social Movements* (New York: Cambridge University Press, 1996), 93–121.

67. Interviews, China, 2005.

68. *Renmin ribao*, October 19, 2005.

69. Voslensky, *Nomenklatura*, 77.

70. Ibid., 240, 441.

71. Ibid., 290; Mervyn Matthews, *Privilege in the Soviet Union: A Study of Elite Life-Styles under Communism* (London: George Allen & Unwin, 1972).

72. See, for example, Li Zhisui, *The Private Life of Chairman Mao: The Memoirs of Mao's Personal Physician* (New York: Random House, 1994; translated by Tai Hung-chao).

73. John Burns, "Rewarding Comrades at the Top in China," in Christopher Hood, Guy Peters, and Grace O. M. Lee, eds., *Reward for High Public Office: Asian and Pacific Rim States* (London: Routledge, 2003), 49–69.

74. *Huasheng bao*, August 14, 2006.

75. Luo Yangjiu, "Jiangxi shengji lingdao 'haohua fuli bieshu' diaocha" (An investigation of the luxurious villas of provincial leaders). Retrieved on November 2, 2005, from http://shbbs. soufun.com/post/1284_19119806_911 9806.htm.

76. *Renmin ribao*, January 31, 2012.

77. Yan Sun, *Corruption and Market in Contemporary China* (Ithaca, NY: Cornell University Press, 2004), 177–178.

78. *Fazhi ribao*, April 8, 2008.

79. Sun, *Corruption and Market in Contemporary China*, 181.

80. Fang Lie and Zhang Le, "Zhengsu guanyuan dubo xianxiang" (Curbing officials' gambling). Retrieved on November 22, 2008, from http://big5.xinhuanet.com/gate/big5 /news.xinhua.com /newscenter/2005-01/07.

81. *Jingji ribao*, September 15, 2007.

82. Ibid.

83. See, among many others, Andrew Wedeman, *Double Paradox: Rapid Growth and Rising Corruption in China* (Ithaca, NY: Cornell University Press, 2012); Minxin Pei, *China's Trapped Transition* (Cambridge, MA: Harvard University Press, 2006); Melanie Manion, *Corruption by Design: Building Clean Government in Mainland China and Hong Kong* (Cambridge, MA: Harvard University Press, 2004); Sun, *Corruption and Market in Contemporary China*; Lü, *Cadres and Corruption*; Ting Gong, *The Politics of Corruption in Contemporary China: An Analysis of Policy Outcomes* (Westport, CT: Praeger Press, 1994).

84. *Hong Kong Economic Journal*, July 15, 2011.

85. Sun, *Corruption and Market in Contemporary China*, chapter 1; Ting Gong, "Forms and Characteristics of China's Corruption in the 1980s: Change with Continuity," *Communist and Post-Communist Studies* 30, 4 (1997): 277–278.

86. Wedeman, *Double Paradox*.

87. *Zhongguo jiancha nianjian* (Procuratorial Yearbook of China), for year 2000, 343; for year 2011, 622.

88. For example, in 1998, there were 640,000 construction projects across the country. *Renmin ribao*, March 15, 1999.

89. In Henan province, three consecutive heads of the provincial bureau of transportation were jailed for corruption between 1997 and 2003. *Jiancha ribao*, June 22, 2004.

90. *21 shiji jingji baodao*, January 22, 2013.

91. Manion, *Corruption by Design*, 117.

92. Dali Yang, *Remaking the Chinese Leviathan: Market Transition and the Politics of Governance in China* (Stanford, CA: Stanford University Press, 2004).

93. Yan Sun, "Cadre Recruitment and Corruption: What Goes Wong?" *Crime, Law and Social Change*, 49, 1 (2008): 61–79.

94. Xie Zhiqiang and Qing Nianbin, "Yingxiang ganbu zhiwu shengqian de zhuyao yuanyin" (Major factors affecting cadres' promotion), *Zhongguo xingzheng guanli* (China Public Administration), 2 (1999): 27–29.

95. Xiao Tangbiao, "Zhongguo zhengzhi gaige de tizhinei ziyuan" (Internal driving forces for political reform in China), *Dangdai zhongguo yanjiu* (Research on Contemporary China), 3 (2005): 35–51.

96. Ibid.

97. See also Victor Shih, Christopher Adolph, and Mingxing Liu, "Getting Ahead in the Communist Party: Explaining the Advancement of Central

Committee Members in China," *American Political Science Review* 106, 1 (2012): 166–187.

98. Voslensky, *Nomenklatura*, 189–191.

99. These people are Zhu Youwen (Henan); Wang Huaizhong, Wang Zhaoyao, Xiao Zuoxin (Anhui); Xing Dangying, Xu Guojian, Zhao Xuefeng, Wang Wulong (Jiangsu); Ouyang De, Yan Wenyao (Guangdong); Chen Tongqing, Yu Yunhong (Fujian); Li Dalun, Sun Chuyan (Hunan); Mu Suixing (Liaoning); Ma De (Heilongjiang); Li Chenglong (Guangxi); Wang Jun (Gansu); Hu Xuejian, Wang Suwen (Shandong).

100. Zhu Yuchen and Sun Zhan, "Quanguo zuida maiguan an diaocha" (Investigation of the biggest case of office selling in China), *Zhongguo xinwen zhoukan* (Chinese News Weekly), April 7, 2005; see also Jiangnan Zhu, "Why Are Offices for Sale in China? A Case Study of the Office-Selling Chain in Heilongjiang Province," *Asian Survey* 48, 4 (2008): 558–579.

101. More than fifty-five of them accepted bribes over job transfers and promotions of lower-level officials. These cases include: Anhui (eighteen cases); Henan (four); Guangxi (five); Fujian (four); Sichuan (four); Guangdong (three); Hubei (three); Shanxi (three); Jiangsu (two); Zhejiang (two); Hainan (two); Liaoning (two); Jilin (one); Hunan (one); Inner Mongolia (one); Shandong (one); Shaanxi (one); Yunnan (one); Jiangxi (one); and Heilongjiang (one).

102. Chen Xianfa and Bao Yonghui, "Xianwei shuji gangwei yuanhe chengwei fubai zhongzai qu" (Why party secretaries are among the most seriously corrupt), *Liaowang* (Perspective), June 19, 2005.

103. *Minzhu yu fazhi shibao*, October 14, 2006.

104. *Zhongguo qingnian bao*, May 21, 2005.

105. *Huaxi dushibao*, September 24, 2005.

106. Ibid.

107. See also Sun, *Corruption and Market in Contemporary China*, 145–147.

108. *Nanfang zhoumo*, October 26, 2006.

109. Sun, "Cadre Recruitment and Corruption."

110. Li Yongzhong, "Fubai 'wushi'" (Five losses due to corruption), *Liaowang dongfang* (Oriental Outlook), March 11, 2004.

111. Ibid.

112. Interview, China, 2005.

113 Zhu and Sun, "Quanguo zuida maiguan an diaocha" (Investigation of the largest case of post selling in China).

114. Interview, China, 2005.

115. *Beijing yule xinbao*, March 2, 2004.

116. Ye Xianming and Li Lifeng, "Pinkunxian li de 'hongbao' shuji" (Corrupt Party secretary in a poverty-stricken county), *Fazhi yu xinwen* (Law and news) 7 (2003): 48–49.

117. *Jiangnan shibao*, November 20, 2005.

118. The Document Research Office of the CCP Central Committee, *Shisanda yilai zhongguo wenxian xuanbian* (Selection of documents after the 13th Party Congress), 447.

119. Zhang Bin, "Xiyang wuxianhao, mozuo huanghun wu" (Life after retirement is good, do not miss it), *Jiangsu jijian* (Jiangsu Discipline Inspection) 7 (1999): 29–30.

Notes to Chapter Three

1. Li Yongzhong, "Fubai 'wushi'" (Five losses due to corruption), *Liaowang dongfang* (Oriental Outlook), March 11, 2004.

2. Melanie Manion, *Corruption by Design: Building Clean Government in Mainland China and Hong Kong* (Cambridge, MA: Harvard University Press, 2004), chapter 5; Xiaobo Lü, *Cadres and Corruption: The Organizational Involution of the Chinese Communist party* (Stanford, CA: Stanford University Press, 2000); Frederick Teiwes, *Politics and Purges in China*, 2nd ed. (Armonk, NY: M. E. Sharpe, 1993).

3. Manion, *Corruption by Design*, chapter 5.

4. Lü, *Cadres and Corruption*, chapter 2.

5. The Editorial Committee, *Shanglin Xianzhi* (Shanglin county gazette) (Nanning: Guangxi renmin chubanshe, 1989), 386.

6. Lu Xueyi (ed.), *Dangdai zhongguo shehui liudong* (Social mobility in contemporary China) (Beijing: Shehui kexue wenxian chubanshe, 2004), 231.

7. The Editorial Committee, *Changwu xianzhi* (Changwu County Gazette) (Xi'an: Shaanxi renmin chubanshe, 2000), 564.

8. The Discipline Inspection Committee and the Supervision Bureau of Guangdong Province (ed.), *Guangdong jijian jiancha zhi* (A record of discipline inspection in Guangdong) (Guangzhou: Guangdong renmin chubanshe, 1999), 162–169.

9. Lu, *Dangdai zhongguo shehui liudong*, 42.

10. Ibid., 75.

11. Manion, *Corruption by Design*, 160.

12. Teiwes, *Politics and Purges in China*, 489.

13. Ibid.

14. Manion, *Corruption by Design*, chapter 5.

15. The Editorial Committee, *Jiangning xianzhi* (Jiangning County Gazette) (Beijing: Dang'an chubanshe, 1989), 553.

16. See Manion, *Corruption by Design*; Yan Sun, *Corruption and Market in Contemporary China* (Ithaca, NY: Cornell University Press, 2004), 168–171; Ting Gong, "The CCP's Discipline Inspection in China: Its Evolving Trajectory and Embedded Dilemmas," *Crime, Law and Social Change*, 49, 2 (2008): 139–152.

17. For a discussion on disciplinary agencies, mainly DICs, see Gong, "The CCP's Discipline Inspection in China"; Stephen Ma, "The Dual Nature of Anticorruption Agencies in China," *Crime, Law, and Social Change* 49, 2 (2008): 153–165; Andrew Wedeman, "The Intensification of Corruption in China," *China Quarterly* 4 (2004): 895–921; Graham Yang, "Control and Style: Discipline Inspection Commissions since the 11th Congress," *China Quarterly* 97 (1984): 24–52; Lawrence Sullivan, "The Role of the Control Organs in the Chinese Communist Party, 1977–1983," *Asian Survey* 24: 6 (1984): 597–667.

18. In Guangdong in 1995, the number of such cadres reached 16,190. The Discipline Inspection Committee and the Supervision Bureau of Guangdong Province (eds.), *Guangdong jijian jiancha zhi:1950–1995* (A record of discipline inspection in Guangdong province: 1950–1995), 395–399.

19. Interviews, China, 2006, 2007, 2008; Sun, *Corruption and Market in Contemporary China*, 168–171.

20. Gong, "The CCP's Discipline Inspection in China."

21. *Xinjing bao*, June 10, 2011.

22. *Nanfang dushi bao*, December 26, 2011.

23. Interviews, China, 2010, 2011.

24. Melanie Manion, "The Cadre Management System, Post-Mao: The Appointment, Promotion, Transfer, and Removal of Party and State Leaders," *China Quarterly* 102 (1985): 203–233; John Burns, "Strengthening CCP Control of Leadership Selection: The 1990 Nomenklatura," *China Quarterly* 138 (194): 458–491; Yasheng Huang, "Administrative Monitoring in China," *China Quarterly* 143 (1995): 828–844.

25. Manion, *Corruption by Design*; Gong, "The Party Discipline Inspection in China"; Sun, *Corruption and Market in Contemporary China*; Lü, *Cadres and Corruption*.

26. "Woguo youhua xian dangzheng zhengzhi duiwu jiegou yi 45 sui zuoyou wei zhuti" (The government is improving the structure of county leadership, with major leaders being around 45 years old). Retrieved on January 26, 2006, from http://news.sina. com.cn/c/2006-01-26/2134808961s.shtml.

27. Yongshun Cai, "Power Structure and Regime Resilience: Contentious Politics in China," *British Journal of Political Science* 38, 3 (2008): 411–432.

28. Steven Solnick, *Stealing the State: Control and Collapse in Soviet Institutions* (Cambridge, MA: Harvard University Press, 1998), 7.

29. Cai, "Power Structure and Regime Resilience."

30. Richard Baum, "Burying Mao: Chinese Politics in the Age of Deng Xiaoping" (Princeton, NJ: Princeton University Press, 1996); Lucian Pye, "Factions and the Politics of Guanxi: Paradoxes in Chinese Administrative and Political Behaviour," *The China Journal* 34 (1995): 35–53; also see Victor Shih, Christopher Adolph, and Mingxing Liu, "Getting Ahead in the Communist Party: Explaining the Advancement of Central Committee Members in China," *American Political Science Review* 106, 1 (2012): 166–187.

31. *Ming Pao*, February 10, 2010.

32. Procedures serve as an important way of protecting power holders' interests. See, for example, Terry Moe, "The Political Structure of Agencies," in John Chubb and Paul Peterson, eds., *Can the Government Govern?* (Washington, DC: Brookings Institution, 1989), 267–329; Mathew McCubbins, Roger Noll, and Barry Weingast, "Administrative Procedures as Instruments of Political Control," *Journal of Law, Economics, and Organization* 3 (1987): 243–277.

33. Li Zhilun, "Congyan zhidang zhizheng, qieshi zhuahao fanfubai renwu de luoshi," *Zhongguo jiancha* (China Discipline Inspection) 4 (2000): 5–7.

34. Edwin Hollander, "Conformity, Status, and Idiosyncrasy Credit," *Psychological Review* 65, 2 (1958): 117–127.

35. *Jiancha ribao*, May 4, 2000.

36. Yin Guo'an, "Xi 'renmin bu yao wo dang yao wo'" (An analysis of the phenomenon that 'the people do not need me but the Party accepts me'), *Jiangsu jijian* (Discipline Inspection in Jiangsu) 7 (2000): 52–53.

37. Michel Voslensky, *Nomenklatura: The Soviet Ruling Class* (New York: Doubleday & Company), 97.

38. Yu Peiqing and Zhang Qiao, "Zoujin Lu Liying" (A close talk with Liu Liying), *Jiangsu jijian* (Discipline Inspection in Jiangsu) 4 (1998): 4–7.

39. Zhang Chaoqun and Xu Renzhang (eds.), *Zhongguo guojia gongwuyuan zhidu gailun* (On the public servant system in China) (Shenyang: Dongbie caijing daxue chubanshe, 1996), 111–112; Jin Qiantai, *Zhongguo gongchandang jilu xue* (Study on the party discipline of the Chinese Communist Party) (Beijing: Hongqi chubanshe, 1993), 408–415.

40. Interviews, China, 2007.

41. The Party has regulations on the many circumstances under which a member must be expelled from the Party. A member can be expelled if the DIC has indisputable evidence showing that the person has severely violated Party rules or the law before the court trial. At other times, a member is expelled from the Party after the person is tried and convicted in court, which often occurs when the DIC and the procuratorate differ in their accusations against a suspect. Interviews, China, 2013.

42. Li Zhilun, "Fanfu changlian biaoben jiazhi" (Anticorruption through all means), *Ziguangge* (Ziguang attic) 9 (2005): 4–6.

43. Interview, China, 2007.

44. Interviews, China, 2006, 2008.

45. Five of the twelve departments are responsible for the disciplining of officials at the administrative rank of vice minister (*fu bu ji*) and above in central government agencies and large state-owned enterprises. The other seven departments are responsible for cases involving local leaders of the administrative rank of vice governor (*fu sheng ji*). *Laonian shibao*, August 6, 2009; *Nanfang dushi bao*, March 18, 2014.

46. It is competitive also because the number of employees or quota in the state sector is strictly controlled by the state. Kjeld Erik Brodsgaard, "Institutional Reform and the *Bianzhi* System in China," *China Quarterly*, 170 (2002), 361–386; John Burns, "'Downsizing' the Chinese State: Government Retrenchment in the 1990s," *China Quarterly* 175 (2003): 775–802.

47. Li Peilin, Zhang Ji, Zhao Yandong, and Liang Dong, *Shehui chongtu yu jiejiyishi* (Social conflict and class consciousness) (Beijing: Shehui kexue wenxian chubanshe, 2005), 203, 207.

48. Ying Qianwei, Luo Danglun, and Liao Junping, "Shui huode le gengduo de yinxing shouru" (Who has received the most hidden income), manuscript, 2011.

49. Voslensky, *Nomenklatura*, chapter 5.

50. As mentioned in Chapter One, most public servants work in state agencies at the county and township levels (61.5 percent in 2003). Tang Jun, "'Min guanbi' zhenxiang" (The truth about the ratio between the population and the number of officials), *Nanfengchuang* (South Reviews) 9 (2005): 26–27.

51. Disciplinary agencies also have an organizational interest in investigating corrupt agents. Investigating cases requires financial resources, and many local governments are short of such resources. DICs are allowed to keep the money confiscated from corrupt cadres for the purpose of investigating cases. This serves as an incentive for local DICs because investigating some cases not only shows their performance but also brings them economic benefits. Interviews, China, 2007, 2008.

52. Ma, "The Dual Nature of Anti-Corruption Agencies in China"; some officials of disciplinary agencies are also corrupt. For example, the secretary of a city DIC in Hunan Province abused the "two-regulated" method to detain local private business people who were not even Party members and forced them to offer bribes to be released. *Yangcheng wanbao*, April 14, 2007.

53. In a county in Jiangsu Province, a cadre of the county Electricity Supply Bureau was beaten to death in the county Anticorruption Bureau in 2007. *Nanfang dushibao*, November 13, 2007.

54. Solnick, *Stealing the State*, 5.

55. Thomas Larrison, "Reform, Corruption, and Growth: Why Corruption Is More Devastating in Russia Than in China," *Communist and Post-Communist Studies* 39 (2006): 265–281.

Notes to Chapter Four

1. *Zhongguo jiancha nianjian* (Procuratorial Yearbook of China) (1999–2011).

2. *Yunnan jiancha nianjian* (Procuratorial Yearbook of Yunnan Province) (1999, 205; 2001, 278).

3. *Zhongguo jiancha nianjian* (Procuratorial Yearbook of China) (1999–2011).

4. Tang Jun, "'Min guanbi' zhenxiang" (The truth about the ratio between the population and the number of officials), *Nanfengchuang* (South Reviews) 9 (2005): 26–27.

5. Interviews, China, 2006, 2007.

6. Sun Chunlong, "Shanxi yi fushizhang luoma" (A vice mayor in Shanxi was arrested), *Liaowang dongfang zhoukan* (Oriental Outlook Weekly), January 23, 2008.

7. *Dongfang zaobao*, May 10, 2007.

8. According to the police department, a collective action involving more than 500 participants is regarded as a large-scale action, and an action involving more than 1,000 participants is regarded as an especially large-scale action. Chen Jinsheng, *Quntixingshijian yanjiu baogao* (Research report on instances of collective action) (Beijing: Qunzhong chubanshe, 2004), 32.

9. Yongshun Cai, *Collective Resistance in China: Why Popular Protests Succeed or Fail* (Stanford, CA: Stanford University Press, 2010), chapter 6.

10. Thomas Bernstein and Xiaobo Lu, *Taxation without Representation in Contemporary Rural China* (New York: Cambridge University Press, 2003).

11. Wu Ran, "Qingshanqiao zhen 11.9 shijian yinfa zhongyang gaoceng guanzhu" (The Qingshanqiao 11.9 incident attracted attention from the higher-level authorities), *Dadi* (Land) 4 (2000): 12–15.

12. As a warning, the central government released such reports to local governments annually or every six months before 2004. Retrieved on June 17, 2005, from www.ah.gov.cn/ zfgb/gbcontent. asp?id=2367.

13. *Zhongguo jingji shibao*, June 20, 2005.

14. *Qiaobao*, December 16, 2005.

15. *South China Morning Post*, January 4, 2005.

16. *Jiancha ribao*, December 25, 2007.

17. The messages could actually be more numerous because some were blocked by the website. The comments were posted on Sohu.com on May 21 and 22, 2004. Retrieved on May 22, 2004, from http://comment.news.sohu.com/comment/ topic. Jsp?id=220147758.

18. *Nanfang zhoumo*, April 8, 2010.

19. "Jianshebu, Hunan shengwei yancha Jiahe chaiqian an, xianzhang shuji beiche" (The Ministry of Construction and the Provincial Party Committee of Hunan conducted a serious investigation of the housing demolition case in Jiahe, and the county head and the party secretary were removed). Retrieved on March 21, 2005, from http://news.sina.com.cn/c/2004-06-04/20442719546s.shtml.

20. *Fazhi ribao*, November 9, 2008.

21. Zhang Chuanjiu, "Gao kaifa, yao shoufa, yao yongdi, xian zhengdi" (Development has to be based on law; land use needs to follow the legal procedures of land acquisition), *Zhongguo tudi* (China Land) 12 (2003): 15–17.

22. *Keji ribao*, August 11, 2003.

23. *Xinjingbao*, July 24, 2008; *Yunnan ribao*, July 20, 2008.

24. *Jinghua shibao*, June 12, 2009.

25. *Xiandai kuaibao*, July 30, 2010.

26. *Nanfang dushibao*, July 2, 2005.

27. *Jiancha ribao*, December 28, 2007.

28. *Tianjin ribao*, April, 10, 2012.

29. Including two heads of two national government agencies (that is, the National Environmental Protection Bureau and the National Food and Drug Agency).

30. On November 25, 1979, an offshore drilling rig of the Ministry of Oil sank at sea, killing seventy-two people and causing a loss of 37 million yuan. As a result, the Minister of Oil was dismissed, and a vice premier in charge of the oil industry was given the administrative discipline of "misconduct highlighted." The head of the Bureau of Ocean Oil Exploration was sentenced to three years in jail under the charge of dereliction of duty, and another three cadres were also sentenced to jail for the same reason. Chen Ji and Niu Fenghe, "Bohai erhao zuanjingchuan zai tuohangzhong fanchen" (The Number 2 Bohai Drilling Rig sank), *Chuanmei* (Media) 6 (1999): 35–39.

31. The four categories of accidents in terms of the number of deaths are: ≤ 3, 3 to 10, 10 to 30, and ≥ 30.

32. Zhu Wenyi, "Duojiaodu shenshi Nandan kuangnan de zhujue Li Dongming" (A comprehensive view of Li Dongming, the main actor in the Nandan mine tragedy), *Sanlian shenghuo zhoukan* (Sanlian Life Weekly), May 30, 2002.

33. Chen Jin, "11.24 Yantai teda Hainan jishi" (A record of the 11.24 ship accident), *Haiyang kaifa yu guanli* (Ocean Exploration and Management) 1 (2000): 76–80.

34. Zou Wei and Lu Xiaoyu, "Xiangfen yuan xianwei shuji Kang Haiyin xianzhang Li Xuejun bei xingju" (The former county Party secretary of Xiangfen, Kang Haiyin, and Li Xuejun, the former county head, were both detained). Retrieved on November 25, 2008, from http://news.163.com/08/0924/22/4MLoPPCL0001124J.html.

35. *Xinjingbao*, June 10, 2011.

36. Kevin O'Brien and Lianjiang Li, "Selective Policy Implementation in Rural China," *Comparative Politics* 31, 2 (1999): 167–186.

37. *Xinjingbao*, April 16, 2006.

38. "80% weifa yongdi mianji de weifa zhuti shi zhengfu" (The government occupied 80 percent of the illegally used land). Retrieved on July 13, 2007, from http://news.sina.com.cn/c/2007-07-12/121513431900.shtml.

39. *Renmin ribao*, April 12, 2003; *Jingji ribao*, April 27, 2002; *Beijing chenbao*, March 24, 2004; *Fazhi ribao*, April 17, 2005.

40. *Nanfang zhoumo*, October 18, 2006.

41. Elizabeth Economy, *The River Runs Black: The Environmental Challenges to China's Future* (Ithaca, NY: Cornell University Press, 2004).

42. *Ta Kung Pao*, December 11, 2005.

43. *China Daily*, October 10, 2008.

44. *Nanfang dushibao*, December 3, 2011.

45. *Xiandai kuaibao*, March 22, 2009.

46. *Handan wanbao*, October 28, 2011.

47. Li Song, *Zhongguo yinxing quanli diaocha* (Survey of hidden power in China) (Beijing: Huaxia chubanshe, 2011), 67.

48. *Fazhi zhoumo*, December 14, 2011.

49. Interview, China, 2011.

50. Interview, China, 2011.

51. *Xinjingbao*, November 27, 2008.

52. *Wenweipo*, February 13, 2009.

53. *Nanfang zhoumo*, March 24, 2005.

54. Chinese Central Television, *Dangjin zhongguo jiuda redian wenti* (Nine hot issues in China today) (Beijing: Zhongyang minzudaxue chubanshe, 2004), 57.

55. Interview, China, 2010.

56. *Zhongguo jijian jiancha bao*, April 13, 2012.

57. Ibid.

58. Interview, China, 2011.
59. Samuel Huntington, *Political Order in Changing Societies* (New Haven, CT: Yale University Press, 1968), 1.
60. Steven Solnick, "The Breakdown of Hierarchies in the Soviet Union and China: A Neo-Institutional Perspective," *World Politics* 48, 2 (1996): 209–238.
61. Steven Solnick, *Stealing the State: Control and Collapse in Soviet Institutions* (Cambridge, MA: Harvard University Press, 1988), 7.
62. Maria Edin, "State Capacity and Local Agent Control in China: CCP Cadre Management from a Township Perspective," *China Quarterly*: 173 (2003): 35–52.

Notes to Chapter Five

1. Susan Rose-Ackerman, *Corruption and Government: Causes, Consequences, and Reform* (New York: Cambridge University Press, 1999), 52.
2. Steven Solnick, *Stealing the State: Control and Collapse in Soviet Institutions* (Cambridge, MA: Harvard University Press, 1998), 244.
3. Melanie Manion, *Corruption by Design: Building Clean Government in Mainland China and Hong Kong* (Cambridge, MA: Harvard University Press, 2004).
4. Rose-Ackerman, *Corruption and Government*.
5. Manion, *Corruption by Design*, 165–166.
6. *Minzhu yu fazhi shibao*, June 30, 2008.
7. Yong Guo, "Corruption in Transitional China: An Empirical Analysis," *China Quarterly* 194 (2008): 349–364.
8. Interviews, China, 2007.
9. *Renmin ribao*, July 21, 1998.
10. The 2001 Work Report of the Supreme Procuratorate. The work reports (1980–2008) are available at the website of the Supreme Procuratorate. Retrieved on October 20, 2010, from www.spp.gov.cn/site2006/region/00018.html.
11. Also see Manion, *Corruption by Design*, 131–132.
12. The 1998 work report of the Supreme Procuratorate.
13. *Fazhi ribao*, June 13, 2007.
14. The 1992 work report of the Supreme Procuratorate.
15. The 1998 work report of the Supreme Procuratorate.
16. Interviews, China, 2013.
17. Some of the reasons are written as formal instructions, and others are not written but are norms. Interviews, China, 2006, 2007.
18. *Sichuan Yearbook 1997*, p. 37.
19. Interviews, China, 2012, 2013.
20. *Beijing qingnian bao*, July 7, 2000.

21. *Xinhua ribao*, June 25, 2008.
22. Wu Danhong, "Jubaoren falu baohu de shizheng yanjiu" (On the protection of citizens who submit reports), *Fazhi luntan* (Legal forum) 3 (2007): 12–17. *Xinjingbao*, June 15, 2007.
23. *Jiancha ribao*, June 25, 2013.
24. Interviews, China, 2013.
25. Independent Commission Against Corruption of Hong Kong, *Annual Report* (1989–2006).
26. Wu Danhong, "Jubaoren falu baohu de shizheng yanjiu" (On the protection of citizens who submit reports).
27. Li Peilin, Zhang Ji, Zhao Yandong, and Liang Dong, *Shehui chongtu yu jiejiyishi* (Social conflict and class consciousness) (Beijing: Shehui kexue wenxian chubanshe, 2005), 203, 207.
28. Wu Danhong, "Jubaoren falu baohu de shizheng yanjiu" (On the protection of citizens who submit reports).
29. *Renmin ribao*, March 29, 1992.
30. *Fazhi ribao*, August 4, 2007.
31. *Minzhu yu fazhi shibao*, June 30, 2008.
32. *Nanfang zhoumo*, January 18, 2002.
33. *Ningxia ribao*, November 12, 2005.
34. *Nanfang zhoumo*, January 17, 2002.
35. *Fazhi ribao*, September 24, 2007.
36. Also see Manion, *Corruption by Design*, Chapter 2.
37. Nie Zhenguang, Lu Ruifeng, and Zeng Yingming, *Xianggang lianzheng* (Anticorruption in Hong Kong) (Hong Kong: Zhonghua shuju, 1990), 173.
38. Ibid.
39. Interviews, China, 2011, 2012, 2013.
40. Interviews, China, 2012, 2013.
41. Interviews, China, 2013.
42. Interviews, China, 2013.
43. Interviews, China, 2013.
44. The sources of information of the central DIC consist of tips that are received by the complaint office from citizens, instructions of central leaders and cases forwarded by the central Party, government agencies, and legal departments. In 2003, the central DIC and the Ministry of Organization established six inspection groups, and the number was increased to eleven in subsequent years. These inspection groups are responsible for checking the discipline enforcement in the provinces. An inspection group often stays in a particular province for two to three months and meets about 100 to 200 local officials. Their responsibility is to find problems rather than investigate cases. They submit reports to the central

DIC and the Ministry of Organization that in turn send the reports to the central DIC or the major central leaders. *Laonian shibao*, August 6, 2009.

45. If the central DIC decides to investigate an official, the investigation normally goes through eight phases: (1) the collection and management of information on a case, (2) the initial verification, (3) the filing of a case for investigation, (4) the collection of evidence, (5) the trial of the case, (6) the enforcement of discipline, (7) the defense or appeal of the accused, and (8) the supervision of case settlement. In urgent circumstances, a case may be put directly on file for investigation. Ibid.

46. Interview, China, 2007.

47. *Nanfang zhoumo*, October 25, 2006.

48. Interviews, China, 2010. Also see Feng Junqi, "Zhongxian ganbu" (Cadres in Zhong county), PhD dissertation, 2010, Department of Sociology, Beijing University.

49. Ibid., 181.

50. Interviews, China, 2010.

51. Interviews, China, 2013.

52. *Renmin ribao*, December 6, 2005.

53. This is particularly true for high-ranking officials. Interviews, China, 2005, 2006.

54. Pan Zefu, "Shanxi Huozhou 128 ming lao ganbu 5 nian gaodao shiwei shuji" (It took five years for 128 retired officials in Huozhou in Shanxi to win a case against the city Party secretary). Retrieved on September 19, 2013, from http://news.xinhuanet.com/legal/2013-09/18/c_125409066.htm.

55. Xiaobo Lü, *Cadres and Corruption: The Organizational Involution of the Chinese Communist Party* (Stanford, CA: Stanford University Press, 2000).

56. Mathew McCubbins, Roger Noll, and Barry Weingast, "Structure and Process, Politics and Policy: Administrative Arrangements and the Political Control of Agencies," *Virginia Law Review* 75 (1989): 431–482.

57. Shi Po and Liu Zhiming, "Lian sha 14 ren zhiwei chu tanguan?" (Killing 14 people to fight against corruption?), *Nanfengchuang* (South Reviews), February 27, 2002.

58. Ren Yanfang, *Minyuan* (People's complaints) (Beijing: Zhongguo wenlian chubanshe, 1999).

59. Andrew Wedeman, "Win, Lose, or Draw? China's War on Corruption," *Crime, Law and Social Change* 49, 1 (2008): 7–26.

60. Wedeman, "Win, Lose, or Draw?"; Minxin Pei, *China's Trapped Transition* (Cambridge, MA: Harvard University Press, 2006), 150–152; Yan Sun, *Corruption and Market in Contemporary China* (Ithaca, NY: Cornell University Press, 2004), 47.

61. *Nanfang zhoumo*, October 25, 2006.

62. *Laonian shibao*, August 6, 2009.

63. I wish to thank an anonymous reviewer for pointing this out.

64. *Zhongguo jiancha nianjian* (Procuratorial Yearbook of China) (1999–2011).

65. Andrew Wedeman, *Double Paradox: Rapid Growth and Rising Corruption in China* (Ithaca, NY: Cornell University Press, 2012), chapter 6.

66. Yongshun Cai, "Power Structure and Regime Resilience: Contentious Politics in China," *British Journal of Political Science* 38, 3 (2008): 411–432.

67. For the data collection, see Yongshun Cai and Lin Zhu, "Punishing Corrupt Officials in China," manuscript, 2013.

68. According to Chinese Criminal Law, corruption takes different forms (see Chapter Two). The criterion for including a case in the data is whether a suspect is convicted of any of those crimes.

69. According to the Chinese Civil Servant Law, eleven categories of administrative ranks exist for civil servants, ranging from staff and clerk (the lowest) to national leaders (the highest). In the data set, the number of corrupt officials in the top three ranks is very small, and they are therefore included in the administrative rank of "vice governor (*fu bu ji*) or higher." Thus, officials are divided into eight categories or ranks in this analysis: (1) staff and clerk; (2) deputy township head or equivalent (*fu ke ji*); (3) township head or equivalent (*ke ji*); (4) deputy county magistrate or equivalent (*fu chu ji*); (5) county magistrate or equivalent (*chu ji*); (6) deputy prefecture mayor or equivalent (*fu ting ji*); (7) prefecture mayor or equivalent (*ting ji*); and (8) vice governor or equivalent (*fu bu ji*) and higher.

70. According to Chinese Criminal Law, accepting bribes and embezzlement are more serious crimes than others, such as misappropriation, giving bribes, and failing to explain the sources of a large amount of income. The empirical analysis includes both the type of corruption and its magnitude in terms of the amount of money involved.

71. In this analysis, the values of all the control variables are set as the mean when applicable. Several specifications apply in this analysis. Officials are assumed to receive a bribe amounting to one million Chinese yuan but without committing other crimes, and they are likewise assumed not to have confessed. In addition, the secretary of the DIC is neither in the first year of office nor locally promoted.

72. Stephen Rosoff, "Physicians as Criminal Defendants," *Law and Human Behavior* 13, 2 (1989): 231–236.

228 *Notes to Chapter Five*

73. "Bai yu ming shengbu ji gaoguan de tanfu zhilu" (The corruption of more than 100 ministry-level officials). Retrieved on May 5, 2012, from: http://news.xinhuanet.com/legal/2012-03/29/c_122906150.htm.

74. *Nanfang zhoumo*, August 14, 2003.

75. Linda Klebe Trevino, "The Social Effects of Punishment in Organizations: A Justice Perspective," *The Academy of Management Review* 17, 4 (1992): 647–676.

76. For example, the arrest of Shanghai party secretary Chen Liangyu in 2006 has been interpreted by some people as the result of the power struggle in China before the 17th Party Congress. See, for example, Joseph Kahn, "Shanghai Party Boss Held for Corruption in Crackdown by President against Opponents," *New York Times*, September 25, 2006.

77. *Yangzi wanbao*, July 16, 2009.

78. Interviews, China, 2005.

79. *Nanjing chenbao*, April 8, 2005.

80. Manion, *Corruption by Design*, Chapter 6.

81. Lee Kuan Yew, *From Third World to First: The Singapore Story 1965–2000* (Singapore: Times Media, 2000), 182–184.

82. Jon Quah, "Singapore's Anti-Corruption Strategy." In John Kidd and Frank-Jurgen Richter, eds., *Corruption and Governance in Asia* (Basingstoke, UK: Palgrave Macmillan, 2003), 180–197.

83. The 2008 work report of the Supreme Procuratorate.

84. *Xinjingbao*, September 7, 2006.

85. *Guangming ribao*, November, 29, 2013.

Notes to Chapter Six

1. Barry Ames, *Political Survival: Politicians and Public Policy in Latin America* (Berkeley: University of California Press, 1987), 1.

2. Kent Weaver, "The Politics of Blame Avoidance," *Journal of Public Policy* 6, 4 (1986): 371–398.

3. Kathleen McGraw, "Avoiding Blame: An Experimental Investigation of Political Excuses and Justifications," *British Journal of Political Science* 20, 1 (1990): 119–131.

4. Ames, *Political Survival*; Robert Bates, *Markets and States in Tropical Africa: The Political Basis of Agricultural Policies* (Berkeley: University of California Press, 1984).

5. Bates, *Markets and States in Tropical Africa*.

6. Paul Pierson, *Dismantling the Welfare State? Reagan, Thatcher, and the Politics of Retrenchment* (New York: Cambridge University Press, 1994).

7. Douglas Arnold, *The Logic of Congressional Action* (New Haven, CT: Yale University Press, 1990), 47.

8. Ibid., 100–104.

9. Interview, China, 2011.

10. John Hood, *Selling Dreams: Why Advertising Is Good Business* (New York: Praeger, 2005).

11. Kathleen McGraw, "Political Accounts and Attribution Processes," in James Kuklinksi, ed., *Citizens and Politics: Perspectives from Political Psychology* (New York: Cambridge University Press, 2001), 160–197.

12. Pierson, *Dismantling the Welfare State?*

13. Lucian Pye, "Factions and Poltiics of Guanxi: Paradoxes in Chinese Administrative and Political Behavior," *China Journal* 34 (1995): 35–53.

14. Yan Sun, *Corruption and Market in Contemporary China* (Ithaca, NY: Cornell University Press, 2004), 188.

15. Zhang Shufan, "Xinyang shijian: yige chentong de lishijiaoxun" (Xinyang incident: A serious historical lesson), *Bainian chao* (Century Stream) 12 (1999): 39–44.

16. Shaoguang Wang, "Regulating Death at Coalmines: Changing Mode of Governance in China," *Journal of Contemporary China* 15, 46 (2006): 1–30.

17. For example, in August 2005, an accident in a coal mine in Guangdong province claimed 123 lives. In 2004, China's coal output accounted for 33.2 percent of the total world output, but its death toll accounted for 80 percent of the total, reaching 6,027. That year, there were 3.96 deaths for every million tons of coal produced in China, whereas there were 0.039 in the United States, 0.42 in India, 0.34 in Russia, and 0.13 in South Africa. *Fazhi ribao*, March 8, 2005.

18. Zhu Guodong, "Caikuanye chulu zai hefang" (How to manage the mining industry), *Liaowang dongfang* (Oriental Outlook), November 10, 2005.

19. For a discussion on miners' lack of choice, see Tim Wright, "The Political Economy of Coal Mine Disasters in China: 'Your Rice Bowl or Your Life,'" *China Quarterly* 179 (2004): 629–646.

20. *Beijing yule xinbao*, November 2, 2005.

21. By October 24, 2005, more than 3,200 government employees and cadres of public firms in twenty provinces were ordered to withdraw their shares from coal mines. *Beijing chenbao*, October 25, 2005.

22. Sun Chunlong, "Guanmei chanyelian heimu" (Behind the nexus between officials and coal mines), *Liaowang dongfang* (Oriental Outlook), November 10, 2005.

23. *Henan shangbao*, August 16, 2005.

24. Zhu Wenyi, "Duojiaodu shenshi Nandan kuangnan de zhujue Li Dongming" (A comprehensive view of Li Dongming, the main actor in the Nandan mine tragedy), *Sanlian shenghuo zhoukan* (Sanlian Life Weekly), May 30, 2002.

25. Jiang An, "Xinwenyulun jiandu yu zongbianji de xiuyang" (Media supervision and the role of the editor-in-chief), *Xinwenshijie* (News World) 3 (2001): 11–12.

26. Zeng Yabo, "Yulun jiandu zaoyu fanji" (The supervision of public opinion meets resistance), *Shi yu xu* (Truth and Falsity) 1 (2000): 38–40.

27. *Zhongguo qingnian bao*, December 9, 2001.

28. *Zhongguo qingnian bao*, August 23, 2000.

29. Zhen Fangjie, "Jiaodian fangtan heyi chengwei qiandong zhongguo gaoceng yu baixing de jiaodian" (Why has "Focus" become the focal point of both the Chinese high-level officials and the masses?), *Zhonghua yingcai* (Chinese Talents) 2 (1999): 21–24; Liu Jianming, *Tianli minxin* (Justice and legitimacy) (Beijing: Jinri zhongguo chubanshe, 1998), 190–194; Ni Ming, "'Jiaodian fangtan' menwai de liangzhi gongguan duiwu" (Two lines outside "Focus"), *Neibu canyue* (Internal References) 8 (1999): 15–16.

30. *Nanfang dushi bao*, September 17, 2003.

31. Qiao Yunxia, Hu Lianli, and Wang Junjie, "Zhongguo xinwen yulun jiandu xianzhuang diaocha fenxi" (A survey and analysis of the media's supervision in China), *Xinwen yu chuanbo yanjiu* (News and Communication Studies) 4 (2002): 21–28.

32. *Renmin ribao*, September 3, 2000.

33. Ibid.

34. *Nanfang zhoumo*, January 11, 2001.

35. Yongshun Cai, "Managed Participation in China," *Political Science Quarterly* 119, 3 (2004): 425–451.

36. See Lianjiang Li, Mingxing Liu, and Kevin O'Brien, "Petitioning Beijing: The High Tide of 2003–2006," *China Quarterly* 210 (2012): 313–334; Cai, "Managed Participation in China."

37. *Jiancha ribao*, June 26, 2002.

38. Wang Mian, Zhou Wei, and Wang Shengzhi, "Huaqian 'xiaohao' jingbao 'xinfang xunzu'luanxiang" (Deleting the records of petitions by offering money reveals rent-seeking in petition management), *Ban yuetan* (Biweekly Forum) 15 (2009): 10–13.

39. Cai, "Managed Participation in China."

40. Liao Yiwu, *Zhongguo shangfangcun* (Village of petitioners in China) (New York: Mingjing chubanshe, 2005): 320–323.

41. When they saw petitioners, they would try to find out their places of residence by, for example, asking them to show their identification cards. If the

petitioners were from their province, they would be sent back; if they were from other provinces, local officials might tell their "comrades" from other provinces. The number of such "petition stoppers" was particularly large when important functions, such as the People's Congress or the Political Consultative Conference, were held in Beijing. *Jiangnan shibao*, November 16, 2004.

42. *Nanfang zhoumo*, May 12, 2005.
43. *Nanfang dushi bao*, September 24, 2010.
44. *Nanfang dushi bao*, March 28, 2012.
45. Wang, Zhou, and Wang, "Huaqian 'xiaohao' jingbao 'xinfang xunzu'luanxiang" (Deleting the records of petitions by offering money reveals rent-seeking in petition management).
46. Interview, China, 2004.
47. *Huashang bao*, September 30, 2006.
48. Interview, China, 2004, 2005.
49. Interview, China, 2006.
50. *Huanshang bao*, November 10, 2000.
51. *Sichuan ribao*, May 3, 2005.
52. Interview, China, 2005.
53. Talk with Zhao Shukai, 2005, Hong Kong. Also see Zhao Shukai, "Xiangzhen zhengfu de yingchou shenghuo) (Township officials' life of reception), *Zhongguo gaige* (China Reform) 7 (2005): 53–55.
54. Ibid.
55. James Kai-sing Kung and Chen Shuo, "The Tragedy of the *Nomenklatura*: Career Incentives and Political Radicalism during China's Great Leap Famine," *American Political Science Review* 105, 1 (2011): 27–45.
56. Yang Jisheng, *Mubei: Zhongguo dajihuang jishi 1958–1962* (Tombstone: A record of the great famine in China 1958–1962) (Hong Kong: Tiandi Press, 2008), 1056.
57. Ibid., 78–88.
58. Ibid.
59. *Zhongguo qingnian bao*, June 22, 2004.
60. Yongshun Cai, "Local Governments and the Suppression of Popular Resistance in China," *China Quarterly* 193 (2008): 24–42.
61. Yang Qingsheng and Dang Jianjun, "Guangxi baming juzhong chongji guojia jiguan he feifa youxing xianfan shoushen" (Eight people accused of attacking state agencies and holding illegal demonstrations were tried in Guangxi). Retrieved on May 22, 2004, from http://dailynews.sina. com.cn/s43438.html.
62. *Zhejiang laonian bao*, August 2, 2006.
63. Michael Lev, "China Sentences Labor Protest Leaders," *Chicago Tribune*, May 10, 2003.

64. McGraw, "Political Accounts and Attribution Processes," 174.
65. *Nanfang ribao*, December 11, 2005.
66. Mayfair Yang, *Gifts, Favors and Banquets: The Art of Social Relationships in China* (Ithaca, NY: Cornell University Press, 1994), 465.
67. Ji An, "Sifa fubai: yige chenzhong de huati (Corruption in the legal system: A serious issue), *Ganbu dangyuan rencai* (Cadres, Party Members, and Talents) 6 (2000): 43–44.
68. Zhuang Huining, "Zengqiang sifa huodong de gongxinli" (Strengthening the authority of legal practice), *Liaowang* (Perspectives) 1 (2002): 34–35.
69. Victor Shih, Christopher Adolph, and Mingxing Liu, "Getting Ahead in the Communist Party: Explaining the Advancement of Central Committee Members in China," *American Political Science Review* 106, 1 (2012): 166–187.
70. John Burns, *The Chinese Communist Party's Nomenklarura System: A Documentary Study of Party Control of Leadership Selection, 1979–1984* (New York: M. E. Sharpe, 1989), xxxii.
71. Xiao Tangbiao, "Zhongguo zhengzhi gaige de tizhinei ziyuan" (Internal driving forces for political reform in China), *Dangdai zhongguo yanjiu* (Research on Contemporary China) 3 (2005): 35–51.
72. Ibid.
73. Interview, China, 2008.
74. *Nanfang zhoumo*, October 25, 2006.
75. Interviews, China, 2008.
76. Sun, *Corruption and Market in Contemporary China*, 188.
77. Feng Junqi, "Zhongxian ganbu" (Cadres in Zhong County), PhD dissertation, 2010; Department of Sociology, Beijing University, 182.
78. Interview, China, 2011.
79. Wang Hongliang, "Liu Zhijun he Liu Zhixiang: liang xiongdi de shitu he mingyun" (Liu Zhijun and Liu Zhixiang: The two brothers' careers and fates), *Sanlian shenghuo zhoukan* (Sanlian Life Weekly), March 7, 2011.
80. An investigator of Yao's case recalled: "When we arrived in the county, locals visited us in dozens every day for more than one month. Some knelt down and cried before us. When we promised to investigate Yao's case and punish him if we found evidence, there were fireworks outside. The judges of the county court shook hands with us, saying that it was their second liberation." Ruan Xiaoyu, "Sanmang yuanzhang beihou you xinwen" (The story of a court president), *Tuoling* (Camel Bell) 8 (2000): 32–38.
81. N. Machiavelli, *The Prince* (Middlesex, UK: Penguin Books, 1995), 59.
82. Pierson, *Dismantling the Welfare State?*
83. *Qilu wanbao*, January 11, 2013.

Notes to Chapter Seven

1. See, for example, Jean Oi, *Rural China Takes Off: Institutional Foundations of Economic Reform* (Berkeley: University of California Press, 1999).
2. Chen Guidi and Chun Tao, *Zhongguo nongmin diaocha* (Survey of Chinese peasants) (Beijing: Renmin wenxue chubanshe, 2003).
3. Samuel Huntington, *Political Order in Changing Societies* (New Haven, CT: Yale University Press, 1968), 345.
4. Federick Barghoon, *Politics in Russia* (Boston: Little, Brown, 1972), 308.
5. Huntington, *Political Order in Changing Societies*, 345.
6. Ibid.
7. Barbara Geddes, "A Game Theoretic Model of Reform in Latin America," *American Political Science Review* 85, 2 (1991): 371–392.
8. Paul Pierson, *Dismantling the Welfare State* (New York: Cambridge University Press, 1994), 8.
9. Ibid., 23.
10. Kent Weaver, "The Politics of Blame Avoidance," *Journal of Public Policy* 6, 4 (1986): 371–398.
11. Also see Melanie Manion, *Retirement of Revolutionaries in China: Public Policies, Social Norms, Private Interests* (Princeton, NJ: Princeton University Press, 1993).
12. Interview, China, 2004.
13. The Editorial Committee, *Qidian* (The starting point) (Hefei: Anhui jiaoyu chubanshe, 1997), 327.
14. Ibid., 161–162.
15. Yu Jintao, "Zhongguo difang zhenggai chongdong" (Local political innovations in China), *Liaowang dongfang zhoukan* (Oriental Outlook), July 22, 2004.
16. Interview, China, 2007.
17. These people include Chen Guang, Lu Rizhou, Qiu He, Song Yaping, Zhang Jingming, Li Zhongbin, Xia Yisong, Ma Yinlu, Dong Yang, Li Changping, Wei Shengduo. Wang Yongzhi and Ouyang Bin, "Dalu 'gaigemingxing' shitu fenxi" (An analysis of the career paths of the reformers in China), *Fenghuang zhoukan* (Phoenix Weekly), April 25, 2004; Author's collection.
18. Interview, China, 2003.
19. *Nongmin ribao*, April 13, 1998.
20. *Fazhi ribao*, August 5, 2001.
21. Talk with Li Changping, Hong Kong, November 16, 2004.
22. Wang and Ouyang, "Dalu 'gaigemingxing' shitu fenxi" (An analysis of the career paths of the reformers in China).

23. Wang Kewen, "Xingzheng shenpi zhidu de gaige yu lifa" (The reform and legislation of administrative approval), *Zhengzhi yu falu* (Politics and Law) 2 (2002): 37–44.

24. The Expert Group, *Xianshi de xuanze: guoyou xiao qiye gaige shijian de chubu zongjie* (Realistic choices: A preliminary sum-up of the reform experience of small SOEs) (Shanghai: Shanghai Yuandong chubanshe, 1997).

25. Lianjiang Li, "The Politics of Introducing Direct Township Elections in China," *China Quarterly* 171 (2002): 704–723.

26. Barbara Geddes, *Politicians' Dilemma: Building State Capacity in Latin America* (Berkeley: University of California Press, 1994).

27. Samuel Huntington, *The Third Wave: Democratization in the Late Twentieth Century* (Norman: University of Oklahoma Press, 1991), 127–129.

28. Dennis Chong, *Collective Action and Civil Rights Movements* (Chicago: University of Chicago Press, 1991), 122.

29. Zhang Li, "Zhongguo zui shou zhengyi de shiwei shuji" (The most controversial city party secretary in China), *Zhoumo wenhui* (Weekend Digest) 5 (2004): 40–47.

30. Ouyang Bin, "Juwai Lu Rizhou" (Lu Rizhou as an outsider), *Fenghuang zhoukan* (Phoenix Weekly), April 25, 2004.

31. For example, some research finds that, between 1999 and 2008, the chance of promotion for provincial Party secretaries is less than 15 percent in a particular year, and it was about 11 percent for city Party secretaries and around 5 percent for county Party secretaries. Ting Chen and James Kung: "Behind the 'China Miracle': Revenue versus Promotion Incentive of Local Leaders," manuscript, 2012.

32. For reports on this case, see *Gongren ribao*, May 25, 2009; *Nanfang ribao*, September 19, 2010; Chen Lei, "Guo Baocheng: renhe yige xian dou neng gao quanmin mianfei yiliao" (Guo Baocheng: Any county can adopt the free medical care scheme), *Nanfang renwu zhoukan* (Southern People Weekly), September 20, 2010.

33. Chen, "Guo Baocheng: renhe yige xian dou neng gao quanmin mianfei yiliao" (Guo Baocheng: Any county can adopt the free medical care scheme)."

34. Wang and Ouyang, "Dalu 'gaigemingxing' shitu fenxi" (An analysis of the career paths of the reformers in China).

35. Pierson, *Dismantling the Welfare State?*

36. Zhang, "Zhongguo zuishou zhengyi de shiwei shuji" (The most controversial city party secretary in China).

37. The Editorial Committee, *Qidian* (The starting point), 26, 314, 318.

38. Li, "The Politics of Introducing Direct Township Elections in China"; Dong Lisheng, "Direct Township Elections in China: Latest Developments and Prospects," *Journal of Contemporary China* 48, 15 (2006): 503–515.

39. Yu Jintao, "Tansuo ke caozuo de gaige" (Exploring applicable reform measures), *Liaowang dongfang zhoukan* (Oriental Outlook), June 22, 2004. For a discussion of the election, also see Baogang He and Youxing Lang, "China's First Direct Election of the Township Head: A Case Study of Buyun," *Japanese Journal of Political Science* 2, 1 (2001): 1–22; Joseph Cheng, "Direct Elections of Township and Township Heads in China: The Dapeng and Buyun Experiments," *China Information* XV, 1 (2001): 104–137.

40. According to Lianjiang Li, who talked to Zhang, Zhang said that had she not carried out the reform, she would have been promoted sooner. Talk with Lianjiang Li, Harvard University, October 31, 2004.

41. Ma Ya, "Haineiwai gejie guanzhu Pingba zhixuan" (Direct elections in Pingba received domestic and international attention), *Fenghuang zhoukan* (Phoenix Weekly), February 25, 2004.

42. Gao Yingxiong, "Quanguo zuidaguimo xiangzheng zhixuan zai Yunnan honghe zhou qi dong" (The largest-scale township direct elections were carried out in Honghe of Yunnan Province), *Xinzhoubao* (New Weekly), November 25, 2004.

43. Mao Yushi (ed.), *Gongzheng touming* (Fairness and transparency) (Beijing: Falu chubanshe, 2004), 313–342.

44. Susan Shirk, *The Political Logic of Economic Reform in China* (Berkeley: University of California Press, 1993).

45. Bao Yonghui and Xu Shousong, "Qiu He shengqian de tupo yiyi" (The significance of the promotion of Qiu He), *Liaowang* (Outlook) 30 (2006): 34–36.

46. Thomas Bernstein and Xiaobo Lu, *Taxation without Representation in Contemporary Rural China* (New York: Cambridge University Press, 2003).

47. *Zhongguo gaige bao*, September 2, 1999.

48. The number for 1993 was not included because it was not available. Li Maolan, *Zhongguo nongmin fudan wenti yanjiu* (Research on peasants' financial burdens in China) (Taiyuan: Shanxi jingji chubanshe, 1996), 127.

49. Ethan Michelson, "Causes and Consequences of Grievances in Rural China," manuscript, 2004.

50. An official of the State Council reported in an interview that a prominent research officer of the State Council had proposed the abolition of rural taxes to central leaders as early as 1999. Interview, Beijing, 2006.

51. For a description of the reform process in Anhui and Hebei, see Chen Guidi and Chun Tao, *Zhongguo nongmin diaocha* (Survey of Chinese peasants) (Beijing: Renmin wenxue chubanshe, 2003).

52. *Zhongguo jinying bao*, December 12, 2004.
53. *Tianjin ribao*, November 1, 2003.
54. *Zhongguo jingji shibao*, February 24, 2001.
55. *Tianjin ribao*, November 1, 2003.
56. *Zhongguo jingji shibao*, February 24, 2001.
57. *Tianjin ribao*, November 1, 2003.
58. *Zhongguo jingji shibao*, February 24, 2001.
59. One important reason was that if peasants paid this amount of acceptable tax, they would no longer be disturbed by local cadres. Talk by He Kaiyin, Chinese University of Hong Kong, November 4, 2004.
60. Chen and Chun, *Zhongguo nongmin diaocha*, 312–313.
61. Ibid., 353.
62. *Zhongguo jingji shibao*, February 13, 2003.
63. *Zhongguo jingji shibao*, February 24, 2001.
64. This governor was Hui Liangyu, who was later promoted to vice premier in charge of agriculture.
65. *Nanfang zhoumo*, November 18, 2004.
66. Paul DiMaggio and Walter Powell, "The Iron Cage Revisited: Institutional Isomorphism and Collective Rationality in Organization Field," *American Sociological Review* 48, 2 (1983): 147–160.
67. The Editorial Committee, *Qidian* (Starting point), 318.
68. Sheng Huaren, "Yifa zuohao xianxiang liangji renda huanjie xuanju gongzuo" (Doing a good job in the selection of leaders at the township and county levels in light of the law), *Qiushi* (Seeking the truth) 16 (2006): 37–42.
69. For the problems, see The Ministry of Agriculture, *Zhongguo nongcun yanjiu baogao* (Research report on rural China) (Beijing: Zhongguo caizheng jingji chubanshe, 1999), 215–228.
70. Chen and Chun, *Zhongguo nongmin diaocha* (Survey of Chinese peasants), 340–347.
71. The National Statistical Bureau, *Xin zhongguo 50 nian tongji ziliao* (A compilation of the statistics of socialist China over the past 50 years) (Beijing: Zhongguo tongji chubanshe, 1999).
72. Yongshun Cai, "Relaxing the Constraints from Above: Politics of Privatizing Public Enterprises in China," *Asian Journal of Political Science* 10, 2 (2002): 94–121.
73. James Fishkin, Baogang He, Robert Luskin, and Alice Siu, "Deliberative Democracy in an Unlikely Place: Deliberative Polling in China," *British Journal of Political Science* 40, 2 (2010): 435–448.
74. Pierson, *Dismantling the Welfare State*.

75. Alexis de Tocqueville, *The Old Regime and the French Revolution* (New York: Anchor Books, 1955), 176–177.

Notes to Chapter Eight

1. Samuel Huntington, *Political Order in Changing Societies* (New Haven, CT: Yale University Press, 1968), 5.
2. Theda Skocpol, "Bringing the State Back In: The Strategies of Analysis in Current Research," in Peter Evans, Dietrich Rueschemeyer, and Theda Skocpol (eds.), *Bringing the State Back In* (New York: Cambridge University Press, 1985), 3–43.
3. Anthony Downs, *Inside Bureaucracy* (Glenview, IL: Scott, Foresman and Company, 1967), 88.
4. Steven Solnick, *Stealing the State: Control and Collapse in Soviet Institutions* (Cambridge, MA: Harvard University Press, 1998), 5.
5. Yongshun Cai, "Civil Resistance and Rule of Law in China: the Case of Defending Home Owners' Rights," in Elizabeth Perry and Merle Goldman (eds.), *Grassroots Politics in China* (Cambridge, MA: Harvard University Press, 2007), 174–195.
6. "Jiaoshi baoguang guanyuan quan chai luyin" (A school teacher released the tape recording officials' persuading her to agree to housing demolition). Retrieved on May 1, 2011, from http://news.ifeng.com/society/2/201003/0323_344_1583956.shtml.
7. *Nanfang zhoumo*, December 1, 2009.
8. *Nanfang zhoumo*, April 8, 2010.
9. Ibid.
10. Roderick MacFarquhar, "In China, Fear at the Top," *New York Times*, May 20, 2012.
11. Yan Sun, "Cadre Recruitment and Corruption: What Goes Wong?" *Crime, Law and Social Change* 49, 1 (2008): 61–79.
12. *Yangcheng wanbao*, October 11, 2013.
13. Interview, China, 2011.
14. *Xinjingbao*, April 29, 2012.
15. David Barboza and Sharon LaFraniere, "'Princelings in China Use Family Ties to Gain Riches," *New York Times*, May 18, 2012.
16. Interview, China, 2011.
17. Andrew Jacobs, "Challenge for U.S. after Escape by China Activist," *New York Times*, April 27, 2012.
18. *Lianhe zaobao*, April 3, 2012.
19. *Hong Kong Economic Journal*, April 23, 2012.

20. Vivienne Shue, *The Reach of the State: Sketches of the Chinese Body Politic* (Stanford, CA: Stanford University Press, 1988).

21. See, for example, Baogang He and Mark Warren, "Authoritarian Deliberation: The Deliberative Turn in Chinese Political Development," *Perspectives on Politics* 9, 2 (2011): 268–289.

22. Such measures include norm-bound succession, merit-based promotion, the differentiation and functional specialization of institutions, and the establishment of institutions for political participation. Andrew Nathan, "Authoritarian Resilience," *Journal of Democracy* 14, 1 (2003): 6–17.

23. Minxin Pei, "Is CCP Rule Fragile or Resilient," *Journal of Democracy* 23, 1 (2012): 27–41.

24. Dali Yang, *Remaking the Chinese Leviathan: Market Transition and the Politics of Governance in China* (Stanford, CA: Stanford University Press, 2004), 313.

25. Solnick, *Stealing the State*, 234.

26. Ibid., 235.

27. William Gamson, *Power and Discontent* (Homewood, IL: Dosey Press, 1968), 180.

28. Wenfang Tang, *Public Opinion and Political Change in China* (Stanford, CA: Stanford University Press, 2005), 55–78; Zhengxu Wang, "Before the Emergence of Critical Citizens: Economic and Political Trust in China," *International Review of Sociology* 15 (2005): 155–171; Jie Chen, *Popular Political Support in Urban China* (Stanford, CA: Stanford University Press, 2004), 21–53.

29. Mathew McCubbins, Roger Noll, and Barry Weingast, "Structure and Process, Politics and Policy: Administrative Arrangements and the Political Control of Agencies," *Virginia Law Review* 75 (1989): 431–482.

30. Yang, *Remaking the Chinese Leviathan*.

31. Guobin Yang, *The Power of the Internet: Citizen Activism Online* (New York: Columbia University Press, 2011); Yongnian Zheng, *Technological Empowerment: The Internet, State, and Society in China* (Stanford, CA: Stanford University Press, 2008); Yuezhi Zhao, *Media, Market, and Democracy in China* (Urbana: University of Illinois Press, 1998).

32. Charles Hutzler, "Beijing Tells Media to Toe Party Line," *Asian Wall Street Journal*, July 31, 2001.

33. *Nanfang ribao*, December 20, 2011.

34. *Beijing qingnian bao*, June 10, 2004.

35. *Shanxi wanbao*, August 1, 2007.

36. *Hong Kong Economic Journal*, December 4, 2012.

37. Christopher Kedzie, "Communication and Democracy: Coincident Revolutions and the Emergent Dictators." Retrieved on June 2010, from http://www.rand.org/pubs/rgs_dissertations/RGSD127/index.html.

38. *Hong Kong Economic Journal*, May 7, 2012.

39. Edward Wong and Chris Buckley, "Tentative Deal Reported in Chinese Censorship Dispute," *New York Times*, January 8, 2013.

40. Andrew McFarland, "Interest Groups and the Policy Making Process: Sources of Countervailing Power in America," in Mark Petracca (ed.), *The Politics of Interests: Interest Groups Transformed* (Boulder, CO: Westview Press, 1992), 58–79.

41. Daron Acemoglu and James Robinson, *Economic Origins of Dictatorship and Democracy* (New York: Cambridge University Press, 2006), 118.

42. Kevin O'Brien and Lianjiang Li, *Rightful Resistance in Rural China* (New York: Cambridge University Press, 2006); Yongshun Cai, *Collective Resistance in China: Why Popular Protests Succeed or Fail* (Stanford, CA: Stanford University Press, 2010).

43. Edward Wong, "Deposed Politician's City Lists Names for Meeting on China's Next Leaders," *New York Times*, May 24, 2012.

44. Steven Solnick, "The Breakdown of Hierarchies in the Soviet Union and China: A Neo-Institutional Perspective," *World Politics* 48, 2 (1996): 209–238.

Index

abuse of power (*lanyong zhiquan*), 101, 108, 125; in dealing with citizens, 62, 109, 112–13, 182–83, 187–88; by disciplinary agencies, 68–69; as persistent, 13, 16; for personal gain, 21, 24–25, 37, 71, 188, 193–94; for policy implementation, 21, 24, 25–28, 29, 77–78, 81–82, 182–84; in promotion, 46; punishment for, 74, 85

accountability of state agents, 4–9, 72, 189–94; in authoritarian vs. democratic governments, 4, 6, 47, 134, 135–36, 161; cadre responsibility system, 9–10; and delegation of power, 4–5; and information technology, 67, 190–92; relationship to regime legitimacy, 7–9, 11–12, 15, 57, 58, 191; role of "fire alarms" in, 6; role of media exposure in, 2, 62, 63, 73, 79, 84, 85, 100, 106, 140, 141, 146, 147–48, 150, 164, 190–92; role of "police patrols" in, 5, 6; role of punishment in, 3, 5, 9, 10–14; role of rewards in, 5, 9, 181; role of selective/differentiated discipline in, 4, 10, 13–14, 15–16, 18, 69–70, 186–87. *See also* blame avoidance; promotion; punishment

Acemoglu, Daron, 193

agricultural tax, 27, 30, 81, 175, 176

All-China Federation of Trade Unions, 56

Ames, Barry, 20, 134, 135

Anhui Province: Chizhou, 89; collective farming system in, 162, 169; corruption cases in, 43, 124, 128, 130; fake milk powder incident in, 150, 191; Fuyang, 34, 150, 191; Household Responsibility System (HRS) in, 169, 171, 177; poverty in, 169; punishment of Party members in, 43, 89; social conflict in, 89, 206n10; Taihe County, 174–75; tax collection in, 163, 172–75, 178; Woyang County, 173–76; Xinxin township, 173–76; Yingshang County, 173

"Antirightists Movement," 53

Anyuanding, 145–46

Arnold, Douglas, 135

authoritarian governments: anticorruption policies of, 131–32; vs. democratic governments, 4, 6, 36, 47, 96, 102, 134, 135–36, 157, 161, 168, 179–80, 181, 192–93; punishment of agents in, 4, 6–9; and reform, 160; regime collapse, 7–9; regime legitimacy, 7–9, 11–12, 15, 189–90; reliance on agents in, 6–9; state authority, 11–12, 189. *See also* Chinese party-state; Soviet Union

Azerbaijan: selling of posts in, 42–43

241

Beijing: corruption in, 129; land-dependent revenue in, 27; petitioners in, 144–46; Procuratorate of, 110; SARS crisis in, 93, 96, 97
Beijing Youth News, 147–48
blame avoidance: blocking of information, 136, 137–49; regarding coal mine accidents, 138–41; complication of traceability chain, 135, 136; coverups, 14, 18, 57, 58, 67, 72, 136, 138, 139, 140–41, 144, 147, 157, 158; dealing with inspections, 146–49; detaining of petitioners, 144–46; higher-ranking vs. lower-ranking officials regarding, 77–78, 93; obfuscation, 136; prevention of media coverage, 139–40, 141–43, 157, 158; role of justifications and excuses in, 136, 152–53; role of politicization of protesters in, 152; role of private safety companies in, 145–46; role of repression in, 151–52; role of social networks (*guanxi*) in, 136–37, 153–57, 184, 185; underreporting, 93, 136, 138, 139, 140–41, 147, 164; use of scapegoats, 13, 18, 58, 91, 96, 98, 136, 149–51
Bo Xilai, 184
budgeting process, 33, 188
Burns, John, 37, 154

casualty-producing incidents, 34, 58, 72, 79, 81–85, 88, 92–94, 222n30; in coal mine industry, 77, 92–93, 139–40, 229n17; investigated by central authorities, 93, 153; involving tax and fee collection, 78, 81–83, 172
central authorities, 38, 48, 54, 81, 87, 111, 117, 118, 120, 143, 158, 235n50; blame avoidance by, 149–50; and coal mine accidents, 93, 138, 139, 140; collective leadership of, 45, 98; commitment to anticorruption among, 18, 122–23, 127–28, 129, 131, 132–33, 184–85; consensus building among, 61, 66–67, 160, 171, 175, 177, 193; family planning policies, 22, 25–26, 28–29, 147–48, 183; investigation of high-casualty incidents by, 93, 153; investigation teams sent by, 55–56, 84, 93–94, 100, 140, 146–47, 150–51, 156–57, 191, 225n44; number of public servants as, 14; and popular contention, 192–93; positional responsibilities of, 12; power struggles among, 129, 184, 228n76; promotion of subordinates by, 42; punishment of, 73, 75, 76, 92, 96, 124–25, 127–28, 184, 191, 193–94, 203, 222nn29,30; regime legitimacy as priority of, 11, 15, 41, 57, 58, 67, 79, 91, 122–23, 133, 172, 189–90, 193, 194; relations with upper-level local authorities, 10, 14, 15–16, 32–33, 57, 67, 94–95, 100, 114, 122–23, 182–83, 184–85, 187, 188, 189, 191; role in reform initiatives, 160, 172, 175, 176, 177–79, 180; social stability as priority of, 3, 27, 36, 78, 79, 86, 89–90, 95, 102, 144, 193; tolerance of malfeasance by, 59–60, 188, 193–94
Changsha, 146
Chen Guangcheng, 187, 192
Chen Jinsheng, 221n8
Chen Kejie, 128
Chen Liangyu, 114, 121, 129, 184, 228n76
Chen, Shuo, 15
Chen, Ting, 234n31
Chen Tonghai, 130–31
Chen Xitong, 129, 184
Cheng Weigao, 129
China Petroleum and Chemical Corporation, 130
Chinese Central Television (CCTV), 85, 158, 167, 191; *Focus*, 142
Chinese party-state: authority of, 3, 4, 7, 10, 11–12, 14–16, 18, 49, 56, 57, 58, 67, 69, 122, 133, 189, 190, 193; Budget Law, 33; Bureau of Industry and Commerce, 55; Bureau of Ocean Oil Exploration, 222n30; Bureau of Quality Inspection, 55; cadres (*ganbu*) in, 9–10, 17, 73, 76, 98, 210n78; Central Party Committee, 32–33; Chinese Civil Ser-

vant Law, 227n69; Chinese Criminal Law, 39, 130, 131, 227nn68,70; Civil Servants Law, 17; Ministry of Agriculture, 36, 55; Ministry of Construction, 33; Ministry of Education, 10, 185; Ministry of Health, 55, 96; Ministry of Land and Resources, 94, 128; Ministry of Oil, 222n30; Ministry of Organization, 56, 225n44; Ministry of Public Security, 36, 55, 56, 128; Ministry of Railways, 41, 156; Ministry of Supervision, 54, 61; Ministry of Urban and Rural Housing Construction, 56; National Bureau of Compilation and Translation, 191; National Bureau of Environmental Protection, 96, 97, 222n29; National Bureau of Production Safety, 56; National Commission of Development and Reform, 97; National Complaints Bureau, 35, 86, 145, 172; National Food and Drug Agency, 55, 96, 128, 222n29; National People's Congress, 128, 177, 189; National Security Bureau, 170; National Supervision Bureau, 56, 90; National Tax Bureau, 38; official ideology, 36, 37, 48, 184; Party standing committees, 45, 46, 55, 56, 61, 76, 87, 88, 97, 100, 115, 133, 170; People's Bank, 39; People's Congress, 231n41; Politburo, 45, 114, 184, 186; Political Consultative Conference, 231n41; regime legitimacy, 7–9, 11–12, 15, 37, 41, 79, 91, 104, 122, 133, 138, 182, 184, 186, 189–90, 191, 193, 194; resilience of, 188–89, 194, 238n22; vs. Soviet Union, 36–37, 57, 68, 69, 102–3, 189, 192; State Council, 31, 55–56, 93–94, 97, 120, 139, 148, 150–51, 157, 178, 235n50; Supreme Court, 154; Supreme Procuratorate, 107, 109, 113. *See also* central authorities; city-level authorities; county-level authorities; disciplinary agencies; government heads; Party secretaries; province-level authorities; township-level authorities; village-level authorities

Chongqing, 39, 170, 192; taxi drivers' strike in, 86
city-level authorities, 1, 2–3, 14, 42, 56, 62, 86, 111, 143, 144, 148–49, 164, 167, 234n31; corruption among, 39, 112–13, 117, 118–19, 142, 220n52; and external investment, 27; mayors, 28, 31–32, 73, 74, 75, 77, 84, 88, 90, 91, 92, 93, 94, 95, 96, 97, 115, 127, 142, 150, 155, 227n69; number of public servants as, 14; Party secretaries, 31, 43, 44, 45–46, 73, 74, 75, 84, 88, 91, 92, 93, 94, 95, 96, 99, 114, 115, 117, 121, 129, 131, 142, 165, 168, 171, 173, 234n31; punishment of, 34–35, 38–39, 44, 63, 73, 74, 75, 77, 88, 89, 90–91, 92, 93, 94, 95, 96, 97, 100, 127, 129, 150, 153, 191; role in promotion, 45–46; role in reform initiatives, 163, 169, 170, 171, 173, 176
coal mining accidents, 77, 92–93, 138–41, 229nn17,21
collective actions, 27, 79, 84, 86, 151, 165, 191, 221n8
collective farming system, 162, 169
consensus building: among central authorities, 61, 66–67, 160, 171, 175, 177, 193; regarding punishment of malfeasance, 6–7, 12, 50, 59, 60–61, 115, 132, 193; regarding reforms, 171, 175, 177
construction sector, 41, 163
consumer price index, 125, 126
corruption, 35, 57, 88, 227n69; bribery, 22, 39, 40–41, 43–44, 51, 52n52, 66, 107, 119, 122, 125, 126, 128, 129, 130, 131, 138, 141, 153, 163, 168, 203, 216nn99,101, 227nn70,71; in Chinese Criminal Law, 39, 130, 131, 227nn68,70; in coal mining industry, 138–39; collection and processing of information regarding, 105–21; defined, 39–40, 104, 227n68; and dissolute lifestyles, 38–39; vs. duty-related malfeasance, 47, 104, 109, 132, 157, 186; embezzlement, 1–2, 22, 38–39, 40, 41, 51, 52, 107, 118, 122, 126, 129,

corruption (*continued*)
130, 131, 227n70; identification of tip providers by corrupt officials, 111–13; investigation of, 104, 105, 106–7, 108–9, 110–12, 113, 114–16, 117, 118, 119–21, 122, 123, 129, 132, 133, 141, 220n51; misappropriation of public funds, 38–39, 40, 41, 51, 52, 107, 122, 126, 227n70; persistence of, 16, 17–18, 21, 39–41, 47–48, 111, 132, 133, 182, 184; political considerations regarding, 113–17, 131; in promotion, 42–44, 45, 47; punishment for, 18, 22, 25, 34, 41, 53, 54, 55, 63, 64, 65, 84–85, 89–90, 94–95, 104, 105, 119, 122–32, 156, 168, 184–85, 186, 191, 215n89; revealed by other cases, 106–7, 109, 117, 155; role of disciplinary agencies in anticorruption, 105–33; seriousness of, 58, 124, 125, 126, 130, 131; sources for cases of, 200–202; tips regarding, 53, 106–19, 184; tolerance of, 18, 59–60, 98, 104, 114, 133, 184
Corruption Perceptions Index, 132
county-level authorities, 1, 2–3, 14, 28–29, 42, 52, 54, 55, 56, 111, 145, 148–49, 168; and coal mine accidents, 139, 140–41; corruption among, 43, 44, 63, 88, 112, 117, 141; and external investment, 27; magistrates, 25, 40, 45, 74, 75, 77, 82, 83, 85, 87, 91, 93, 97, 115, 116, 117, 126, 136, 140, 141, 173–74, 183, 227n69; number of public servants as, 14, 220n50; Party secretaries, 3, 37, 38, 43, 44, 46–47, 73, 74, 75, 77, 82, 83, 84–85, 87, 88, 91, 93, 97, 99, 115, 117, 137, 140–41, 144, 150, 154–55, 162, 164, 166, 167, 168–70, 173–74, 182–83, 185, 234n31, 235n40; punishment of, 53, 73, 74, 75, 76, 77, 82, 83, 85, 86, 87, 91, 93, 97, 112, 117, 124, 126, 127, 140–41, 150–51, 156–57, 163, 222n19, 232n80; role in promotion, 45–47; role in reform initiatives, 163, 166–70, 173–75, 176

credit claiming, 98, 134, 135
Cultural Revolution, 21, 51, 52, 69

democratic governments: vs. authoritarian governments, 4, 6, 36, 47, 96, 102, 134, 135–36, 157, 161, 168, 179–80, 181, 192–93; blame avoidance in, 134, 157, 161; and elections, 5–6, 134, 157, 161, 180; and free press, 5; reform in, 161, 168; and rule of law, 5
Deng Xiaoping, 45
disciplinary agencies, 16, 40, 72, 88, 185, 186; abuse of power by, 68–69, 121; discipline inspection committees (DICs), 22, 45, 54–55, 56, 63, 67, 68, 89, 107, 108–9, 110, 111, 114, 115, 116, 117, 118, 119–21, 125, 126, 129, 133, 155, 156, 168, 170, 191, 219n41, 220nn45,51,52, 225n44, 226n45, 227n71; effectiveness of, 12, 16, 40, 48, 49; expansion of, 49, 54–56; in Guangdong Province, 21–23, 54–55, 218n18; influence of Party/government leaders on, 12, 48, 49–50, 55, 56–57, 68, 69–70; and inspection groups, 225n44; political considerations regarding tips, 113–17; positional responsibilities in, 49; role in anticorruption, 105–33; and social connections, 155–56; supervision bureaus, 22, 54, 55, 56, 61, 90, 107, 108, 117, 118, 119, 121; tips to, 53, 106–19, 184, 225n44; two-regulated approach (*shuang gui*) of, 120, 220n52. *See also* investigation teams, ad hoc; procuratorates
Discipline Inspection Commission, 2
dissolute lifestyles, 22, 38–39, 89, 129, 191–92
divide and rule strategy, 135, 161
division of public property, 122, 125
Dong Yang, 163
Downs, Anthony, 20, 181; on climbers vs. conservers, 25; on leakage of authority, 11
Dunn, Delmer, 5

duty-related malfeasance (*duzhi qinquan*), 12, 17, 21, 23, 24–36, 58–60, 62; vs. corruption, 47, 104, 109, 132, 157, 186; defined, 10, 11, 24, 101; favoritism for selfish ends (*xunsi wubi*), 24, 74, 101; neglect of duty (*wanhu zhizhou*), 11, 22, 24, 33–36, 55, 59–60, 74, 89, 101, 107, 110, 125, 129, 182, 222n30; punishment for, 18, 34, 35, 55, 58, 59, 60, 64–65, 66, 71–103, 104, 132, 141, 157, 184, 186; sources for cases of, 198–99. *See also* abuse of power

Easton, David: on regime legitimacy, 7
economic development, 19, 35, 102, 169, 188; GDP growth rate, 9, 26; image-enhancing projects as, 30–33, 44; as priority of local governments, 9, 15, 26, 27, 28, 30–33, 44, 116, 159, 160, 168, 189; and reform, 159, 160
Edin, Maria, 9
environmental pollution, 15, 28, 47, 72, 96, 97, 191

face projects (*mianzi gongcheng*), 30
faction politics, 58, 154, 193
family planning policies, 22, 25–26, 28–29, 147–48, 183
food safety, 34–35, 55, 62, 72, 191
Fuyang city, 34

gambling, 38–39
Gamson, William, 7
Gansu Province: coal mine accidents in, 139; earthquake in 2008, 99; Longnan city, 99–100; riot in 2008, 99–100; tax buying in, 30; Yongdeng County, 139
Geddes, Barbara, 161
gift-sending, 154–55, 185
Gong Fugui, 128
Gorbachev, Mikhail, 8
government heads: political power of, 56, 164; punishment of, 73, 76, 125, 203
Grant, Ruth: on agent accountability, 4
Great Famine, 15, 137, 149–50, 157, 183–84

Great Leap Forward, 15, 51
gross domestic product (GDP), 9, 26
Guangdong Province, 68, 184; Bureau of Agricultural Affairs, 56; Bureau of Civil Affairs, 56; Bureau of Supervision, 56; coal mine accidents in, 93, 229n17; Cultural Revolution in, 52–53; disciplinary agencies in, 21–23, 54–55, 218n18; Guangzhou, 25, 27, 31, 187; Land and Resource Management Bureau, 56; land use dispute in 2005, 153; number of petitions in, 22–23; Organization Department, 56; Propaganda Department, 56; punishment of Party members/officials in, 21–23, 24–25, 37, 38, 39, 53, 54–55; Shenzhen, 31, 34, 107; *Southern Metropolis News*, 145; Stability Maintenance Office, 56; Wukan village protest, 1–3, 56, 187–88, 190–91, 205n3; Zhanjiang, 121; Zhuhai, 31–32
Guangxi, 145; coal mine accidents in, 93, 139, 140–41; Cultural Revolution in, 52; Nandan County, 139, 140–41; Shanglin County, 51–52; social conflict in, 151
Guangzhou, 25, 27, 31, 187
Guizhou Province, 128, 145; Weng'an County, 86–87, 97
gun possession, illegal, 125
Guo Baocheng, 166–68

Haikou, 31
Hangzhou, 27, 38
Hankou Railway Station, 156
heads of the state agency: punishment of, 25, 73, 75
He Kaiyin, 173
health and safety, 93, 95–96
Hebei Province, 100, 116; coal mine accidents in, 77, 139; corruption cases in, 112–13, 128, 129; Dingzhou city, 83–84; Handan County, 139; land disputes in, 83–84, 86; melamine-tainted milk in, 55, 96, 97, 191;

Hebei Province (*continued*)
Shijiazhuang city, 96, 97; Tangshan city, 77; tax collection in, 173, 178; Wu'an city, 139
Heilongjiang Province: coal mine accidents in, 93; corruption in, 131; Harbin, 96; Shuihua city, 43, 131
Henan Province, 28–29, 112, 142, 145; coal mine accidents in, 139–40; corruption in, 124, 215n89; Xinyang incident, 137, 150; Zhengzhou, 95
hierarchy-based blame attribution, 76–78, 90–91, 161
hierarchy-based investigation, 113–17
Hollander, Edwin, 61
Hong Kong, 31, 32; corruption in, 110–11, 113; gambling in, 38–39; Independent Commission Against Corruption (ICAC), 110–11, 113; signed tips in, 110–11, 113
Household Responsibility System (HRS), 169, 171, 176, 177
housing demolition, 85, 88–89, 97, 98, 109, 182–83, 222n19
Hu Changqing, 128, 130
Hubei Province: anonymous tips in, 110; corruption in, 124; Dong Yang in, 163; Li Changping in, 163–64; social conflict in, 163–64
Hui Liangyu, 236n64
Hunan Province, 44, 81, 115, 185, 220n52; census in, 147; coal mine accidents in, 139; housing demolition in, 85, 97, 222n19; Jiahe County, 85, 97, 222n19; Lenshuijiang city, 139
Huntington, Samuel, 102, 160, 181

image-enhancing projects (*xingxiang gongcheng*), 30–33, 44
India: corruption in, 6, 36, 132
Indonesia: corruption in, 36
information asymmetries, 5
Internet, 73, 79, 84, 85, 143, 167, 191–92, 222n17
investigation teams, ad hoc: preparations of lower-level officials for, 148–49; sent by central authorities, 55–56, 84, 93–94, 100, 140, 146–47, 150–51, 156–57, 191, 225n44; sent by provincial-level authorities, 2, 3, 56, 88, 100, 148–49, 170, 190–91

Jiang Chunyun, 175, 176
Jiang Zemin, 62, 156, 175
Jiangsu Province, 38, 121; anonymous tips in, 109–10; corruption cases in, 124, 128, 221n53; Jiangning County, 53; land use disputes in, 86, 97; punishment of Party members in, 53; Qiu He in, 168, 171; Yancheng, 28
Jilin Province, 46, 96, 121
Jinan, 38

Kahn, Joseph, 228n76
Kennan, George, 36–37
Keohane, Robert: on agent accountability, 4
Key, Veron, 5
Kung, James Kai-sing, 15, 234n31
Kuomintang (KMT), 51, 149–50

Landry, Pierre, 10
land use, 29, 72, 94–95, 142; land-dependent revenue, 27; social conflict regarding, 1–3, 27, 81, 83–85, 86, 88–89, 97, 99–100, 109, 153, 187. *See also* housing demolition
Latin American, 134, 135, 160–61
leakage of authority, 11, 14–16, 18, 67, 122–23, 184–85, 189
Lee Kuan Yew, 132
leniency, *ex post*, 13, 18, 59, 60, 72, 97–102, 134–35, 183, 184, 186
Li Changping, 163–64
Li Jiating, 128
Li Jizhou, 128
Li Keqiang, 95
Li Lanqing, 175, 176
Li, Lianjiang, 235n40
Liaoning Province: coal mine accidents in, 93; Liaoyang, 152; Shenyang, 38–39
Limaye, Madhu, 6
Liu Fangren, 128

Liu Zhixiang, 156
Lü, Xiaobo, 118

Ma De, 43, 131
Macau, 32; gambling in, 38–39
MacFarquhar, Roderick, 184
Machiavelli, Niccolò, 157
malfeasance of officials: consequence severity, 4, 12, 13, 18, 49–50, 54, 55, 58–59, 60, 62, 64–65, 69, 71, 72, 77, 78, 79, 80, 81–86, 90, 101, 102–3, 113, 139–40, 151, 182, 186, 222n30; criminal behavior, 13, 24, 34, 43, 55, 58–59; dissolute lifestyle, 22, 37–39; failure in governance, 22, 33–36, 62, 72, 92, 95–96, 184, 191; gambling, 38–39; immoral and illegal self-regarding behavior, 10–11, 12, 13, 17, 18, 21, 22, 23–24, 36–44, 125, 129, 157; as persistent, 11, 13, 15, 16, 17–18, 21, 38, 39–41, 47–48, 69, 111, 132, 133, 182; political mistakes/crimes, 21, 22; predatory behavior, 26–28; responsibility of agent/blame attribution, 4, 12–13, 14, 18, 49–50, 59, 60, 65, 69, 71, 72, 76–78, 79, 80, 82, 90, 98, 102, 103, 182, 186; violations of national policies, 22, 25, 72, 92, 94–95; womanizing/mistresses, 38, 39, 89, 168. *See also* blame avoidance; corruption; duty-related malfeasance; tolerance of malfeasance
Manion, Melanie, 53
Mao Zedong, 149, 150
Maravall, Jose Maria, 6
Marx, Karl, 37
McCubbins, Matthew, 10, 118
McGraw, Kathleen, 134, 153
media exposure, 1, 40, 113, 153, 155, 222n17; prevention of, 139–40, 141–43, 157, 158; role in accountability of state agents, 2, 62, 63, 73, 79, 84, 85, 100, 106, 140, 141, 146, 147–48, 150, 164, 190–92; role in reform initiatives, 167–68; sources for cases of, 197–98
medications, 34

Meng Xuenong, 76, 91, 93, 96, 97
Michelson, Ethan, 172
mistresses, 38, 39, 89, 168
moral hazards, 5
motivation of agents: climbers vs. conservers among officials, 20, 21, 25, 33–34, 166; family welfare, 21, 37, 161–62; keeping position, 20, 21, 25; as mixed, 181; policy preferences, 20, 21; promotion, 9, 15, 20, 21, 25, 27, 161, 164–65, 166; public interest, 21, 161–62, 164, 165–66, 181; self-interest, 9, 15, 20, 21, 22, 24–25, 27, 35, 37, 47, 51, 52, 69, 71, 157, 161–62, 181, 188, 193–94; staying in power, 20–21, 134, 157, 161, 163
murder, 38

Nathan, Andrew, 188, 238n22
nepotism, 185–86
New Beijing Post, The, 192
Noll, Roger, 10

O'Flaherty, Brendan, 5
"Opposing Five Tendencies" campaign, 51

Party secretaries: at city level, 31, 43, 44, 45–46, 73, 74, 75, 84, 88, 91, 92, 93, 94, 95, 96, 99, 114, 115, 117, 121, 129, 131, 142, 165, 168, 171, 173, 234n31; corruption among, 43, 44, 88, 89, 112, 117, 125, 128, 129, 131, 141, 142; at county level, 3, 37, 38, 43, 44, 46–47, 73, 74, 75, 77, 82, 83, 84–85, 87, 88, 91, 93, 97, 99, 115, 117, 137, 140–41, 144, 150, 154–55, 162, 164, 166, 167, 168–70, 173–74, 182–83, 185, 234n31, 235n40; vs. government leaders, 76; Jiang Zemin, 62, 156, 175; political power of, 45–47, 56, 164; at province level, 73, 76, 85, 88, 92, 93, 112–13, 116, 128, 129, 150, 162, 169, 175, 187, 234n31; punishment of, 3, 38, 61, 73, 74, 75, 76, 77, 78, 82, 83, 84–85, 86, 87, 88, 89, 90–91, 92, 93, 94, 95, 96, 97, 99, 100, 125, 128, 129, 131,

Party secretaries: at city level (*continued*) 140–41, 150, 216nn99,101, 222n19, 228n76; role in promotion, 45–47; role in reform initiatives, 164, 165, 166, 167, 168–70, 171, 173–76; at township level, 30, 73, 74, 75, 82, 83, 85, 86, 88, 89, 91, 97, 99, 162, 163–64, 169, 170, 173, 174, 175–76, 183; at village level, 73, 75, 78, 82, 86; Xi Jinping, 194

Pei, Minxin, 188

People's Daily, 140, 142, 143, 147–48, 157, 158

Peres, Shimon, 192

performance assessment, 20, 78, 90; cadre evaluation system, 9–10; image-enhancing projects, 30–33, 44; one-item veto system, 26, 144, 147; relationship to promotion, 42

performance projects (*zhengji gongcheng*), 30, 33

personal connections (*guanxi*). *See* social networks

personal gain, 22, 51, 52, 69, 125, 157, 165; abuse of power for, 21, 24–25, 37, 71, 188, 193–94; selling of posts for, 41, 42–44, 216n101. *See also* corruption

personal income, 9, 27, 35, 37, 43, 64, 66, 68, 184; as unexplained, 39, 122, 126, 130, 131, 203, 227n70

petitions from citizens, 22–23, 27, 35–36, 99, 144–46, 175, 230n41, 231n45

PetroChina, 96

Philippines: corruption in, 116

Pierson, Paul, 161

police departments, 121, 151–52, 153, 221n8

policy implementation, 57, 193; abuse of power for, 21, 24, 25–28, 29, 77–78, 81–82, 182–84; policy distortion, 28–30, 189; role of inspections in, 146–49; as selective, 10, 189

policy preferences, 20, 21, 36

political campaigns, 49, 50–53, 69

popular contention. *See* social conflict

positional responsibilities, 12, 49, 57, 58, 69, 193

power struggles, 129, 184, 228n76

predatory behavior, 26–28

principal-agents relations: and delegation of power, 4–5; and leakage of authority, 11, 14–16, 18, 67, 122–23, 184–85, 189; as patron-client relations, 57–58, 136–37, 154. *See also* central authorities; hierarchy-based blame attribution; hierarchy-based investigation; scapegoats; upper-level local authorities

prioritization of responsibilities, 10, 14–15

private distribution of confiscated property, 39

private distribution of state-owned assets, 38–39

privatization of public enterprises, 178–79

procuratorates, 54, 75, 85, 129, 130, 151, 168, 225n44; anticorruption bureaus, 119, 121, 155–56, 221n53; cases filed by, 24, 34, 39–40, 71, 101, 107–8, 110, 120, 122, 123; cases investigated by, 24, 34, 38, 40, 41, 52, 55, 64, 65, 68, 71, 101, 107–9, 110, 112, 122, 123; Supreme Procuratorate, 107, 109, 113; tips to, 107, 111–12. *See also* disciplinary agencies

Procuratorial Daily, 123

production safety, 55, 77, 90, 96, 138, 191

promotion, 25, 63, 98, 102, 142, 155, 163, 170, 171, 235n40, 238n22; as agent incentive, 9, 15, 20, 21, 27, 161, 164–65, 166, 179; corruption in, 42–44, 45, 47; of DIC secretary, 125, 126; nepotism in, 185–86; for Party secretaries, 234n31; relationship to local politics, 44–47, 186–87; role of age in, 167–68; role of bribery in, 43–44; role of education in, 42; role of expertise in, 42; role of opportunities in, 42; role of performance in, 42; role of social networks in, 42, 57–58, 60–61, 154, 186; selling of posts, 41, 42–44, 216n101

province-level authorities, 38, 81, 84, 86, 94, 111, 114, 137, 138, 144, 145, 150, 153, 167, 187–88, 205n3, 227n69; corruption among, 112–13, 123–24, 128,

129, 130; DIC, 89, 115, 121, 125, 126, 155; governors, 73, 74, 75, 85, 92, 93, 95, 97, 128, 130, 175, 176, 236n64; investigation of, 120–21; investigation teams sent by, 2, 3, 56, 88, 100, 148–49, 170, 190–91; number of public servants as, 14; Party secretaries, 73, 76, 85, 88, 92, 93, 112–13, 116, 128, 129, 150, 162, 169, 175, 187, 234n31; people's congress, 174, 176; and promotions, 45–46; punishment of, 41, 62, 63, 73, 75, 89, 92–93, 95, 96, 97, 124–25, 127, 128, 130, 185, 191, 203, 206n10, 215n89; role in reform initiatives, 162, 168–69, 170, 171, 174–75, 176, 178, 236n64; Wukan village protests investigated by, 2, 3, 56

public attention, 12, 15, 57, 58, 59–60, 62, 67. *See also* media exposure

punishment: administrative discipline (*zhengji chufen*), 13, 63–64, 65, 82, 86, 92, 93–94, 95, 96, 107, 112, 122, 150, 191, 222n30; costs of discipline, 3, 4, 7, 12, 13, 15, 18, 49, 50, 57–58, 59–63, 66, 69–70, 103, 104, 116, 122, 127, 182, 190, 193; death penalty, 84, 85, 89, 100, 112, 124, 127, 128, 130, 132, 141, 150, 156, 203; death penalty with reprieve, 84, 89, 124, 127, 128, 130–31, 203; as demoralizing, 6, 58, 69; for duty-related malfeasance (*duzhi qinquan*), 18, 34, 35, 55, 58, 59, 60, 64–65, 66, 71–103, 104, 132, 141, 157, 184, 186; exemption from, 3, 13, 14, 50, 59, 60, 66, 67, 70, 72, 80, 84, 85–86, 94, 95, 100, 101, 102, 103, 105, 114, 129, 131, 133, 159, 186; expulsion from Party, 13, 39, 63, 65, 66, 82, 129, 137, 162, 219n41; fixed term of imprisonment, 124, 127, 128, 129, 131, 141, 157; of higher-ranking officials, 60–63, 67, 70, 72, 73–76, 77–78, 81–83, 84–85, 86, 87, 88, 89, 90–96, 97, 102–3, 105, 114, 116, 117, 124–31, 132, 184–85, 191–92, 203; inconsistency in, 128–31, 133; institutionalization of discipline, 6–7, 49, 51, 53, 54–56, 69, 181, 188, 193; job transfers, 9, 64, 66, 81, 100, 162, 163–64, 165, 167–68, 174, 216n101; legal sanctions, 13, 24, 34, 43, 55, 59, 63, 64, 65–66, 74, 75, 82, 84, 85, 89, 90, 93, 100, 104, 107, 112, 122, 123–31, 137, 141, 150, 151–52, 203; leniency in, 13, 18, 59, 60, 72, 97–102, 134–35, 183, 184, 186; life imprisonment, 124, 127, 128, 130, 203; of lower-ranking officials, 1, 3, 67, 73, 74, 75–78, 79, 81–83, 97, 102, 114, 116, 117, 124–28; organizational discipline (*zuzhi zhufen*), 13, 63, 64, 65–66; Party discipline (*dangji chufen*), 13, 63, 64, 65–66, 74, 77, 82, 85, 86, 93, 94, 95, 96, 107, 112, 122, 129, 150, 153, 162, 191; of Party officials vs. government officials, 76, 135–36; and positional responsibilities, 12, 57, 58, 69, 193; of protesters, 1, 2, 83, 87, 144, 151–52; of reformers, 162, 162–63, 165, 167–68; relationship to agent responsibility, 4, 12–13, 49–50, 59, 60, 65, 76–78, 79, 80, 82, 90–91, 92, 98, 102, 103, 182, 186; relationship to consequence severity, 4, 12, 13, 49–50, 54, 58–59, 60, 62, 64–65, 79, 81–90, 91, 92–94, 101, 102–3, 182, 186, 222n30; relationship to cooperative attitude, 130–31; relationship to magnitude of corruption/money involved, 58, 124, 125, 126, 130, 131; removal from office, 1, 13, 39, 45, 63, 64, 65, 66, 72, 74, 77, 82, 85, 86, 87, 88, 89, 93–94, 95, 96, 97–99, 100, 103, 150, 153, 162, 163, 167, 170, 185, 186, 222n19, 222n30; role in accountability of agents, 5, 9, 10–14; role of political campaigns in, 49, 50–53, 69; selective/differentiated discipline, 4, 10, 13–14, 15–16, 18, 50, 57–58, 59–66, 78, 85–86, 89–90, 103, 104, 122–23, 182, 186–87, 193; severity of punishment, 13, 63–65, 74–78, 81–83, 89, 90–91, 122, 123–31, 156, 184–85, 186; threat of, 3, 4, 14, 16, 50, 66–69, 72, 86, 101–2, 103, 105, 118, 119, 122–23,

punishment: administrative discipline (*continued*)
   127–28, 133, 134, 141, 158, 182, 185, 186; vs. tolerance, 3, 4, 71, 80, 85–86, 182, 186; types of discipline, 4, 5, 10–11, 63–66. *See also* blame avoidance; corruption; disciplinary agencies
Pye, Lucian, 137

Qiu He, 168, 171
Qiushi, 177–78

reappointment, 72, 97–99, 102, 103, 186
reform: diffusion of, 175, 176–80; and economic development, 159, 160; Household Responsibility System (HRS), 169, 171, 176, 177; as institutional, 9, 41, 49, 53, 54–56, 69, 159, 171, 190, 193; medical care reform, 166–68, 177; political repercussions of, 160; privatization of public enterprises, 178–79; punishment of reformers, 162, 163–64, 165, 167–68; relationship to violations of laws/regulations, 16, 19, 159, 161, 162, 165, 171, 175, 178, 180; risks of, 159, 160–66, 168, 173, 175–76, 177, 179–80, 235n40; role of local initiatives in, 16, 19, 159–60, 161–68; tax-for-fee reform, 16, 171–76, 178, 235n50, 236n59; as tolerated/supported by upper-level authorities, 16, 159–60, 166, 167, 168–71, 172, 173–75, 176, 179, 180; township head elections, 164, 169–71, 177–78
regime collapse, 7–9, 69, 180, 192, 194
regime legitimacy, 3, 37, 182; as damaged by malfeasance of officials, 7, 11, 104, 138, 184, 186; as priority of central authorities, 11, 15, 41, 57, 58, 67, 79, 91, 122–23, 133, 172, 189–90, 193, 194; relationship to accountability of state agents, 7–9, 11–12, 15, 57, 58, 191
regime resilience, 188–89, 194, 238n22
regime transition, 165, 180
resignation of officials, 64, 98, 163–64
revenue generation, 26–28, 29–30
Robinson, James, 193
Rose-Ackerman, Susan, 104

rule of law, 5, 16
Russia, 132

SARS (severe acute respiratory syndrome), 93, 96, 97
Saxonberg, Steven: on regime legitimacy, 7
scapegoats, 13, 18, 58, 91, 96, 98, 161
selling of posts, 41, 42–44, 47, 216n101
severe acute respiratory syndrome (SARS), 93, 96, 97
Shaanxi Province: census in, 147; coal mine accidents in, 93, 139; corruption in, 38, 191; disciplinary actions in, 100–101, 191; Huangling County, 139; illegal coal mining in, 138; medical care reform in, 166–68, 177; Shenmu County, 166–68, 177
Shandong Province, 187; Jinan, 38; ship accident in 1999, 93
Shanghai, 114, 228n76; anonymous tips in, 110; fire in Jing'an district, 55–56, 93–94; land-dependent revenue in, 27
Shanwei city government, 1–2
Shanxi Province, 28, 34, 143; child labor in, 191; coal mine accidents in, 92–93, 139; corruption in, 117, 142, 156–57, 232n80; Fanshi County, 139; Hejin city, 139; Linfen city, 139; mud-rock flow accident in 2008, 93, 97; Ningwu County, 139; village cadres killed in, 118; Zuoyun County, 139
sheltering criminals, 125
Shenzhen, 31, 34, 107
Sichuan Province, 145, 162; census in, 148; Chengdu, 183; dereliction of duty in, 59–60; earthquake in 2008, 59–60, 99; false accusations in, 109; fee collection in, 82; Hanyuan County, 84; land use dispute in, 84–85; township head elections in, 170
Simis, Konstantin, 8
Singapore, 132
social conflict, 15, 22, 47, 144, 192–93; casualties in, 79, 81–85; as collective action, 27, 79, 84, 86, 151, 165, 191, 221n8; regarding housing demolition, 85, 88–89, 97, 98, 109, 182–83,

222n19; regarding irresponsiveness of local officials, 2, 3, 24, 34, 35–36, 51, 87; labor conflict, 86, 90; regarding land use, 1–3, 27, 81, 83–85, 86, 88–89, 97, 99–100, 109, 153, 187; management of, 3, 18, 71, 78–90, 188, 193, 199–200, 206n10; between peasants and local cadres, 1–3, 23, 26, 35, 78, 81–85; punishment of officials in cases of, 3, 18, 71, 78–90, 85–86, 151, 199–200, 206n10; punishment of protesters, 1, 2, 83, 87, 144, 151–52; relationship to abuse of power, 16, 182; responsibility attribution in, 79; state-citizen vs. civil disputes, 78, 79; regarding tax collection and fees, 81–83, 163, 172
social movements, 164, 192–93
social networks (*guanxi*), 12, 14, 29, 115, 146, 171; role in blame avoidance, 136–37, 153–57, 184, 185; role in promotion, 42, 57–58, 60–61, 154, 186
Sohu.com, 85, 222n17
Solnick, Steven, 4, 104–5; on Soviet Union, 8, 57, 69, 102–3, 181, 207n35
Sondi, Sunil, 6
Southern Weekend, 192
Soviet Union: vs. China, 36–37, 57, 68, 69, 102–3, 189, 192; collapse of, 8–9, 69, 192; Communist Party, 8, 36, 37; corruption in, 7–9; *nomenklatura* system in, 17, 37, 210n74; officials in, 17, 36–37, 37, 57, 68, 181, 189, 210n74; Solnick on, 8, 57, 69, 102–3, 181, 207n35; spontaneous privatization in, 102; state authority in, 57
state-owned enterprises, 17, 102, 123, 138, 155–56, 164, 178–79, 186
Streeck, Wolfgang, 28
Suihua city, 43
Sun, Yan, 44, 155
Sun Zhigang, 191
Suzhou, 88–89

tax and fee collection, 98, 183; agricultural tax, 27, 30, 81, 175, 176; casualty-producing incidents involving, 78, 81–83, 172; illegal tax breaks, 47; social conflict regarding, 81–83, 163, 172; tax buying, 29–30; tax-for-fee reform, 16, 171–76, 178, 235n50, 236n59; by township-level authorities, 26–27, 28–30
Thelen, Kathleen, 28
"Three Oppositions" campaign, 51
Tian Fengshan, 128
Tiananmen protests, 60, 188
Tianjin, 35
time trend, 125, 126
tips, 225n44; regarding corruption, 53, 106–19, 184; political considerations regarding, 113–17; signed vs. unsigned, 109–11, 113, 117
tolerance of malfeasance, 12–14, 28, 48, 59–60, 118–19, 122–23, 138, 157, 189, 193, 207n35; exemption from punishment, 3, 13, 14, 50, 59, 60, 66, 67, 70, 72, 80, 84, 85–86, 94, 95, 100, 101, 102, 103, 105, 114, 129, 131, 133, 159, 186; as *ex post* leniency, 13, 18, 60, 72, 97–102, 134–35, 183, 184, 186; and leakage of authority, 11, 15–16; and nice man theory (*haoren zhuyi*), 62; political reasons for, 61, 98; vs. punishment, 3, 4, 18, 71, 80, 85–86, 182–84, 186–87; relationship to cost of punishment, 7, 12, 15–16, 49, 50, 57–58, 59, 103, 116, 122; relationship to idiosyncrasy credits, 61; relationship to persistence of malfeasance, 13, 16; in Soviet Union, 7–9
township-level authorities, 1, 2–3, 42, 54, 115, 118, 138–39, 148–49, 227n69; corruption among, 39, 43; election of township heads, 164, 169–71, 177–78; number of public servants as, 14, 220n50; Party secretaries, 30, 73, 74, 75, 82, 83, 85, 86, 88, 89, 91, 97, 99, 162, 163–64, 169, 170, 173, 174, 175–76, 183; punishment of, 24, 62, 63, 73, 74, 75, 76, 81–83, 85, 86, 88–89, 91, 97, 99, 124, 125, 127, 163; role in reform initiatives, 169, 173–74, 175–76; role in rural development, 9; tax collection by, 26–27, 28–30

two-regulated approach (*shuang gui*), 120, 220n52

unexplained personal income, 122, 126, 130, 131
upper-level local authorities, 25, 35–36, 133; positional responsibilities of, 12; promotion of subordinates by, 42; punishment of, 122–23, 125; relations with central authorities, 10, 14, 15–16, 32–33, 57, 67, 94–95, 98–99, 114, 119, 122–23, 182–83, 184–85, 187, 188, 189, 191, 193–94; relations with subordinates, 9, 14, 15, 42, 45, 67, 98–99, 100–101, 118–19, 122–23, 133, 155, 186–87; role in reform, 16, 163–64, 165, 167–69

vice government heads: punishment of, 73, 75
Vietnam, 132
village-level authorities: corruption among, 1–2, 118, 187; election of, 187, 193; number of public servants as, 14; Party secretaries, 73, 75, 78, 82, 86; punishment of, 1, 73, 75, 76, 78, 81–83, 187; role in rural development, 9; tax collection by, 26; Wukan village protest against, 1–3, 56, 187–88, 190–91, 205n3
violation of citizens' rights, 74, 101, 108
Voslensky, Michel, 36, 37

Wan Li, 162, 169
Wang Huaizhong, 128, 130
Weaver, Kent, 134
Weber, Max: *Politics as a Vocation*, 20
Weingast, Barry, 10
Wen Jiabao, 81, 142, 175, 176
Whiting, Susan, 9
Wu Zhipu, 150
Wukan village protest, 1–3, 56, 187–88, 190–91, 205n3

Xi Jinping, 194
Xie Zhenhua, 96, 97
Xinhua News Agency, 140, 156, 157, 158
Xinyang incident, 137, 150

Yang, Dali, 41, 153, 189
Yunnan Province: cases of duty-related malfeasance in, 74, 101; corruption cases in, 122, 123, 128, 130; Menglian County, 88; procuratorate of, 122, 123; township head elections in, 170–71

Zartman, William: on regime collapse, 7
Zhang Wenkang, 96
Zhejiang Province, 121, 124, 152
Zheng Xiaoyu, 128
Zhou Yongkang, 184
Zhu, Lin, 126
Zhu Rongji, 32, 163–64, 175, 176, 178
Zhuhai city airport, 31–32